The Talking Ape

In loving memory of
Anne Hvenekilde.
Min beste venn.

The Talking Ape

HOW LANGUAGE EVOLVED

ROBBINS BURLING

OXFORD
UNIVERSITY PRESS

OXFORD

UNIVERSITY PRESS

Great Clarendon Street, Oxford OX2 6DP

Oxford University Press is a department of the University of Oxford.
It furthers the University's objective of excellence in research, scholarship,
and education by publishing worldwide in

Oxford New York

Auckland Cape Town Dar es Salaam Hong Kong Karachi
Kuala Lumpur Madrid Melbourne Mexico City Nairobi
New Delhi Shanghai Taipei Toronto

With offices in

Argentina Austria Brazil Chile Czech Republic France Greece
Guatemala Hungary Italy Japan Poland Portugal Singapore
South Korea Switzerland Thailand Turkey Ukraine Vietnam

Oxford is a registered trade mark of Oxford University Press
in the UK and in certain other countries

Published in the United States
by Oxford University Press Inc., New York

© Robbins Burling 2005

The moral rights of the author have been asserted
Database right Oxford University Press (maker)

First published 2005

British Library Cataloguing in Publication Data

Data available

Library of Congress Cataloging in Publication Data

Data available

Typeset by SPI Publisher Services, Pondicherry, India
Printed in Great Britain on acid-free paper by Biddles Ltd., King's Lynn

ISBN 0-19-927940-3   978-0-19-927940-1

10 9 8 7 6 5 4 3 2 1

Contents

Publisher's note

This is the fifth book to appear in the Oxford University Press series *Studies in the Evolution of Language*, whose editors are Professor James R. Hurford of the University of Edinburgh and Professor Frederick J. Newmeyer of the University of Washington.

Preface

My fascination with language origins goes back at least to the 1980s when some students and faculty members from the Department of Anthropology at the University of Michigan used to get together periodically for very informal evening seminars on topics of human evolution. More than once, archeologists turned to me, the only linguist in the group, and asked "When did language begin?" I could do nothing except look blank and say "I dunno," but the question prodded me into thinking about how it all might have started. This book is the result of that thinking.

Over the years, many friends, colleagues, and correspondents offered their wise counsel as I worked on various articles on the subject (some of which form the basis of sections in the book and are listed in the Acknowledgements below) and I must again give my thanks to A. L. Becker, Derek Bickerton, Paul Bloom, Loring Brace, William Croft, Iain Davidson, Penelope Eckert, Mark V. Flinn, Allan Gibbard, Virginia Guilford, Barbara King, Chris Knight, Frank Livingstone, Bruce Mannheim, John Mitani, Thomas Moylan, Emanuel Polioudakis, Ernst Pulgram, Roy Rappaport, Robert Seyfarth, Michael Tomasello, Virginia Vitzthum, Ron Wallace, and Richard Wrangham.

Some of these same people, and many others as well, have helped in one way or another with the book itself. I will never overcome my astonishment at the generosity of scholars, several of whom I know only through e-mail, who have responded to my pleas for help. Simon Kirby and Jim Hurford have on several occasions done their best to help me understand work on the computer simulation of language evolution. Judy Kegl not only answered my questions and sent me papers, but sent me a stunning tape about young Nicaraguan signers. Another stunning tape, this one about bonobos, was sent by Sue Savage-Rumbaugh. Adam Kendon helped me to understand the differences between various kinds of gestures. William Irons brought me up to date on the relation between status and reproductive success, and Judith Irvine did the same for the relation between status and valued forms of language. Ruth Lesser educated me about aphasia. Karin Schmidt helped me with the relationship between human and animal gestures. Simon Frasier did his best to untangle my confusion about the FOXP2 gene. Bruce Richman guided my reading on music. Judith Becker instructed me about the rhythm and metrics of both music and language. Paula Berwanger guided my reading on sign language. Over the years, Barbara King has cheerfully responded to numerous queries on matters primatological. Iain Davidson has sent me countless e-mail messages, hoping to straighten out my notions of prehistory and much else. For two decades, Milford Wolpoff has never stopped arguing with me, always hoping to educate me. Among many other acts of generosity, he supplied the data from which Illustration 7 was constructed.

Anne Hvenekilde was able to read early drafts of two chapters and, as always, she made sharp criticism even while encouraging me to continue. Allan Gibbard and Robert Whallon read and offered helpful comments about parts of the manuscript at later stages. Three good friends read the whole thing. Thomas Trautmann was the first of these and, along with numerous astute criticisms and suggestions, he gave me the confidence to continue. Sheila Procter and Derek Brereton read later drafts and both helped me in all sorts of ways toward both good sense and clarity. Recruited by OUP, Frederick Newmeyer reviewed the penultimate draft. He not only saved me from several embarrassing errors but pushed me to clear up some of my more murky prose.

These thoughtful friends did their best to set me straight. Where I have failed to learn from them, blame me.

Robbins Burling
Ann Arbor, Michigan
March 2005

Acknowledgements

Several of the chapters in the book grew, in part, from earlier articles. I first suggested that we should pay more attention to comprehension in an article called "Comprehension, Production and Conventionalization in the Origins of Language" in *The Evolutionary Emergence of Language*, edited by Chris Knight, Michael Studdert-Kennedy, and James R. Hurford and published by Cambridge University Press in 2000. This is reflected most closely in Chapter 1, but this entire book is, in a sense, an expansion of that article. Parts of Chapters 2 and 3 appeared in a rather different form in "Primate Calls, Human Language, and Nonverbal Communication" in 1993 in volume 14 of *Current Anthropology*, pages 25–37, and published by The Wenner-Gren Foundation for Anthropological Research. A first attempt to organize the ideas in Chapter 4 appeared in 1999 in volume 10, section 32 of the electronic journal *Psycoloquy* as "The cognitive prerequisites for language". Parts of Chapters 5 and 6 are adapted from "Motivation, Arbitrariness, and Conventionality" that appeared in 1999 in *The Origins of Language: What Nonhuman Primates Can Tell Us*, edited by Barbara J. King and published by the School of American Research, Santa Fe. The first half of Chapter 10, is based on "The selective advantage of complex language," which appeared in 1986 in pages 1–16 of volume 7 of *Ethology and Sociobiology*, published by Elsevier Science Publishing Co. Inc.

1

In the beginning

Few topics about which scholars have puzzled can be quite so intriguing and so tantalizing, but at the same time so frustrating, as the evolution of the human capacity for language. Nothing so decisively sets us apart from our primate cousins as our constant chatter. It is no exaggeration to credit language for the very humanity that distinguishes us from the beasts from which we sprang. If we are even a tiny bit curious about our own origins, we have to be curious about the origins of language.

This is why it so frustrating to have no direct evidence for the language of our early ancestors. Fading as soon as it is uttered, spoken language leaves no trace. A few of our remote forebears left their bones in places where we could find them, and as more and more of these bones have been moved to museums, we have gained a clearer understanding of the several million years of evolution during which our bodies diverged from those of chimpanzees. The tools that early humans knocked from stones have survived in their thousands, and they tell us a good deal about early technology. But it was only after writing was invented, a mere five or six thousand years ago, that earlier languages could leave any trace. By then, the human capacity for spoken language had already had a very long history. Not even the earliest writing can tell us anything about the far more ancient periods when people first began to talk.

The lack of direct evidence for such a crucial part of our heritage has left the topic open to speculation, some of it reasonable, some that might be called "imaginative," and some downright crazy, and this has brought the subject a certain disrepute. Every student of linguistics is told about the famous prohibition of the Linguistic Society of Paris that, in 1866, banned the topic of language origins as a subject unfit for the Society's meetings. The ban is often cited as a sorry example of intellectual censorship, but anyone who has read widely in the literature on language origins cannot escape a sneaking sympathy with the Paris linguists. Reams of nonsense have been written on the subject.

Nevertheless, we cannot forever taboo a topic of such great interest, and even if we have no direct evidence, enough indirect evidence has accumulated since the prohibition of Paris to invite us to think carefully about what the early forms of language might have been like. In the last two decades, scholars of apparently sound mind from such serious disciplines as paleontology, primatology, cognitive science, archeology, and linguistics have once more turned their curiosity to the origins of language.

Any attempt to figure out how language evolved does have two reasonably solid anchor points. To get an idea about where it all began, we can observe the behavior of our closest primate cousins, the chimpanzees and bonobos. The latter, once rather misleadingly called "pygmy chimpanzees," are now recognized as a separate species. For the ending point, we can look at our own languages. We want to know how animals with something similar to the capacities of chimps and bonobos could have evolved into animals that could talk. Right away, we need to qualify. That "something similar" is important, for we did not evolve from chimps or bonobos, but only from "something similar" to them. These two closely related, but strangely different, species split from each other about three million years ago. Their common ancestor, in turn, split from the human line two or three million years before that. Since the time of that earlier separation, chimps and bonobos have had just as long to evolve as we have, so we certainly did not evolve from the apes we know today, and the differences between chimpanzees and bonobos show us that they have also evolved. Nevertheless, in the time since we separated, our ape cousins have changed their living circumstances much less than we have, and they have probably changed their bodies and behavior much less as well. Gorillas are considerably further from us genealogically than chimpanzees and bonobos. Orangutans are even more distant, and they probably split off from the rest of us at least thirteen million years ago, perhaps more. (See Illustration 1.) In spite of this great phylogenetic distance, gorillas and orangs share more of their behavior with chimps and bonobos than they do with us.

All the great apes have their own special characteristics, of course, the legacy of their own millions of years of separate evolution. All of us have evolved, in our diverging directions, away from our distant common ancestor, but where the apes show common features in their anatomy or behavior, it is a good bet that their, and our, common ancestor had that trait too. Since all the apes are so much hairier than we are, for example, we can be reasonably confident that it is we who have lost our hair rather than the apes who have acquired theirs. Since we can talk and they cannot, we can be equally confident that it is we who have acquired language, not they who have lost it. The apes, especially the chimpanzees and bonobos, give us the best idea we have about the behavior of our common ancestor. We can use the behavior of these apes, cautiously, as a plausible starting point.

Our other anchor is modern human language. We can listen to people talk and try to figure out how language works. Even here we know less than we would like. We have only a primitive idea of how the brain processes language, for example, and we know much more about

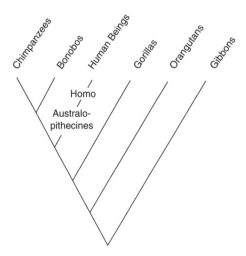

Illustration 1. Phylogenetic Relationships among Humans and Apes

how the vocal tract produces the sounds of speech than about how our ears and brains manage to interpret them. Still, we do know a good deal about the sounds, words, and grammar of our languages, so the question that has to be asked by anyone interested in the origin of language is "How did we get from an ordinary primate that could not talk to the strange human primate that can't shut up?"

Between our two anchors we have stones and bones. The fossil record of human bones has grown wonderfully richer in the past half century. We now have a reasonable understanding of how our bodies evolved from an ape that was much better than we are at clambering around trees, but not as good as us at walking on two legs. We also know more about how, some millions of years after leaving the trees, the serious expansion of the brain got underway. We can make some plausible inferences about what these bodily changes implied for behavior. We can also inspect a couple of million years of glacially slow development of stone tool technology and then the sudden speeding up of technological change in the last hundred thousand years. From the evidence of stones and bones, we can infer less about communication than about technology and subsistence, but the technology gives us some idea of the cultural context within which language grew.

The central argument of this book is that comprehension, rather than production, was the driving force for the evolution of the human ability to use language. To put comprehension first bumps up against a widespread, but barely recognized, bias that usually consigns comprehension to second place. We always act as if speaking is what really matters. We are more likely to ask a friend "Can you speak French?" than "Can you understand French?" Statistics tell us how many "speakers" each language has. They never count up the "understanders." We have no less than four common words that refer specifically to the production of spoken language: "speak," "say," "talk," and "tell," but not a single word for what happens when language reaches our ears. We make do with "listen," "hear," "receive," "understand," or "comprehend" but none of these is specific to language. We can hear or listen to music or to the passing traffic as well to language.

"Understand" and "comprehend" are no better since, unlike "speak," "say," and "talk," they are used for more than language. We can "understand" something as nonlinguistic as the workings of a mouse-trap. Our language makes it seem that when we "speak" or "talk" we do something special that can only apply to language. When we "understand" or "listen" we seem to use ordinary skills that serve many other purposes than just language.

Grammars that describe the world's languages are packed with rules that explain how words are built up from prefixes, bases, and suffixes. Other rules show how words are joined to form sentences. You must search out very specialized literature to find suggestions about how a sentence might be decomposed into its words, or how the words can be taken apart into their smaller bits. Speaking, admittedly, is much easier to study than comprehension. We just listen to what people say, or even peer into our own minds to find out what we can say ourselves, and then try to figure out how in the world we do it. That is how linguists spend most of their time. It is much more difficult to know how, or even whether, people understand.

Nevertheless, speaking is only one half of the communicative process. Language needs a listener as much as it needs a speaker, and whenever we pay close attention to understanding, we find that everyone—children, adults, and even animals—can understand more than they can say. Comprehension always surpasses the ability to produce. Sometimes, we can even interpret another's actions when he would much rather we understood nothing at all. Consider some examples.

Children. Children learn their first language with what seems, to adoring parents, like magical ease. Parents eagerly follow the steps by which their children learn to use words, first alone and then in increasingly complex combinations. Linguists can scribble the child's words and sentences on paper or record them on tape, and then use the records of paper and tape to build up a picture of their step-by-step progress toward a mature ability to speak. It is much harder to know just how much children understand, but parents quickly discover that those little ears can pick up far more than the child could possibly say. Astonished by their baby's precocious understanding, parents quickly learn to guard their tongues.

Linguists have not always shared the parental confidence in their children's ability to understand. Linguistic skepticism derives, in part, from a vaguely behaviorist bias that makes the "behavior" of speaking seem more important than mere "passive" comprehension, but they have a better reason than this for doubting the reports of doting parents. Comprehension is very difficult to study. How do we know what a child understands? How much does she grasp from the language and how much from the wider context? Hold out a cookie to a child and ask "Do you want a cookie?" When she eagerly responds with gurgles and outstretched hands, it would be foolish to leap to the conclusion that she understands the inquiring words. No one can doubt that she understands the situation.

Distinguishing what a child learns by means of the words from what she picks up with the help of the context is so difficult that linguists, to say nothing of hard-nosed experimental psychologists, are always tempted to turn to the active part of communication, to the "behavior" that can be listened to and recorded. The linguist can even point out that children, now and then, use a word that they do not seem able to understand. Sometimes they even produce a grammatically impeccable construction where its meaning seems out of place. If they can learn words or bits of grammar before they grasp what they mean, it can seem as if production can actually come before comprehension. That, however, is a misinterpretation of what is going on.

To master a word, a child needs to know two things, both its meaning and its pronunciation. Children occasionally learn to pronounce a word without having learned its meaning. This can give the illusion that production is possible without comprehension, but it is really pronunciation that has been learned without meaning. A child who can pronounce a word has certainly heard that pronunciation often enough to recognize it even if he has not yet learned what the word means. By the time a child uses a word with its correct meaning, he has certainly learned to understand its meaning. Pronunciation can be learned before meaning, but children cannot use a word with its correct meaning before being able to recognize the meaning when they hear the word. What goes for words also goes for grammar. Children may use a grammatical form in an inappropriate place because they have not yet learned to understand its meaning. They need to be able to understand its meaning before they can use it in the correct context.

Parents never doubt that their children understand far more than they can say, and I place my trust in the judgement of parents rather than in the judgement of skeptical linguists. One example is especially vivid to me. My own grandson, then called "Jamie," was very late to talk. At the age of two years and two months, his total productive vocabulary consisted of exactly three words, only one of which was at all frequent: a loud insistent *da-da-da-da* meaning "Give it to me," "I want it." At the same age, however, he was able to point to the right place, not only when asked to show his eye, nose, or mouth, but also when asked about his elbow, knee, or shoulder. He could point not only to a window or door, but also to the wall, ceiling, or floor. He understood the names of dozens of people. He could follow quite elaborate instructions, and his total receptive vocabulary was certainly in the hundreds, if not thousands. A month later he apparently decided that it was time to talk, and he very quickly advanced to full sentences.

Jamie's delay in production was extreme, but not unique. All children so consistently understand more than they can say that we have to conclude that an essential part of language learning takes place silently as children absorb the sounds, the words, and the grammatical patterns of the language that swirls around them. Language starts to be absorbed even before a child is born, as the baby inside becomes familiar with the rhythm and intonation of the language that penetrates from the outside. This, at least, seems to be the only explanation for the ability of four-day-old infants to react differently to their mother's native language (as spoken by someone other than their own mothers) than to other languages. Four-and-a-half-month-old babies react differently when they hear their own names than when they hear another name with the same number of syllables and the same stress pattern, so by the age of four and a half months they have already learned to distinguish at least one word. Halfway through their second year, when most children start to produce words, they have had more than a year and a half of intensive exposure to their language. Starting to speak is a magical moment, but it is not the day when language learning begins.

We ought to regard speaking as only the final step in the long process of acquisition. It is the point at which language that is already understood is finally made active. We may not really know how children learn their language until we know how they learn to understand it. We might do better with second-language instruction if we would more often allow learners to be quiet, at first, while they listen to large amounts of the language.

Adults. Even as adults, we always understand more than we can say. English speakers from the opposite shores of the Atlantic and from the opposite sides of the equator can generally understand each other with no more than an occasional minor hitch, but few of us ever try to speak another dialect. We all understand words that we would not risk using ourselves, not only words from distant dialects, but the slang of other ethnic groups or other generations. We understand technical terms from specialties with which we are only partially familiar. We understand and admire rhetorical styles that we cannot duplicate. In New Guinea, people have a nice way of distinguishing receptive and productive skill. They say "I can hear that language but I cannot talk it," acknowledging that it is possible to have a skilled ability to understand a language without the ability to speak.

Chimpanzees and bonobos. As people, over the years, have labored to teach language to apes, their efforts have most often been directed toward production. Comprehension has generally been an afterthought. One of the most ambitious early experiments was with a chimpanzee named Viki who was born in 1971 and raised by Keith and Catherine Hayes. Viki grew up in the Hayes home and in everything from bottles to diapers, the Hayes did their best to treat Viki like their own child. They subjected her to all sorts of experiments, but the experiment that caught the most attention was an intense effort to teach her to articulate a few words of English. She was coaxed to make word-like noises, but the best she ever managed was four breathy vocalizations that, with charity, could be taken as attempts to say "Mama," "Papa," "cut," and "up."

How much could she understand? Unfortunately, the study of chimpanzee comprehension is even more difficult than the study of comprehension by human beings. Like human children, chimps are skillful at drawing inferences from the context, so it is every bit as hard with apes, as with children, to know how much they grasp from the context and how much they are helped by the language. Responding correctly to "Close the drawer," when a drawer had just been opened and when a gesture accompanies the request, may demonstrate a firm grasp of social routines, but it is hardly proof of a high level of language comprehension. The Hayeses did report that Viki could understand a considerable amount of spoken English but they were so eager to teach her to articulate words that they failed to study her comprehension systematically. Their reports of comprehension are anecdotal, and Viki is always remembered for her failure to speak rather than for her success at understanding. Our behaviorist biases have prevented us from taking "mere" comprehension seriously enough.

Now, however, we can put aside our skepticism about comprehension, for in a report that should have attracted more attention than it has, Sue Savage-Rumbaugh and her colleagues have described how the famous bonobo named Kanzi dramatically confirmed the ability of at least one ape to comprehend a significant amount of spoken English. Kanzi was born in captivity at the Yerkes Primate Center in Georgia in October 1980. Between the ages of six months and two and a half years, he was cared for by his foster mother, Matata, while she was being trained to use lexigrams. These are arbitrary visual symbols that were attached to the keys of a keyboard and that lit up when pressed. Both humans and apes could punch these keys and use them, like words, to communicate with each other. Several chimpanzees and bonobos had learned to recognize and use lexigrams, and while Matata was being trained, her baby Kanzi was allowed to wander about the laboratory. In this way he was regularly exposed both to the lexigrams and to natural spoken human language, but he received no deliberate instruction. He did take a certain delight in punching the buttons on the keyboard with their lexigram labels, but he seemed to punch them quite randomly, and he gave no sign that he had learned their meaning.

When Kanzi was about two and a half years old, Matata was separated from him so as to give her a chance to get pregnant, and Kanzi was left behind. He still visited the laboratory and the familiar people who worked there, and it was then, quite suddenly, that he showed more interest in the lexigrams. To the general astonishment of all who knew him, Kanzi, who had never been given any deliberate training, turned out to have learned a number of the lexigrams. Even more surprisingly, he had also absorbed far more spoken English than anyone had imagined.

Unlike Viki, Kanzi was not home-raised. He was housed with the other bonobos but he spent many of his waking hours with humans. In spite of, or perhaps because of, having received much less deliberate instruction than most language-trained apes, he continued to learn even after his mother had gone. By the time he was eight years old, his apparent ability to understand spoken English called for a careful study, and to give a standard for comparison, a parallel study was made of a human child who appeared to understand approximately as much as Kanzi. When the study began, Kanzi was eight and Alia, the child, was between one and a half and two. Alia's mother was one of Kanzi's caretakers, and Alia had watched the apes through a window, but she had never interacted with them directly. Like Kanzi, she had some experience with lexigrams but, like all children, and like Kanzi, she was learning spoken language by living among talkative people rather than by deliberate instruction. Though differing markedly in age, the study confirmed that they had reached about the same level in their ability to understand spoken English.

Kanzi and Alia were tested in similar home-like laboratories. Each laboratory had a bathroom, TV, refrigerator, and places to sit, and each was provided with food and with other small objects to manipulate. The ape and the child were tested separately but in closely parallel ways. After a period of training that gave Kanzi a chance to become familiar with the procedures, Sue Savage-Rumbaugh gave him a series of instructions from behind a one-way mirror so that she could not inadvertently give visual clues to the meaning. After a similar period of training, Alia's mother, Jeannine Murphy, did the same for Alia. At first, both Kanzi and Alia were uncomfortable about responding to a disembodied voice from an unseen person, but with time and practice they both grew willing to cooperate. Other people were sometimes present so that Kanzi and Alia could interact with them. Sometimes these people covered their eyes so that they could not inadvertently give clues to the subjects, and this, too, was disconcerting to both Kanzi and Alia. Now and then, they both simply refused to cooperate.

Manipulable objects, such as food items and toy animals, could be taken from one place to another in the laboratories or in the yards outside. Once Kanzi and Alia had become comfortable with the situation, the experimenter issued an instruction from behind the one-way mirror: "Put the ball on the pine needles." "Give the lighter to Rose." "Give Rose a hug." "Get Rose with the snake." "Knife the sweet potato." "The surprise is hiding in the dishwasher." "Take the [toy] snake outdoors." "Go to the refrigerator and get a banana." "Go get the carrot that's in the microwave." "Make the doggie bite the snake."

Responses to these instructions ranged from acting promptly, immediately, and correctly; through hesitation; to correct responses only after the instruction had been repeated or clarified; doing what was requested but doing something else in addition; doing only part of what was requested; doing the right thing with the wrong object or using the right object for the wrong thing; performing the parts of a task in the wrong order; refusal to cooperate; and finally, doing something that was completely wrong.

Over the course of the experiment Kanzi was given 415 trials. He performed 246 of these, 59 percent, promptly and correctly. He carried out another 61 instructions correctly but only after some hesitation or after the instruction had been repeated or clarified. 100 were carried out partially but not fully. On 4 trials Kanzi did not respond at all, and 4 responses were totally incorrect. Alia was given 407 blind trials. As Table 1 shows, she made a few more flat-out mistakes than Kanzi did, but overall, her results were not much different.

For both Kanzi and Alia, the results are overwhelmingly better than could have been expected by chance. Dozens of responses might have been made to any of the instructions. Many objects might have been

Table 1. Kanzi's and Alia's Comprehension

	Kanzi		Alia	
	N	%	N	%
Prompt and correct	246	59%	220	54%
Correct after hesitation or a repeated instruction	61	15%	47	11%
Partially correct	100	24%	108	27%
No response	4	1%	8	2%
Completely wrong	4	1%	24	6%

manipulated, many locations were available for the objects, and many different actions could have been performed with each of them. No one would hesitate to attribute Alia's success to her ability to understand English. Can there be any further reason to doubt that an eight-year-old bonobo can understand as much?

To be sure, Alia and Kanzi did not behave in identical ways. During the period of her testing, Alia was rapidly learning not only to understand, but to speak, and unlike Kanzi, she frequently commented verbally on what she was doing. By speaking, she confirmed her ability with English, and since Kanzi did not speak, we cannot look for the same kind of confirmation from him. Nevertheless, it would seem perverse to deny Kanzi's ability to understand a large number of English words representing several parts of speech, and even to use the order of words to infer something about the way they are related. Kanzi was able to go out of the room to retrieve an object from a particular place, even though, when he first heard the request, he could see neither the object nor the place. The circumstances in which natural animal calls are used are narrowly restricted. Alarm calls, for example, are produced only in a situation of danger. Because animals use their calls in such limited ways, many of us have been unwilling to accept them as comparable to words. Kanzi, like Alia, understood words in much more varied circumstances than animals understand alarm calls, and the kind of skepticism that has been directed toward animal calls is no more justified for Kanzi's understanding, than for Alia's.

We do not have to credit either Kanzi or Alia with the ability to understand every word in a sentence or every detail of its syntax. A request such as "Take the sparklers outdoors" might be obeyed correctly with little more than an understanding of "sparklers" and "outdoors." That, itself, is no mean achievement, but we do not have to assume that they understood "the," and even "take" might have been guessed from the context, although other guesses would have been plausible. If only "sparklers" and "outdoors" were understood, the sentence might mean "Look for the sparklers outdoors," or "Bring the sparklers from outdoors."

It is clear that Kanzi, like Alia, could do more than simply understand words. He was able to respond correctly to three types of sentences where word order was significant. He responded correctly to 33 out of 42 examples (79 percent) with forms like "Put the ball on the rock" or "Put the rock on your ball" where word order was crucial. Even his mistakes were not usually simple reversals, but various other kinds of errors. With instructions such as "Take the umbrella out-doors" or "Go outdoors and get the umbrella," Kanzi responded correctly on 38 out of 46 trials. When he heard a sentence of the first kind, he would survey the objects around him, apparently searching, but with sentences of the second kind he would more often move directly to the place instructed without bothering to look at the things nearby. In such sentences, to be sure, the verbs are also different, so that word order is not the only clue to the meaning, but neither Kanzi nor Alia had trouble understanding a considerable number of different words and a variety of sentence types.

Kanzi's receptive skills give better evidence of linguistic ability than has ever been demonstrated by any other nonhuman primate who has been trained to use symbols, whether these were spoken words, deaf signs, plastic chips, or buttons that needed pressing. Indeed, Kanzi's comprehension demonstrates a degree of linguistic competence that linguists have often presumed to be exclusively human. No one need fear that a bonobo, or any other ape, is about to give serious compe-tition to human children. Kanzi, after all, was eight years old when he was tested, while Alia was not yet two. Nevertheless, it is hard to deny that Kanzi had learned a good deal of English.

The pattern is consistent. It is not only humans who understand more than they can say. So does Kanzi. If Kanzi could learn to under-stand so much, it is reasonable to suppose that when our ancestors first separated from the line that led to the chimps and bonobos they would already have been able to understand a good deal. To make use of their abilities, however, they had to wait until there was something to be understood.

Animal signals. It is not only among language-using humans and apes that comprehension runs ahead of production. Comprehension also came first as animal signals became established under the pres-sures of natural selection. The gestures and vocalizations by which animals communicate probably began as purely instrumental acts— movements and vocalizations that are part of the ordinary business of living: moving around, eating, scratching, yawning. Instrumental acts are performed to meet the needs of the animal, but with no intention to communicate. Even without intending to communicate, animals may profit by being able to interpret one another's movements and sounds, but only after some behavior has come to convey a meaning to another animal, can it develop into a specifically communicative signal. The classic example is the retracted lip of a dog's snarl.

At first, the lip must have been drawn back as a simple instrumental gesture. It would have been nothing more than one part of getting ready to bite. A dog that did not want to bite his own lip needed to get the lip out of the way of his teeth. A few million years could have passed before potential victims began to recognize a retracted lip as a sign of an imminent bite, but any victim that was clever enough to read the lip movement as a warning might have had a chance to flee and to avoid the bite. By escaping, an animal would improve his chance of staying alive long enough to reproduce, so natural selection would have insured the spread of skillful comprehension.

Comprehension had to be the first step, but once the instrumental act was understood, a new opportunity was opened to an aggressor. By retracting his lip as if to bite, the aggressor might frighten off his enemy even while avoiding the much riskier activity of really biting. Now it was the turn of natural selection to favor those individuals who were clever enough to pull back their lip in order to scare away their enemies without a fight. From that point on, production and comprehension of the signal could evolve together. To make the sign less ambiguous, aggressors might even develop exaggerated or stereotyped lip movements. The sign would then have evolved from a purely instrumental act into a stereotypic communicative signal.

By evolving into a communicative signal, the retracted lip became useful for both the aggressor and his potential victim. The victim might escape, and the aggressor might avoid a fight. All this happened, of course, under the slow but relentless pressure of natural selection. The end result was to build in a signal, but learning could have nudged the process along. At first, some victims may have been able to learn by experience that lip retraction is likely to be followed by pain. If they also learned that running away was the best way to avoid pain, they would boost their own chance for survival and give their genes a better chance to reach the next generation. Natural selection would favor those who could learn most quickly and easily. Eventually, no more than a slight triggering experience would be needed to persuade a potential victim that bared teeth were a serious matter, and finally, animals might react to the gesture with flight even without needing any experience at all. Potential victims could then be said to have the fear of a curled lip firmly built in.

Like their victims, the earliest lip curlers also probably needed to learn by experience. They would learn that some animals flee at the sight of a retracted lip, and discover how useful the gesture could be even when they had no intention of biting. Again, natural selection would have favored those who could most easily learn how the gesture affected others, but after some thousands of generations the behavior became almost, or fully, automatic. Behavior is not neatly divided into some bits that are learned and other bits that are built in. Rather, some bits are learned more easily and some less easily. The history of the curled lip shows us how hopeless it is to ask whether heredity or environment is to be credited for some behavior. Both are essential.

The process by which natural selection builds in signals is known as "ritualization." The ritualization of the lip twitch turned an instrumental act into a communicative signal, but ritualization could not even begin until the twitch was understood. Other animal signals began much as did the retracted lip. Only after meaning is discovered in instrumental gestures or vocalizations can they be ritualized into stereotypic signals.

I will be returning to comprehension repeatedly in the later chapters of this book, but any discussion of language evolution must also consider many other issues, and I want to clear the ground now by staking out positions on four of these issues: first, whether language evolved from animal calls or as a part of an evolving mind; second, whether technology or social relationships gained the most from language; third, the speed with which language developed, whether gradually or abruptly; and fourth, the relative significance of vocabulary and syntax in the development of language. All four of these issues have been debated more vigorously by students of language origins than has comprehension, but on all of them, opinion has been divided.

Animal calls and the mind. The first kind of evidence to which people turn, when looking for hints about the antecedents of language is, more often than not, the communication of other animals, particularly the communication of our nearest animal kin, the primates. Like most other mammals, primates communicate with their voices as well as by movements and gestures. With their cries, whoops, and chatters they coordinate their activities, call for help, show their anger, make threats, and even warn one another of danger. Since most human languages are also produced with the voice, and since language is also used to coordinate activities, call for help, and show emotions, hardly anyone can resist searching among primate calls for the forerunners of human language. It seems only reasonable to ask how natural selection might have transformed a set of primate calls into the kind of language that humans speak.

Language, however, is organized in such utterly different ways from primate or mammalian calls and it conveys such utterly different kinds of meanings, that I find it impossible to imagine a realistic sequence by which natural or sexual selection could have converted a call system into a language. Human beings, moreover still have a fine set of primate calls that remains quite separate from language. Primate calls have much less in common with human language than with human screams, sighs, sobs, and laughter. Our own audible cries, howls, giggles, and snorts, along with our visible scowls, smiles, and stares, all belong securely to our primate heritage. They form the primate communication of the human primate. We produce our gestures and noises with the same parts of our bodies that other primates use for their signals, and we use them to convey the same kinds of messages. Primate communication and some aspects of human nonverbal communication resemble each other very closely, but human language is different from both of them. We will understand more about the origins of language by considering the ways in which language differs from the cries and gestures of human and nonhuman primates than by looking for ways in which they are alike.

Even if language owes little to primate calls, however, we still have plenty to learn from other primates. Apes, in particular, have minds that resemble our own, sometimes more closely than we find comfortable. Chimps and bonobos show us the kind of mind where the first glimmerings of language must have appeared. In spite of ingenious and energetic efforts by field primatologists, little of what we have learned about wild chimps, bonobos, gorillas, or orangutans suggests that their natural communication is more like human language than is the communication of other, more distantly related mammals. Primate calls and communicative gestures may be a bit more complex than the calls and gestures used by other mammals, but they do not seem to be organized in a different way. Primate minds, on the other hand, share a great deal with ours. We will learn much more about the beginning of language by examining how primates use their minds than by learning how they use their voices. Language, after all, is not only a way to communicate. It has also become a tool that helps us to think clearly. As language has developed, the human mind has been transformed. Human beings also have another kind of communication that remains more like the communication of other animals. I will look on language as one product of the evolving human mind.

Technology and social relations. A second easy assumption about the origin of language is that it developed primarily as an instrument to assist with the business of making a living. Today, language is so essential for technical and practical affairs that we easily presume that, from its earliest days, its main use was to coordinate the hunt, agree on where to meet, tell others where to find ripe fruit, warn about a marauding lion, or instruct the young on how to make a hand-axe. I join others such as the evolutionary psychologists Nicholas Humphrey, Robin Dunbar, and Geoffrey Miller, who argue, instead, that we need language most urgently for dealing with one other. Language has always been used, first of all, for the fine-tuning of social relationships.

Language is more than simply a means of exchanging information. It is also a medium for art, humor, poetry, storytelling, and oratory. It gave our ancestors, as it gives us, a means to display themselves. Language may have helped our ancestors to cooperate, but at least as important, it gave them new ways to compete. With language we have acquired a powerful new tool with which we can try to outmaneuver and outmanipulate one another. If you want to engage in social climbing, you had better hone your language skills. I want to understand the emergence of language as one aspect of the evolution of our minds, and as a means by which our minds can build increasingly complex social relationships. This should mean that the better we understand the evolution of our minds and our social relationships, the better we will understand the emergence of language.

Sudden or gradual emergence. The question of whether language emerged gradually or suddenly has generated more debate than it should have among students of language evolution. Some, particularly linguists, are so impressed by the uniqueness of language and by the interdependence of its parts, that they have argued that it must have arisen quite suddenly. Derek Bickerton once even insisted that the most important aspects of language, in particular its syntax, could only have come about as the result of a single crucial mutation. Others, particularly primatologists who have searched for continuities between ape and human communication, have argued that language must have developed slowly and incrementally. I side with the gradualists, not because I want to derive language from primate calls, but because I believe that this is the way evolution works. Wings distinguish birds from reptiles as sharply as language distinguishes human beings from other primates, and the parts of a wing are as interdependent as the parts of language, but nobody would argue that wings were achieved by a single mutation. Of course we now have fossils that show us some of the steps by which front legs evolved into wings, but even without the fossils we would be certain that there were, once upon a time, animals that were intermediate between walking reptiles and flying birds. We will never have fossil evidence for language, but it makes no more sense to imagine that language arose abruptly than to suppose that wings arose abruptly. There had to be intermediate stages.

Readers familiar with the debates about language evolution will have noticed that I take opposing positions on two issues that are often presumed to be linked. Many of those, especially linguists who have been most impressed by the unique features of language, have been dismissive of the relevance of primate calls, and it is they who have most often argued in favor of the abrupt beginnings of language. Many of those, especially primatologists, who have searched most diligently for language-like features in primate communication, have argued for a slower, more gradual development of language. On the issue of the relevance of primate calls, I side with the linguists, but on the issue of gradualism I side with the primatologists. If wings could evolve through many intermediate steps, so could language, but this does not mean that language had to evolve from calls.

Words and syntax. Linguists, or at least some linguists, love syntax. Their devotion can seem odd to others who have less-than-fond memories of diagraming sentences or of the grammar that came with high-school French. For a certain kind of mind, however, syntax has an intricate beauty. It is extraordinarily complex, but close investigation reveals startling regularities. It is so utterly unlike anything used by other animals that it is easy to draw the conclusion that syntax is what makes language unique.

It is well to remember, however, just what syntax is used for. It is needed to serve the lexicon. We use syntax to arrange our words in efficient and unambiguous ways, and it would have no purpose at all without the words. For most ordinary speakers, if not for linguists, meaning is what language is all about, and while syntax certainly contributes to meaning, words do more. Because syntax needs words, while even single lonely words that have no syntax can easily convey meanings, words must have come first in the course of human evolution.

This is not to dismiss the evolution of the specific capacity for syntax as unimportant. Indeed, its very complexity gives syntactic evolution a special fascination and presents us with special puzzles. Far more scholarly ingenuity has gone into trying to imagine how syntax could have evolved than into puzzling about the evolution of the capacity to use words. We can imagine that vocabulary just needs a lot of cranial storage capacity but that syntax demands some very special cortical circuitry. Nevertheless, words had to came first and I will put a bit more weight on the lexicon than have some others who have shared my interest in language origins.

In the chapters that follow, these four themes will recur, interwoven with the insistence that comprehension always comes before production. Together, these suggest a plausible step-by-step picture of the emergence of language, and of the central role that language played in the evolution of our species.

A puzzle has always hovered over the first appearance of language: If no one else was around with the skills to understand, what could the first speaker have hoped to accomplish with her first words? The puzzle dissolves as soon as we recognize that communication does not begin when someone makes a meaningful vocalization or gesture, but when someone interprets another's behavior as meaningful. The original behavior that was interpreted in a language-like way could not have been intended to communicate anything at all. A lonely producer who experimented with a new kind of signal would surely fail to communicate, but she would be unlikely ever to try. A lonely interpreter, on the other hand, might gain considerable advantage by being able to understand another's actions, even when no communication had been intended. At every stage of evolution, the selective pressures favoring skill at comprehension must have been more insistent than the selective pressures favoring skill at production. Producers often benefit by not giving themselves away. Only profit can result from successful interpretation.

The precocity of comprehension implies that at every point along the evolutionary path toward language, interpretation needed to be at least one step ahead of production. Only when behavior was being interpreted correctly, could an animal deliberately use that behavior as a communicative signal. More precisely: *The only innovations in signal production that can be successful, and so consolidated by natural selection, are those that conform to the pre-existing receptive competence of other individuals.* At every point, production would have been limited by and directed by the interpretive ability that already existed in the population. Only after others had grasped the meaning of some bit of instrumental behavior, would anyone be able to expand his productive repertoire with a new linguistic trick. This disposes of any mystery about the communicative usefulness of the first word-like signs. They would not have been produced with communicative intent. Their communicative value came from the skill of the receiver, not from the intent of the producer.

The question that we should ask, therefore, is not "Why did the first speaker try to communicate if no one was around who shared her talents?" The answer to this is easy: "She didn't. It would have been useless." A much better question is "Why would anyone engage in language-like behavior when she had no intention of communicating?" Here, a plausible answer is that the first acts that could be interpreted in a language-like way were instrumental ones. Everyone has to act instrumentally and others can benefit by being able to interpret their acts. Only as skill at interpretation grew, did the time finally come when actors could conventionalize the actions that others were already understanding, and turn these actions into deliberate communicative signals.

This implies that word-like signs began in the same way as animal signals such as a retracted lip, but from the beginning, proto-words differed from animal signals in one crucial respect. Most animal signals have been ritualized by the long process of natural selection. Early word-like signs, as much as modern words, needed to be learned by each individual within a single lifetime. Our ancestors must have been selected for their ability to give conventional meanings to visible or audible signals, but the conventionalizations of even the earliest words were never passed down by the genes. Rather, they had to be learned anew by the members of each generation. In Chapter 6, I will return to a more detailed consideration of the process by which conventionalized and language-like signals could have begun.

If comprehension must always run ahead of production, not only in the history of each animal sign and in the language abilities of our children, but also at the earliest stages of language, we ought to ask rather different questions than we have usually asked about language origins. We should ask what selective pressures could have driven our prehuman and early human ancestors toward ever greater skill at interpreting the instrumental acts of other individuals. We should ask how, at each later stage, people could have understood the gestures or vocalizations of their fellows in increasingly word-like, and then sentence-like, ways. The origins of comprehension are, after all, considerably less mysterious than the origins of production. Animals, including human animals, have little to lose and a great deal to gain by learning as much as possible from the behavior of others: What is that fellow likely to do? What does she want? Why is she moving off in that direction? What does that grunt mean? The more that an animal can infer from the behavior of others, the more adroitly it can plan its own behavior.

A focus on improved comprehension gives us a different picture of the sequence by which new features enter language than does a focus on production. If, for example, we assume that our forebears used single words before joining them together into orderly sequences, too much attention to production might lead us to puzzle about why anyone would bother to join them. If, instead, we ask how comprehension evolved, we might wonder how understanders could start to make inferences from words that they heard in vague proximity, even when the producer had made no effort to arrange them in any sort of orderly way.

These are questions that arise naturally as soon as we recognize the crucial role of comprehension, and I will return repeatedly to such questions in chapters that follow. Before that, however, I need to establish the beginning and end points, first by describing the various forms of human communication and the place of language among the other forms, and second by showing just how different language is from animal communication. These will be the topics of the next two chapters. Once these topics have been addressed, it will be possible to focus on the steps by which a species without language could have evolved into a species whose members could talk.

2

Smiles, winks, and words

Human beings never run out of talk. We relate the events of the day. We gossip about our acquaintances. We speculate about people and power. Children chatter so incessantly that even their talkative parents lose patience. We explain, we cajole, we schmooze, we harangue, and we flirt, all with the help of language. To be sure, we also convey information in many other ways than by talking. We use our voices not only to speak, but to scream, sigh, laugh, hum, and cry. We show our joy with our smiles, and our anger with our scowls. We threaten by standing tall, and show submission by trying to look small. By the way we touch each other, we can show either fury or love. We even learn something from the way others smell. If we are to ask how language emerged in the human species, we need to start by understanding where it fits among the many other ways, audible, visible, olfactory, and tactile, by which humans communicate.

I had a vivid lesson about our different forms of communication when, as a young man, I landed by small boat at the little port of Marmaris on the southern coast of Turkey. Within half an hour of landing, I found myself negotiating for a room with a woman who ran a small guest house. She and I had no common language but the situation made my needs obvious. We stood in a courtyard and she held out her hand, palm downward, with her fingers together and extended toward me. She then bent her hand sharply so that her fingers turned downward, while the back of her hand remained horizontal, This was clearly a stereotyped gesture, intended to convey a specific meaning to me, but I did not understand what that meaning was.

I could think of two possibilities. Perhaps she wanted me to follow her or, perhaps, she wanted me to wait. I hesitated for just a moment but then decided to make a test. I deliberately took one step backward, and the woman scowled and looked a bit frustrated. I knew immediately that she wanted me to follow her, and she then led me to a room.

The woman had made two communicative gestures, and even then I was startled at how different they were. Her palm-down beckoning gesture, I would later learn, is used everywhere from Turkey through India and on to Southeast Asia, but as my previous ignorance showed, it is by no means universal. It is conventional and it has to be learned. Her scowl, on the other, hand, needed no learning at all. It was part of the heritage that the woman and I shared with every other human being. I could even use her scowl to help me define the meaning of her hand gesture.

The scowl is an example of a large class of signals that are common to all humanity. These signals need little learning and they allow us to communicate in quite subtle ways with people of all cultures. They include many of the ways in which we express ourselves with our faces, voices, hands and arms, and even with the posture and movements of our entire bodies: our laughs, screams, smiles, frowns, and shrugs. I will argue that these gestures and vocalizations, which all humans share, should be seen as forming a second kind of human communication, one that is quite different from language. I need a name for this group of signals and I will call them "gesture-calls". This is, admittedly, a somewhat contrived term, but it is useful as a way of anticipating the next chapter, where I will describe the similarities between these signals and the calls and communicative gestures of other mammals. The word "calls," of course, is not generally used for human signals, but only for the communicative vocalizations of animals. We do not think of human laughs and sobs as "calls" but that is only because we do not usually think of human beings as "animals," but our laughs, sobs, sighs, and screams can be counted among the distinctive calls of the human species just as pant-hoots and long calls are among the distinctive calls of chimpanzees, and just as barks, growls, and howls are among the distinctive calls of dogs. I cannot fully justify the use of the term "gesture-calls" for human beings until the next chapter, but what matters now is to recognize that our human repertory of signals includes many that have meanings that are similar to the signals of other mammals, and that are produced with our voices, our faces, and our postures, just as theirs are.

I will use the word "language" only in its narrow sense, to refer to the system of sounds, words, and sentences to which we give names like "English," "Zulu," or "Chinese." "Body language" is something else. I will begin with an account of some characteristics of language (in this narrow sense) and of the ways in which our other forms of communication are similar to and different from language. These other forms of communication are sometimes referred to simply as our "nonverbal communication," but this expression bundles together too many different kinds of signaling to be very useful. They need to be distinguished not only from language but from one another.

By the end of the next chapter, I will have reached the conclusion that language could not have evolved from any animal-like form of communication, simply because it is so different from all other animal behavior. The headings used in the following pages identify a series of ways in which language differs from other forms of human communication and from the communication used by other species. It is the evolution of these unique characteristics of language that we must understand if we are ever to know how language originated.

Digital and analog communication. Information can be conveyed in either analog or digital form, not only inside a computer, but in any medium at all. The steadily sweeping second hand of a clock, the swinging needle of an automobile speedometer, and a slide rule that can be manipulated into an unlimited number of positions are all analog devices. The meanings of a clock hand, speedometer needle, and slide rule vary in proportion to their positions, and in principle, there is no way to count the number of readings these instruments can give. A digital clock that bumps time abruptly from 8:45 to 8:46 but permits no compromise, presents its information with digital rather than analog signals. So does an abacus where each bead can be positioned either up or down but can never come to rest halfway between. Digital signals have sharp boundaries. They are discrete. Digital devices can assume no more than a finite number of states. The beads of an abacus have a limited number of positions. A pocket calculator has only a finite (though huge) number of possible displays. Human beings communicate with both digital and analog signals.

The sound system of a language, its phonology, is prototypically digital. The meaningless units of our phonological systems are the phonemes that we represent, imperfectly, by the letters of our wretched spelling system. These phonemes are, as linguists say, in "contrast" with one another. This means that it is no more possible to compromise between the *p* and *b* of *pat* and *bat* than between 11:13 and 11:14 on face of a digital clock. There is always a midpoint between any two positions of a speedometer needle even if the midpoints quickly become microscopic. The contrastive sounds of a language can be joined to form the many thousands of words that language users need, and the words, too, are in contrast. Contrasting words, in turn, allow sentences to be in contrast with one another. It is the digital phonological code that allows us to construct an enormous number of words and an unlimited number of sentences, and to keep them all distinct from one another.

Most of our signals, other than language, are graded rather than discrete. A giggle is not sharply distinct from a laugh, nor is a laugh clearly distinct from a guffaw. A sound that is halfway between a giggle and a laugh means something halfway between them as well. Perhaps giggles even grade into snorts, snorts into cries of objection, cries of objection into cries of anguish, and cries of anguish into sobs. This suggests a continuum that runs all the way from laughs to sobs with no sharp break at any point along the way. This is grading with a vengeance, with no boundaries in sight. The continuum may not reach quite all the way from a laugh to a sob, but human gesture-calls do show extensive grading, and this makes them utterly different from language. A halfway point between two words like *single* and *shingle* simply does not exist. A halfway point between a giggle and a laugh is perfectly real and perfectly understandable.

We can't count the number of our gesture-calls. What happens if we try? We have names for some of our gestures and for some of our calls, and these may tempt us to try to count the signals by counting the words: *laugh, snort, smile, frown, cry, sigh, squint, scream, pout, swagger,* and dozens of others. Listing the names is easy enough, but we soon run into problems. Do we count a giggle and a guffaw as different from a laugh? Or are they simply different forms of a single call? What about something halfway between a giggle and a laugh? What about a cry, a sob, and a whimper? There is an indeterminacy here that is intrinsic to an analog system. We can give names to spots or segments along the continuum, but there is no principled way to decide how many spots or segments to name, or where to draw a line between the end of one and the beginning of the next. There is no way to decide how different two signals must be in order to be counted as different.

The digital system that is provided by linguistic contrast allows human languages to be constructed according to profoundly different principles than what I am calling our "gesture-calls". To say that gesture-calls lack contrast is simply another way of saying that both in their meaning and in the manner by which they are produced, smiles, laughs, frowns, and screams vary along continuous scales. Language is digital, gesture-calls are analog.

Immediately, complications need to be acknowledged. The intonation of language, the ups and downs of pitch and emphasis, vary continuously so they form analog signals. On the other hand, the beckoning gesture of the Turkish guest-house keeper had to be sharply distinct from her other gestures. Clearly, it would be too simple to imagine that language is uniformly digital and that everything else is analog. Examples such as these enormously complicate the description and understanding of human communication, and I will need to return to them later and put them in place. In the meantime, we can still recognize that the phonological and syntactic core of language (but not its intonation) is digital, while large parts of the rest of our communication is analog. The difference between digital and analog signals is crucial.

Reference, propositions, and emotions. The digital nature of the phonological code lets us distinguish thousands of words from one another. These words can be used to talk about our ideas, both our ideas about the world and ideas that are pure imagination. With language, we can tell someone where to buy fish. We can extol the virtues of a politician or an applicant for a job. We can whisper a fascinating tidbit about what Velma said to Mervin last night. We can ask questions, make requests, or give orders. We can spin yarns, tell lies, share jokes, and invent imaginary beings. Words give us names, not only for objects but also for actions, qualities, relations, sentiments, and indeed, for anything at all that we can think about. By combining words into sentences we can express propositions, and in this way convey messages about all the things that we name with our words. This kind of propositional information can be easily shared with others, so it conveys information about the state of the world, or at least, about what we imagine the state of the world to be. Our ability to form propositions even allows us to talk about language. We can use language to describe language.

Our analog cries, facial expressions, and postures are of only limited use for describing the world around us. They are much better at conveying delicate shades of emotion and intention. With frowns, smiles, shrugs, sighs, whimpers, and chuckles, we let others know how we feel, and suggest what we are likely to do next. Postures and facial expressions are likely to give a more reliable guide than words about whether to expect a kiss or slap. We use our postures, our gestures, and our facial expressions to ease relationships with others and to show that we know our place in the social world.

We convey many of our feelings more easily, more subtly, and less self-consciously with our calls and facial expressions than we do with language. Many of us dislike discussing serious or sensitive matters over the telephone, in part, at least, because we cannot read the gestures and facial expressions of the person on the other end of the line. We feel crippled by being limited to mere language. We hear one another's words, but we are left uncertain about one another's feelings. Mere language does not make up for the missing gesture-calls.

We can show our anger, our boredom, or our playfulness, with our gesture-calls. We can show others how much we love them. But we cannot tell stories. We cannot describe the difference between a pine tree and an oak, let alone the difference between an odd and even number. We cannot agree on a time and place to meet for lunch. We could easily enough invent gestures with which to plan a lunch date, but the gestures would have to refer to times, places, and events in the world, and in the very act of agreeing on them we would have to devise gestures that have more in common with language than with gesture-calls.

If we find it difficult to form true propositions about the world with our gestures and calls, we find it even more difficult to form false propositions. If we cannot tell true stories, we can hardly tell fairy tales. We cannot lie. We can, to be sure, feign, or at least we can try. The poker player must act as if his cards are different than they really are. The boxer pretends that he is about to hit from the left when he is really planning to hit from the right. We can try to pretend to a happiness we do not really feel or we can try to hide our excitement or pleasure. Feigning emotions, however, is not the same as lying, and most of us are not very good at it. The majority of human beings, who are neither con men nor skilled actors, find it much easier to lie with words than to mislead with gesture-calls.

So the most important thing about language is also the most obvious one. Language allows us, with great ease, to refer to things and events, and to say something about them. Gesture-calls are much better at expressing our emotions and intentions. Nevertheless, the association of digital language with referential messages on the one hand, and analog gestures and calls with emotional messages on the other, while high, is not perfect. Skillful poets can express emotions beautifully with words. Most of us need help from our gesture-calls. When I bite into an apple, my puckered face tells you something about its taste, and my face can also tell you whether something that I have just seen is desirable or frightening. So we can convey some information about the state of the world with our gesture-calls, and we can convey some emotions with language. More often and more easily we use digital language for facts and analog gestures and calls for emotions.

Heredity and environment. I need to begin this hoary subject by insisting on one thing: everything that human beings are or do (or that other animals are or do), everything about our bodies, our minds, and our behavior, comes about by the joint action of heredity and environment. Nothing could develop if the genes did not make it possible, and nothing could develop without a suitable environment. It is nonsense to ask whether heredity or environment should be credited for some human trait like stature, language, rock music, spelling, or intelligence. Both heredity and environment have a role in everything.

We find it easier to accept the interaction of inheritance and experience for physical traits like stature or complexion than for behavioral and intellectual traits like aggression, music, or a sense of humor. We feel comfortable with the idea that stature depends on both the genes we inherited from our parents and the food we ate while growing up. Skin color depends not only on how a particular set of genes has instructed a body to produce pigment, but also on how long that body has been exposed to the sun. We have more trouble recognizing that bashfulness, courting behavior, bicycle riding, spoken language, and literacy also emerge from the interaction of hereditary endowment and environmental opportunities, but our behavior is just as much the result of this interaction as is our body. The way we sit depends on both the way our genes have built our bones and the habits of the society in which we have grown up. The food we enjoy depends not only on the inherited nature of human digestion but on our idiosyncratic experiences with food. Our ability to dance, to catch fish, and to do long division, all require both inherited aptitudes and the right experiences. We ask the wrong question when we ask whether heredity or environment is responsible for a piece of our bodies or a bit of our behavior. We can be certain that both have played a role.

What makes us most uncomfortable is to attribute individual differences in behavior to heredity. We accept hereditary variability in the shape of our noses or the amount of hair on our arms, but many of us would like to believe in human perfectibility, to believe that anyone can learn to do anything if only the opportunities are right. Individual differences in inherited aptitude will not go away simply because we wish they did not exist, however, and the world would really be a much duller place if we all started life exactly alike. To make everyone average would call for a lot of dumbing down as well as smarting up, and you and I would be poorer for having no Darwins, Beethovens, and Picassos to show us what is possible.

What, then, do we do about our strong intuitions that nature is more important for some things and nurture for others? Eye color seems pretty well set by the genes. Whether we call the bottom end of our leg our *foot, pied,* or *Fuss* seems to have everything to do with experience and nothing at all to do with biology. We can deal with this intuition by asking what proportion of the variation that is found in some physical or behavioral trait is due to differences in heredity and what proportion of that variation is due to differences in experience.

A trait whose variability depends on variable genes is said to be "heritable." Variability that results from experience is not. Heritability, however, is not an all or none matter. Different traits show different degrees of heritability. Stature depends on nutrition as well as inheritance, but it does have a high degree of heritability. The particular name that we use for the end of our leg has a very low heritability. We can legitimately ask how much of the variation that we find in some trait is due to differing kinds of experiences and how much is due to differing innate aptitude, but it is simplistic to ask whether it is one or the other.

My insistence that heredity and environment are every bit as intricately interwoven in our behavior as in our bodies, is needed because it is so terribly tempting, but also so terribly wrong, to suppose that our laughter, our cries, our frowns, and our scowls are determined by inheritance while language has to be learned. Of course we need to learn a particular language, but we could not talk at all if we had not inherited a mind that is designed for language learning. Dogs, even dogs that live in Tanzania, never learn Swahili because they have not been given the right kind of minds. Nor do Japanese very often learn Swahili, but this has nothing to do with Japanese genes or minds. To learn Swahili you need both the right kind of inheritance and the right kind of experience.

What is true for language is also true for our gesture-calls. Once past the first few weeks of life, every reasonably normal human being smiles. The magical ability of babies to smile needs both the right kind of inheritance and the environment of womb and cradle that allows a smile to develop. Short of violence or starvation, it is nearly impossible to stop a baby from smiling, but you and I would not smile under exactly the same circumstances had we grown up in a different culture. We must learn the rules laid down by our own society for the appropriate times, places, and circumstances for smiles, and for all our other gesture-calls.

Both our language and our gesture-calls, then, depend on both genes and experience, but the mixtures differ. The variation from one community to another is much greater for language than for gesture-calls, and this can only mean that language is less narrowly constrained by inheritance than are gesture-calls. Gesture-calls such as laughter are highly heritable. Whatever variability distinguishes the laughs of different individuals depends largely on inherited differences, not on variable experience. The contribution of learning is greater for language. A foreigner understands nothing of Chinese without some learning, and it takes a great deal of learning to understand or to say very much. New arrivals in China can understand much of what is conveyed by Chinese laughs and sobs, giggles and snorts, cries of anguish and all the rest of their gesture-calls, from the moment they step off the plane in Beijing. Because humans everywhere are genetically very much alike, our facial expressions, like our cries and laughs, convey much the same meanings everywhere.

Wherever you travel, a smile will suggest more friendliness than a scowl. Nowhere will you find people who habitually laugh when sad but cry in response to a joke. When anthropologists need to find their way in a new community but have not yet learned much of the language, they can easily judge the reactions of their hosts by reading their facial expressions. They do not need language to know whether people are friendly or hostile.

A half century ago, the mind of a newborn baby was often imagined to be a "blank slate." It was supposed to contain little when it first entered the world except an ability to absorb whatever the environment offered. Language, like the rest of our behavior, was then attributed almost entirely to learning. If anything called a "mind" was even considered, it was regarded as a sort of general-purpose learning device that could learn one thing about as easily as another. The mind was thought to be pushed in one direction or another by its experiences, and learning seemed to dominate heredity. Nothing was assumed about the inherited nature of the human brain or mind.

Part of the intellectual upheaval brought about by Noam Chomsky was his challenge to this extreme behaviorism. He has always insisted that human beings come equipped with a mind and brain that are designed, in highly specific ways, for language. He has insisted that a child could not possibly master the fierce complexities of a language in a few short years, if all he had to work with was a blank slate and a generalized ability to learn. Chomsky persuaded a large body of linguists that a successful language learner needs much more built in than generalized learning skills, and he shifted the focus of much of linguistics away from the differences among languages to the universal features that are presumed to arise because of the universal nature of the human mind. The mind came to be thought of as specifically designed for language.

Chomsky succeeded in pushing opinion so far away from the older behaviorism that a few linguists seem almost to have forgotten about learning. Thus, what would otherwise hardly need to be said at all, now needs to be insistently proclaimed: languages do, after all, differ. The differences among them can only result from varying experience, which is to say, from learning. Chomsky is surely right to insist that our genetic inheritance provides us with the capacity to learn a language. It is not simply a metaphor to say that we have a "language instinct." Nevertheless, a vast amount of learning is still needed in order to fulfill the potential of our inheritance. As with all other aspects of our bodies and behavior, we could never speak without both inheritance and learning. Indeed, one of the most interesting questions about human evolution is to ask how our genetic endowment managed to evolve to the point where it lets us learn so much. Our digital and propositional language requires much more learning than our analog and emotional calls and gestures.

A massive vocabulary and duality of patterning. Languages have tens of thousands of words. Every one of us has managed to learn a massive vocabulary. This is so utterly unlike anything found in any other communication system, that it has to count as one of the most distinctive characteristics of language and, indeed, of humanity.

Our huge stock of words would not be possible without the digital phonological code. Most languages have a thousand or more possible syllables, enough to allow a million distinct two-syllable words. By some counts, to be sure, Hawaiian allows only 160 syllables, but it manages easily because most of its words have at least two syllables and many have three or more. Vocabulary size, obviously, is not limited by the phonological code. Every natural language allows its speakers to name thousands upon thousands of objects, actions, and qualities, and to make whatever subtle distinctions in meaning they need or desire. By our nature, we have the capacity to learn both a phonological code and the thousands of words that are formed with this code. Nothing remotely like this is possible with gesture-calls. These give us no names at all, and they are poorly designed to make the kinds of distinctions in meaning that come so easily with language.

It is not quite accurate to say that we have more words than gesture-calls, however. In principle, gesture-calls have infinite variability. Just as a graded slide rule allows an infinite number of positions, so graded gesture-calls allow an infinite variety of laughs. In practice, of course, we cannot discriminate so many kinds of laughter, and it is words that give us real flexibility. We cannot add new gesture-calls to our repertory in the way we can add new words to our language, and gesture-calls permit nothing like the tens of thousands of words that every adult speaker so easily controls. We ought to regard our huge vocabulary as at least as important as syntax in defining our uniqueness.

The phonological code gives language two distinct levels of organization. This has sometimes been called "double articulation" and sometimes "duality of patterning." First, we have the contrasting units of the sound system, the phonemes. These are meaningless, but they can be strung together by one set of patterns into larger chunks to which we assign meanings. These larger bits are the morphemes. They include the prefixes, suffixes, and word bases that are further organized by a different set of patterns into the words, phrases, and sentences that we toss back and forth to one another. No such dual structure characterizes our gesture-calls. Each call has a characteristic sound and each gesture has a characteristic shape and movement, but they are not constructed from smaller, meaningless parts.

Arbitrariness. With the phonological code of our language, we can assign a distinct sequence of sounds to every meaning for which we need a name, and we can assign the sounds to the meanings in entirely arbitrary ways. As long as everyone else calls it a "shovel" you are well advised to do so too, but if everyone agreed, the same object could just as well be called a "snurk" or a "blongsel." The form of a gesture-call such as a laugh might also be called "arbitrary." A laugh does not, in any objective sense, resemble humor, any more than the word "shovel" resembles a shovel. We can imagine a species where sobbing was a sign of humor and where laughter indicated grief, but human beings are simply not the kind of animals that can switch the meaning of these signs. The meaning and the form of laughter and sobs are narrowly set by our inheritance, with convention making only a very modest contribution. "Shovel" is conventional as well as arbitrary. The same object is called by many other names in other languages. Language is pervasively conventional as well as arbitrary.

Syntax and productivity. For many linguists, it is the complexity of syntax that gives the most compelling evidence for the unique character of the human mind. Since gesture-calls are not organized by any sort of syntax, they seem, to these linguists, to have little in common with language. You cannot subordinate, embed, or relativize a gesture-call. It is true that two or more gesture-calls can join to convey more precise or more forceful messages than a single one could convey by itself. We can demonstrate anger by combining the right posture with the right facial expression. We can show both anger and fatigue at the same time. But our gesture-calls simply do not meld into the tight syntactic constructions that are so characteristic of all natural spoken or signed languages.

Syntax allows language to escape the limitation of a fixed number of signals. New words can be invented, but not with complete freedom. You may get through the day without hearing a single word that you had never heard before, but unless you neither speak yourself nor listen to anyone else, you will certainly hear many new sentences before you sleep. It is hardly imaginable that the sentences in this paragraph were ever before uttered or written.

Any language with tens of thousands of words that can be joined into long strings allows astronomical numbers of sentences. In fact, thanks to recursive rules, there is no limit on the number of possible sentences. Rules are called recursive if they can be used repeatedly. The most trivial recursive rule simply lets a word be repeated. We can say that something is *very very very . . . big* with as many *very*s as we want to toss in. A child who speculates about his *great-great-great-great- . . . grandmother* has discovered the joys of a recursive rule. Only slightly more complex are rules that allow sentences to be joined to one another by means of simple conjunctions: *I saw Bill, so I spoke to him, and we talked for a while, but he got tired, and . . .* Such a sentence could, in principle, go on for ever. Languages allow more interesting kinds of recursion than these, and I will return to them in Chapter 9. For now, we need only note that recursive rules, in principle, allow us to produce and use an infinite number of sentences. Recursion is one of the most distinctive characteristics of language.

However subtle our gestures and calls are, they are fixed in form and fixed in meaning. Only over the course of the thousands of generations that are needed for natural selection can a set of gesture-calls be expanded or elaborated. You can never use gesture-calls to say anything that is truly new. Language is open. The system of gesture-calls is closed.

Voluntary control. We have a strong sense of having voluntary control over our language. Voluntary control over our gesture-calls is less secure. The ghastly photographs in which people pretend to smile are a tribute to the difficulty so many of us have in producing gesture-calls on demand. We don't naturally smile at inanimate objects, so it isn't easy to smile at a camera. Only something real can make us smile. On other occasions we find it just as hard not to smile, even when keeping a straight face would be more polite. The relatively involuntary nature of our smiles and of our other gesture-calls means that we are in constant danger of revealing ourselves. When people say one thing with language but send a conflicting message with their faces and bodies, they are likely to be branded as liars. It will not be their language that is believed, but their less voluntary gestures and facial expressions. Our calls and gestures sometimes convey our true emotional state considerably more faithfully than we want them to. If you want to lie, you will be well advised to stick to words and be careful to convey as little as possible with your gesture-calls. Photographers may ask us to pretend to smile, but they know better than to ask us to pretend to laugh.

Immediacy and displacement. Gesture-calls are limited by what might be called their "immediacy." We can use them to express the present state of our emotions and intentions, but not to describe our past or future emotions. They show our reaction to our immediate surroundings but, except when used along with language, we cannot use them to convey our attitude about things that are out of sight or earshot. With language, we can easily describe things that happened long ago or at a great distance, or that never happened at all. This is sometimes described by saying that language allows "displacement" while most other forms of communication do not. Displacement is not totally absent from animal communication. Bees famously tell other bees about where nectar is to be found, but bee dancing is not likely to have much bearing on language. Only with language, did human beings overcome the limitation to the immediate situation that is characteristic of all other primate communication.

Audible and visible mediums. Most people, everywhere, use audible languages, and our dependence on visible signals is sufficiently limited that we find it easy to talk in the dark and equally easy to adapt to a telephone. Deaf people who cannot use audible signals can develop rich and flexible visual languages, so spoken languages and sign languages each require just one medium, either audible or visible. Gesture-calls often use both. Many facial expressions are exclusively visual, but most of our audible gesture-calls can be seen as well as heard. Across a noisy room we have no trouble seeing that someone is laughing. We do not have to hear the sobs to see that a child is crying. The audible and visible parts of our gesture-call system are so similar and are so often joined closely together that I find it artificial to separate them. This is why I use the term "gesture-call." I find it helpful to be reminded that this part of our own communication includes both audible and the visible signals and that many signals are both. Languages are predominantly expressed by one medium or the other. Gesture-calls exploit both mediums more equally. Nevertheless, spoken language is regularly accompanied by waving hands and it is always accompanied by moving lips, so it cannot be said to be completely lacking a visible component. Spoken language is also accompanied by intonation which is more like gesture-calls than most of language, both in being analog rather than digital and in being better at expressing emotion than propositional information. Waving hands, moving lips, and intonation all greatly complicate any description of human communication, and a place will eventually have to be found for each of them.

In summary up to this point: As a first approximation, language is digital and allows easy reference. Large parts of language, including its huge vocabulary, have to be learned and this means that it can vary from one community to another. It is characterized by distinct phonological and syntactic levels of patterning. Its signals are largely arbitrary and conventional, and most languages are predominantly vocal and audible. It can be used productively to describe things distant in time and space. It is subject to a high degree of voluntary control. Our laughs, screams, groans, sobs, scowls, and smiles, like other gesture-calls, form a very different kind of communication. They are analog signals and excellent at conveying emotion. They are less subject to cultural variation than language, and they are less subject to voluntary control.

We need to consider some other forms of human communication that share features of both systems. Deaf signing is a visible language. Signs like the beckoning gesture of the Turkish guest-house keeper are digital rather than analog. The intonation of language is analog although most of language is digital. We need to find a place for all of these, and for several other kinds of signals by which humans communicate.

Deaf signing. For most of us, language is overwhelmingly auditory and vocal. When people with normal hearing learn to read and write, they add a visible form of language to the audible language they started with, but writing is based so closely on spoken language that it needs to be seen as a secondary and specialized skill. Only in very recent times has everyone been expected to become literate, and in some parts of the world literacy is still a minority achievement. Spoken language came first in human history and it comes first for every hearing child.

People who are deaf, however, need a visible language or they will have no language at all. Deaf people find it exceedingly difficult to learn any sort of spoken language. Without one, written language is a terrible challenge, but communities of deaf people are able to devise visible languages that use manual, instead of spoken, words. These manual languages are largely independent of the spoken languages of the wider communities in which they are used, and in the last few decades, we have come to realize that sign languages are as rich in expressive power as spoken languages.

For anyone who can hear well, spoken languages offer several practical advantages. In particular, they interfere less with other activities. We can talk and bathe the baby at the same time. Since a listener does not need to watch the speaker, a spoken language could once have been understood while checking for lions and a spoken language can still be used while keeping one's eyes on the road. Spoken language can even be used in the dark. It is for practical reasons like these, we presume, that communities of hearing people always choose to use a spoken language rather than a manual language as their primary form of communication. Speech is simply more convenient. When the vocal channel is blocked, however, it is now clear that the human mind is every bit as capable of directing language out through the hands and in through the eyes as it is of sending it out of the mouth and in through the ears.

Sign languages share all the essential characteristics that distinguish spoken languages from our gesture-calls. Signs are as referential as spoken words, and the sentences of a sign language can express the same kinds of propositions as the sentences of spoken language. Just as the words of a spoken language contrast, so do deaf signs. The manual signs of a language such as American Sign Language are as safely distinct from one another as are the words of any spoken language, so sign languages, like spoken languages, are digital systems. Contrasting hand shapes, together with contrasting locations, orientations, and motions of the hands and arms join to form signed words, much as the phonemes of a spoken language join to form spoken words. Like spoken languages, signed languages need to be learned, so sign languages differ from one part of the world to another, just as spoken languages do.

Sign languages can be used to convey the full range of meanings that spoken languages convey. Signers, like speakers, can agree on where to meet for lunch, discuss the qualifications of politicians, or report the latest scandal. Signers can lie as easily as speakers, and they can as easily use their language to discuss the language itself. Sign languages are as fully productive as spoken languages. New signs can be coined when new things or new ideas need to be discussed, and sign languages put no more limits than spoken languages on how many new sentences can be constructed. They are just as subject to voluntary control. In all these respects, signing is utterly different from the nonverbal communication of hearing people. Sign languages are nothing like mime or a game of charades. They are complex and conventional systems that take years to master. Signing has just as much right to be called a "language" as does Chinese or Spanish.

Nevertheless, signing and spoken language are organized in somewhat different ways. Signing takes place in three-dimensional space. Unlike spoken language it is not confined to the single temporal dimension, and this both imposes limitations and opens opportunities. Visible signs take a bit longer to produce than the average audible word, but the extra dimensions of visible space allow the signer to do several things simultaneously, and this compensates for the time needed to produce each individual sign. When signing about people or objects that are present, signers point to them. When signing about people who are not present, they often assign each person to a different location within their signing space, and then orient their signs toward these assigned spots. A sign meaning "give" can then move from one spot to another, so both the giver and the recipient are shown simultaneously with the sign for "give."

A visual medium invites a degree of iconicity that is impossible in a spoken language, and a considerable proportion of the signs of American Sign Language resemble, in some way, the object that they stand for. Illustration 2 shows several ASL signs. Those in the top row are almost transparent in meaning. Those in the middle row might not be understood without an explanation, but once their meaning is known, their iconicity is clear: a branched plant growing upward, a stick being broken, an umbrella being opened. Those in the bottom row seem to be entirely arbitrary. Spoken words cannot so easily mimic the things they stand for. *Chickadee* and *bob-white* imitate the calls of birds, but the onomatopoeia of spoken languages is marginal when compared with the iconicity of sign languages, although even the languages used by the deaf have many signs that are fully arbitrary.

Because sign languages exploit the special potentials of vision and space while spoken languages exploit the potentials of sound, they are organized differently, but they share their most essential properties. Human beings can devise rich and versatile languages in either a visible or an audible medium. Sign languages show us that it is the brain, rather than the vocal organs, that has made the most important adaptations for language. The human brain can learn to produce a language with either the tongue or the hands, and it can understand with either the eyes or the ears. Which medium each of us prefers is not much more than a matter of convenience.

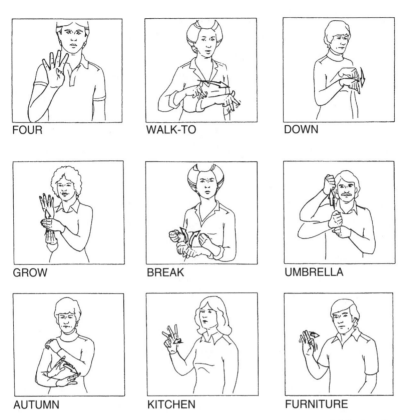

Illustration 2. Signs of American Sign Language. Top row: Highly iconic. Middle row: Semi-iconic. Bottom row: Arbitrary. (Reprinted with permission from T. Humphries, C. Padden, and T. J. O'Rourke, *A Basic Course in American Sign Language, Second Edition* © 1994, T. J. Publishers Inc., Silver Spring, Maryland 20910, USA.)

Quotable gestures. We nod and shake our heads, and we use dozens of hand gestures such as the "okay circle" and the "bye-bye wave." These are meaningful signs, but they have to be learned and they are conventional, so they are very different from our laughs and sobs. These learned and stereotypic gestures have sometimes been called "emblems," but I find the term "quotable gestures" to be particularly apt. Just as we can quote a word or a sentence, so we can also quote an okay circle or a shake of the head simply by making the same sign. The palm-down beckoning gesture that I learned from the Turkish guest-house keeper was a quotable gesture. Her scowl was not. Try quoting a scowl. You might imitate a scowl, but it is hard even to know what it would it mean to "quote" a scowl.

In both their forms and their meanings, quotable gestures are as conventional as words, and they can convey referential meanings that are as well defined as words. Like words, also, they contrast with one another. It is no more possible to compromise between two quotable gestures than between two words. In spite of the similarity of their form—fingers aimed upward—there can be no compromise, in either meaning or form, between the "finger" and a V-for-Victory sign. The conventional hand signals of a referee need to be unambiguously distinct from one another. Nothing can bridge the gap between a nod and a head shake in the way that transitional laughs bridge the gap between a giggle and a guffaw. It is their contrast that allows these gestures to be quoted, for only a contrastive system lets us know for certain whether two gestures are the same or different. We cannot know whether or not two smiles should count as the same but we do know that two head shakes mean the same thing. Quotable gestures need to be learned. Like language, they form a part of the cultural tradition of a community, and they differ from one community to another. In all these respects quotable gestures are very much like words and very different from gesture-calls. Because they are visible rather than audible, however, they cannot be incorporated into either the phonology or the syntax of spoken language.

Quotable gestures resemble the individual signs of a sign language more closely than they resemble spoken words. Everything that they share with spoken words, they also share with the signs of sign language, but in addition they are, like deaf signs, made with the hands and arms, sometimes with the assistance of facial expressions. Indeed, quotable gestures of the hearing community are sometimes incorporated into the signed languages of the deaf. The usual way to negate a sentence in American Sign Language is with a head shake. Head shakes cannot be incorporated into the audible language of a hearing community, but they can be incorporated into the grammar of sign language, and they can be used systematically within its sentences. In that way, a head shake becomes a word, one among the thousands of other signed words of American Sign Language.

Even for those of us who use spoken languages, the clear meanings and conventionality of quotable gestures make them more like words than like gesture-calls. Although they cannot be used as a part of spoken language, they deserve to be grouped with language in any typology of human communication.

Quotable vocalizations. Everyone who uses a spoken language also uses a few expressions such as *oh-oh, tsk-tsk, m-hm,* and *uh-uh* that are meaningful vocal noises, but not really words. These expressions are difficult to spell because they don't conform to ordinary English sound patterns, but these four should be recognizable as meaning "oh dear," "shame on you," "yes," and "no." They have consistent sounds and consistent meanings, but in addition to violating the usual phonological patterns of the language, they cannot be incorporated into its syntax. They don't fit into sentences. We do not have many of these vocalizations, perhaps a dozen or so, but they are unlike any of our other communicative signals. They are discrete rather than graded, for it is no more possible to compromise between the *m-hm* that means "yes" and the *uh-uh* that means "no," than it is to compromise between *yes* and *no* or between a nod and a head shake. Their sounds and meanings are conventional and they have to be learned. All this makes them so much like quotable gestures that they deserve a parallel name, and I will call them "quotable vocalizations." Like quotable gestures, these quotable vocalizations are more like words than like gesture-calls, and they belong on the language-like side of our communication.

Since neither quotable vocalizations nor quotable gestures enter the syntactic constructions of spoken language, they cannot contribute to the kind of productivity that syntax gives to all languages. We can, however, add new quotable gestures to our repertory. We do not often do so, but the V-for-Victory sign was invented only during the Second World War. It is not difficult to learn the quotable gestures of another culture. It would also be possible to add new quotable vocalizations to our repertory, though this must be even less common than adding quotable gestures. Adding to our existing stock of gesture-calls is impossible.

We can lie with either quotable gestures or quotable vocalizations just as we can lie with language. A nod or a *m-hm* is as surely a lie as is "yes," if the nodder or vocalizer really believes the correct answer should be a head shake or an *uh-uh*. If you try to deceive by shaking your head, you lie; if you laugh at a joke that you do not find funny, you do not. Quotable vocalizations are almost words. They are subject to roughly the same degree of deliberate control as language or quotable gestures, and like words, they have to be learned by participation in the community where they are used. Since quotable vocalizations are produced with the same vocal machinery as spoken language, we usually think of them as closer to language than a shake of the head or a wink of the eye, but the two kinds of quotables are used in almost identical ways, and both exhibit full contrast. In all these respects, both quotable gestures and quotable vocalizations differ from our analog gesture-calls, and both belong with spoken and signed language on the language-like side of our communication.

Gesticulation, intonation, and instrumental acts. We communicate with several other kinds of gestures and vocalizations, including the intonations of the voice, the gesticulations of the hands, and even with instrumental gestures that are not intended to communicate at all. These will be considered at greater length in Chapter 5, but to round out the picture, they need to be introduced briefly right now.

"Gesticulation" refers to the way we wave our arms and shape our hands as we speak. This hand waving is very different both from the gestural component of our gesture-call system and from quotable gestures, and it is different, also, from the manual gestures of sign language. That gives us four distinct kinds of communicative gestures, and still omits instrumental gestures which are meant for something else than communication. All this makes the word "gesture," if used alone, hopelessly ambiguous. From now on, therefore, I will avoid using "gesture" without qualification, but will, instead, use more specific terms: "gesture-calls," "quotable gestures," "gesticulation," "signing," or "instrumental gesture." Gesticulation differs from the others in its intimate association with speech. It might almost be regarded as a part of language, but its visibility and silence set it apart.

"Intonation" refers to the rhythm, stress, and ups and downs in pitch that accompany ordinary spoken language. Like gesticulation, intonation is used simultaneously with the words and sentences of language, and it is intimately related to them. Generally, we think of intonation as an integral part of language, and it is hardly conventional to set it apart, but it works so differently from the rest of the sound system that it needs special treatment.

Intonation conveys less propositional information than words and sentences generally do, but it reveals more about the attitudes and emotions of the speaker. Intonation also differs from the rest of language in being largely analog rather than digital. Both in its meaning and in its analog form, therefore, intonation is more like our gesture-calls than is the rest of language. Intonation has much in common with gesticulation. Since gesticulation is manual, it seems to be more distinct from spoken language than vocal intonation is, but intonation and gesticulation are closely linked to each other, and they have parallel kinds of involvement with language. It is even difficult to define intonation in a way that makes it a part of language without dragging in gesticulation along with it. Gesticulation and some parts of intonation have sometimes been grouped together as "paralanguage," meaning that they are used "alongside" language. The term recognizes their close connection with language, but still sets them apart. They will both be considered more carefully in Chapter 5.

Finally, we need to leave a place for instrumental acts that are not even meant to be communicative, but that can still be interpreted as meaningful by an observing individual. The business of living requires us to stand up, walk around, search for food, eat, sleep, cooperate, fight, look for mates, and engage in any number of other mundane activities. Our footsteps, our grunts, and even our breathing, can all be heard. Other people can see us and hear us as we perform these activities. These instrumental acts are meant for practical purposes, not for communication, but even if the actors would rather not be seen or heard, others may still be able to glean useful bits of information by watching and listening.

Behavior that starts instrumentally sometimes becomes conventionalized. The arms-up gesture by which babies ask to be picked up starts as an instrumental gesture that allows older hands to slip easily under the baby's arms. Children do not learn this gesture by imitation because older folks never ask a baby to pick them up, and a baby may never see another baby holding out its arms. Instead, each child conventionalizes the gesture by habit, and then exaggerates it to get attention. Adults, in turn, learn to recognize the gesture as a request.

The gesture-calls of animals, such as the retracted lip that warns of a bite, also began as instrumental acts. I will return to instrumental actions in Chapter 5 and propose that they must also have been important at the earliest stages of language.

Illustration 3 shows our various kinds of communication in a way that is intended to highlight both their similarities and their differences. The Illustration has two columns, one for visible, and the other for audible, signals, but the dividing line does not extend all the way to the top. This reflects the close association of the visual and audible parts of gesture-calls. Across the middle of the Illustration is a horizontal line that divides the analog gesture-call-like forms that are best at conveying emotions and intentions at the top, from the language-like digital communication that is best at conveying referential meaning below. The gesture-call system at the very top is the component of

		Visible	Audible
Emotional-Analog	Mammalian	Gesture-call System	
	Paralinguistic	Gesticulation	Intonation, Tone of voice
Referential-Digital	Quotable	Quotable Gestures	Quotable Vocalizations
	Linguistic	Sign Language	Spoken Language

Illustration 3. Varieties of Human Communication.

our communication that is most like that of other mammals and least like language. Language, at the bottom, is the most distinctively human. Both the top and bottom halves of the Illustration are further divided, and the two forms just above the central line and the two just below it all share some features of both language and gesture-calls. Quotable gestures and vocalizations are very much like words but they are not pulled into either the syntax or phonology of language. Gesticulation and intonation are both used more intimately with language than are either quotable gestures or vocalizations, but they are analog signals and thus quite different from the other parts of language. Instrumental acts are left out of the Illustration because they are not intended to be communicative at all.

One purpose of Illustration 3 is to show how very similar to each other audible and visible communication are. Most of what we can do in one modality we can do equally well in the other. The distinctiveness of human communication lies not in our specific ability to use vocal language, but rather in our ability to use language, whether audible or visible, to convey referential and propositional meaning, and to do so by means of principles that are very different from our own gesture-calls as well as from any form of animal communication. Linguistic contrast, syntax, and a massive vocabulary are all unique to language but they are just as characteristic of visible language as of audible language. It is our minds that changed most profoundly as our ability to use language evolved.

3

Truths and lies

We can view the path along which the capacity for language evolved from either of two directions, forward from a starting point somewhat like that of the living primates, or backward from the form of our own languages. The primates that we know, especially the chimpanzees and bonobos, give us a plausible model for the anatomy and behavior of our earliest hominin ancestors, and we can ask how such a species would have had to change in order to gain linguistic competence. Understandably, this is the perspective from which primatologists have generally looked at human evolution. Just as understandably, linguists have tended to start from language and look backward. Gazing from opposite directions across the gap that separates humans and apes, linguists and primatologists start with very different assumptions, and they often fail to appreciate the assumptions made by those on the other side. Primatologists know that their monkeys and apes are highly vocal animals that use their calls for all sorts of useful communicative purposes, so of course, they search these calls for anticipations of human language. Linguists, having immersed themselves in the enormous complexities of language, have been more inclined to dismiss primate calls as too impoverished to have any relevance at all for the way humans talk.

As a linguist, I am as impressed as any other linguist by the differences between human language and animal calls. Those differences, by themselves, however, do not rule out primate calls as a possible source for language. Even the most exotic trait of body or behavior had to grow out of something, and animal calls are a reasonable place to look for hints of language. What I believe is more damaging to the hope of finding anticipations of language in animal calls is the very good primate call system that we still have, and that is manifestly homologous to the call systems of other primates. We do not usually think of our nonverbal cries, screams, and laughter as constituting a call system, but along with many of our facial expressions, postures, and manual gestures, they constitute the human version of the primate communication system. If language had developed out of our own ancestral gesture-calls, it would have been very odd for us to retain such an intact and typical primate system.

When birds acquired wings, they did not hang onto forelimbs like those of their reptilian ancestors. Rather the wings of birds *are* their forelimbs. Although flight transformed these forelimbs in both their form and their function, wings are obviously homologous to the forelimbs of other vertebrates. If language had developed from gesture-calls, we should expect to find a human gesture-call system that had been as radically transformed by language as reptilian forelimbs were transformed by flight. Of course the particular gestures and calls of every species are unique, and we should not expect any human call or gesture to be precisely duplicated in another species, but the varieties of calls and gestures that we use, and the purposes for which we use them, are very much like those of other primates. Several of our gestures and calls are clearly homologous to those of apes. They are derived from the same ancestral gestures and calls.

Human beings, moreover, have another organ that is deeply involved in language and that has evolved dramatically away from the organ's more typical primate form. Language helped to transform the human mind and the human brain, just as flight transformed reptilian forelimbs. Our brains, and the minds that our brains make possible, are clearly homologous to the brains and minds of other primates, just as the wings of birds are homologous to the forelimbs of reptiles. The remaining chapters of this book will address the question of how language developed as one part of an evolving mind, and how, in the process, it helped to transform that mind.

First, however, I need to show how little our gesture-calls have been disturbed by all the other changes that evolution has brought to humankind. In the previous chapter, I did my best to persuade the reader that human beings have two very different forms of communication: language and what I named our "gesture-call system." I now need to justify that name by showing how closely our cries and gestures resemble the signals used by animals, and especially, those used by primates.

Like other primates, we communicate with our voices, with our facial expressions, and with the postures of our body. When we look closely at the characteristics of our communication, we see not only how similar human gesture-calls are to those of other animals, but how different both forms of gesture-calls are from language.

Reference and emotion. We use words as names for objects, qualities, and actions, and we use these names to call one another's attention to what we are thinking about. Primatologists have searched for hints that primate calls resemble names, and the most famous of their searches was conducted in Kenya among a species of small arboreal African monkeys known as "vervets." Building on earlier work by Peter Marler and T. T. Struhsaker, Dorothy Cheney and Robert Seyfarth conducted a series of ingenious experiments that showed that vervets make three distinct alarm calls. One of these warns of birds of prey, one warns of leopards, and the third warns of snakes. All three of these animals prey on vervets, and all pose serious threats. Cheney and Seyfarth recorded the alarm calls on tape and later played them back when no real predators were nearby. On hearing a recorded eagle alarm call, the vervets ran for the brush where eagles cannot penetrate. The leopard alarm caused them to climb high into the trees. That would be a dangerous place in an attack from an eagle, but the outer branches are too thin to support a leopard's weight so the vervets are safe from leopards there. Hearing a snake alarm the vervets stood up and looked around, presumably searching for a python. With the recorded calls, Cheney and Seyfarth demonstrated that a vervet does not need to see a predator himself in order to react appropriately to another's alarm call. Alarm calls, unquestionably, save many vervet lives.

In less detail, Cheney and Seyfarth also describe a series of distinctive vervet grunts. Vervets grunt in one way when approaching an animal whose status is higher than their own, but they grunt in a different way when approaching a subordinate. By showing deference, one vervet avoids attack. By asserting dominance, another vervet gets more food or mates. The grunts are difficult for humans to distinguish, and the first human observers who listened to them did not even notice that vervets adjusted their grunts to fit another's status. Vervet grunts warn us that we may have badly underestimated the complexities of animal signals. If vervets don't pick up the subtleties of human language, we should not be surprised if we have trouble with the subtleties of their calls.

With their alarm calls and their grunts, vervets communicate important facts about the world in which they live, both about the danger of predators, and about the nature of their social system. Animal calls are not limited, as had sometimes been supposed, to expressing their emotions or indicating their intentions. Whatever the emotions felt by alarmed or grunting vervets, Cheney and Seyfarth demonstrated beyond any possible doubt that animals are capable of communicating vital factual information about their environment.

Like vervet alarm calls, human gesture-calls can also convey referential information. If I withdraw my hand quickly after grazing it against a metal stove, I tell you that the stove is hot. Even from the other side of a room filled with a noisy crowd of strangers, we can often make a good guess about which man is a partner of which woman simply by watching the way they stand and move in relation to one another. Our smiles must show at least as much about our social relationships as do vervet grunts.

Our ability to convey factual environmental information with gesture-calls was made vivid to me one day as I stood waiting for an intercity bus on the campus of the University of Michigan. The bus stopped just in front of me and I watched several people climb down the steps. Among them was a young woman whose eyes darted tensely around the crowd that stood waiting on the sidewalk. Her eyes then locked onto something off to one side, something that I had not yet seen, and I watched the young woman's face melt into a smile of recognition. Her posture softened as the tension flowed from her body. From her posture and her face alone, I felt certain that this young woman, a woman whom I had never seen before, had caught sight of a young man, and I was equally certain that he was not her brother. Only then did I follow the direction of her gaze. I saw the young man, and then watched them greet each other warmly and walk away, shoulders bumping and in animated conversation. I did not have to ask whether they were brother and sister.

The nonverbal communication of this young woman told me something about the external world. The details of her darting eyes, her warm smile, and her melting posture conveyed information that was comparable, in every way, to the information conveyed by a grunting vervet. To the young man, it must have come as a confirmation of their friendship. To me, a bystander, it expressed something about the kind of individual she recognized, even though I had not, at that moment, seen him. Her smile and posture, we can presume, were expressions of her emotion, but we know that only because we can so readily empathize with her. Only the most deprived among us have failed to experience similar emotions. We cannot as easily empathize with the emotions of a grunting vervet. We cannot feel what a vervet feels when approaching a superior, but we should probably be cautious about dismissing too casually the emotional component of a vervet grunt simply because it also conveys other information. Nor did the emotion reflected in the young woman's smile deny the information that the smile conveyed. Certainly that smile told me about something I was likely to find in the world around me. Like a vervet searching for a snake, I could search for a boyfriend.

We would not call that smile of recognition a "word" however, and vervet grunts and alarm calls are no more like words than the smile was. If alarm calls were words, what would they mean: "leopard," "bird of prey," and "dangerous snake?" They might, instead, be commands meaning "run for the outer branches," "run for the brush," and "look around." No alarm call can ever be used to announce "The bird has flown away," to ask "have you seen any leopards?" or to reassure one's neighbors that "No snakes have been seen." Animal calls simply do not name things in the way words do. We can use the English word "leopard" to call attention to the idea of a leopard, whether or not a real leopard is present. A vervet cannot do that. An alarm call is more like a scream than a word. Like those of animals, our own gesture-calls can convey important information about the environment, but not in the same way or with the same subtlety as language. More often, our gesture-calls tell others about our emotions and intentions.

With the words of our massive vocabulary we can show others what we are thinking about and induce them to think about the same thing. With syntax we join words together and freely express propositions— factual statements that refer to some real or imagined situation. Nothing remotely approaching propositions is possible for either human or animal gesture-calls. Human gesture-calls, like those of animals, are much better at expressing emotions and intentions than propositions. Often they can express emotions with more subtlety than language can. It is our gesture-calls, not our words, that resemble primate communication.

Digital and analog communication. In the previous chapter, I described the pervasively digital nature of human languages, and contrasted this with the extensive grading of our gesture-calls. Most mammalian calls are graded, but some, like vervet alarm calls, are discrete. Much labor has been invested in charting the extent to which animal calls are graded and the extent to which they are discrete, but this linguist must confess that he has found this literature difficult to interpret, even when it deals with primates, and still more so when other mammals and birds enter the picture. It is not even clear that when students of animal behavior talk about "discreteness" in animal calls and when linguists talk about "contrast" in language that that they are talking about the same thing.

Most of us have too little experience with primates to allow us to judge the degree of discreteness or grading in their calls, but since we have all had experience with dogs, we can get a sense of the problems by thinking about their barks, growls, and howls. These three vocalizations seem reasonably discrete. At least they are different enough to have been given different names. Nevertheless, barks can come singly or with incessant repetition or with anything in-between. Growls can be short or long, quiet or loud. So there is considerable grading within these signals and, as in any analog system, the meaning of a signal is proportional to its point along the graded continuum. Fierce barking is more menacing than a few quiet yaps. Somewhat fierce barking is somewhat menacing. Clearly, we find plenty of graded variation here, but what about the differences between barks, growls, and howls? When a long growl is periodically punctuated by a soft bark does it mean that a growl can even grade into a bark, or are these two distinct signals that are being used together? Are yelps and barks discrete? It is difficult to give confident answers, even for the most familiar of animals.

The vervet alarm calls appear to be truly discrete. Vervets do not, it seems, make alarm calls that are intermediate in both sound and meaning. That's a good thing for the vervets. Running to the small branches is a good defense against a leopard but it's likely to be fatal when the danger comes from an eagle. The alarm calls are different enough that neither vervets nor human observers confuse them. Does their discreteness bring them close to language?

There are three reasons to doubt whether discrete animal signals have much significance for language. Most important is the vastly greater extent of discreteness in language. The pervasively contrastive phonological system lets every language have thousands of words that are fully discrete. We find nothing like this among either animal calls or human calls such as laughs or cries.

Second, the signaling systems of the great apes, the animals that are phylogenetically closest to us, appear to be even more consistently graded than those of many other animals, even monkeys. This suggests that discrete signals probably had little part in the signaling system of our immediate ancestors. In its degree of discreteness, our own gesture-call system may not be so different from the signaling system used by the common ancestors of humans and the great apes. It has nothing remotely like the contrastive phonology of every spoken or signed language.

Finally, to whatever extent animal gesture-calls are discrete, that discreteness is determined primarily by the inherited nature of the animal. Human beings certainly inherit the ability to learn and use contrastive phonology, but the particular contrasts that each of us needs depend on the language of our community. We know of no discrete signals in primate communication that need to be acquired by learning.

While a few gesture-calls of any particular species are likely to be distinct from one another, the extent of discreteness is tiny by comparison with the pervasive contrast of all human languages. This is what it means to insist that the communication of nonhuman mammals, including that of primates, is predominantly analog in form.

There are, to be sure, important analog elements in human communication, but these are not found in the phonological and syntactic core of language. The digital principles that pervade language set it as sharply apart from animal communication as from our own gesture-calls. To call both alarm calls and the words of a language "discrete" hides their differences but hardly demonstrates their similarities.

Heredity and environment. Languages need a lot of learning. Neither human gesture-calls nor any other form of mammalian communication needs as much. Here again it is not language, but our gesture-calls, that resemble animal communication. To be sure, experience contributes something to both human and animal gesture-calls. Of course, an animal needs to grow up in normal healthy conditions if its calls are to develop properly. Beyond this, young birds of many species never sing properly unless they first hear the adult forms of the calls. The songs of some cetaceans, notably those of humpback whales, differ from one population to another and change through time. These differences would not be possible without learning.

Evidence for learned and traditional behavior has been much harder to find among nonhuman primates than among birds and cetaceans, though the search has been intense. Hints of learned communicative behavior have appeared regularly, but if differences between the vocalizations of different groups exist at all, they are very subtle. We know of nothing among primates that comes close to the learned and traditional component of bird songs. Many of the primatologists who have had long field experience among wild chimpanzees are convinced that some learned behavior such as tool-making habits, and some details of their calls are, in fact, handed down within local groups, and better evidence for variation in communication may still emerge. In the meantime, it seems that the degree of cultural flexibility of chimpanzee and other primate gesture-calls is no greater, and perhaps considerably less, than the cultural flexibility of human gesture-calls. Language, once again, is worlds apart from both.

Arbitrariness and conventionality. The meaning of some animal signals can be called "arbitrary," but as with "discrete" it is not clear that "arbitrary" means the same thing when applied to animal signals as when it is used for words. A vervet grunt or alarm call is certainly arbitrary in the sense that it does not resemble the thing it stands for.

The vervet call that warns of a dangerous bird has been described as a "cough-like sound" while the warning for a snake has been called a "chutter." Whatever "cough-like" and "chutter" are supposed to suggest, neither resembles a predator, and it seems that nothing more than an arbitrary assignment gives the chutter to a snake and the cough to a bird. We can imagine, easily enough, a species where the assignments were the other way round. The swishing tail of a cat warns of aggression, while the wagging tail of a dog invites play. Both tails move from side to side, but they mean different things. That looks arbitrary.

When they insist on the arbitrary relation between the sounds of words and their meanings, however, linguists have something more in mind than the different meanings of waving tails. The examples they give are always conventional as well as arbitrary. We know that *bread* is an arbitrary symbol for the stuff we use to make toast because other languages use other words: *pain* in French, *roti* in Hindi, and other words in other languages. It is our ability to relate the meaning and the form of a word by convention that clinches its arbitrary nature. Whatever arbitrariness we find in animal gestures and calls depends on the inherited capacity of the animal, not on a learned convention. The vervet's chutter that warns of a snake or the cough that warns of a dangerous bird have nothing to do with differing conventions and everything to do with the nature of vervets. Human laughs and sobs, like vervet alarm calls, depend primarily on the nature of the human animal and to only a minor extent on convention. We cannot set the meaning of a sob by convention any more than a vervet can set the meaning of a chutter by convention. Once again, animal and human gesture-calls are more like each other than either is like language. It may be correct to call some animal signals "arbitrary," but that does not make them resemble language.

Syntax. Does animal communication ever exhibit anything like syntax? The awesome songs that humpback whales liberate into the ocean may come as close to having syntax as any form of animal communication. Short phrases of several notes are repeated to form themes, and these in turn are strung together to form what have been called "songs." Songs have been heard to continue for as long as thirty-five minutes, although eight to sixteen minutes is more usual. Songs can follow one another for hours, and under favorable conditions, they can be heard over thousands of square kilometers.

The most remarkable thing about the songs is that each population of whales constructs them from different phrases and themes, and with the passing of months, the phrases, themes, and songs of each population gradually change. Clearly there is some sort of imitative learning going on that allows the members of each population to conform to one another, even as their songs change. Presumably the songs serve as markers of the group, and perhaps they attract females. The way in which shorter parts of these songs are joined to form larger parts looks a bit like linguistic syntax, but there is no hint that the individual parts of the songs have meanings, or that the meaning of the whole is built up from the meaning of its parts.

Gibbons, and even gelada baboons, engage in calls that are complex enough to have been called "songs," but these do not have the kind of learned variability of bird songs or the songs of whales, and in that respect they are less like language. Nothing in the communicative behavior of primates, and nothing in human gesture-calls, resembles the productive syntax of language.

Voluntary control. Cheney and Seyfarth ask whether vervet alarm calls are produced voluntarily or are simply involuntary responses to external stimuli. They tell us that vervets, like many other animals, are freer with their alarm calls when other animals are present, and they are especially likely to sound alarms in the presence of kin. Vervets, in other words, take account of who is listening, and Cheney and Seyfarth suggest that this might imply voluntary control by the caller. I am puzzled by this suggestion. If the presence of a predator could evoke an involuntary call, I would suppose that the presence of other vervets, especially kin, could involuntarily lower the threshold at which the involuntary call is produced. I do not mean to argue against the voluntary nature of vervet calls, but I do not understand why reacting to the presence of kin implies voluntary control while reacting to the presence of a predator does not.

Even more, however, I wonder if the very concern about the voluntary nature of a call does not reflect a preoccupation with human language. We have a strong intuition that we have voluntary control over what we say and how we want to say it. Since language seems to be voluntary, animal signals would be more like language if they were voluntary, too. Would we be equally concerned about the voluntary nature of animal calls if we compared them to our own gesture-calls instead of to language? Was the smile of recognition of the young woman whom I watched as she climbed off a bus voluntary? Perhaps it was, but how could we know? Does it matter? We cannot doubt that our own gesture-calls are less subject to deliberate control than is language. Sometimes we try to control them but sometimes they overwhelm us. We may laugh or cry in spite of our best efforts to be silent or to hold back the tears. Mostly we just give our gesture-calls less deliberate attention than we give to language.

We have a privileged understanding of our own laughs and sobs, and they show us that voluntary control is by no means an all-or-none matter. We would, I believe, gain more insight into the gesture-calls of other animals by comparing them to our laughs and cries, than by searching for their similarities to language. We cannot have the same intuitive understanding of the gesture-calls of other species that we have for our own, but a good guess might be that vervet grunts and alarm calls are subject to about the same degree of voluntary control as is a smile of recognition.

Medium. The gesture-calls of most mammals, including all the monkeys and apes, combine audible and visible signals. Good primates that we are, most of our audible cries are also visible. Perhaps some closed-mouth sighs should count as invisible calls, but laughs and cries, like barks and pant-hoots, can be seen as well as heard. Language is more narrowly confined to just one medium. It is true that the shape of the lips can help us to understand language and that we regularly mold our hands and wave our arms as we speak. It can even be tempting to consider manual gesticulation to form the visible part of spoken language, but even if we were to do so, it would be an easily separable part. People everywhere can easily talk in the dark. If you peel away the intonation from vocal language, the resulting monotone sounds awful. Peel away the gesticulation, as we do with the telephone, and we carry on with little trouble. The audible component of language can stand on its own.

Because spoken language requires only a single medium, we can translate this language from its natural auditory medium to an invented visible one, from speech to writing. Our writing does not represent gesticulation at all, and it represents intonation only poorly. Deafness restricts sign language users to a single medium, but gestures, though silent, give deaf signals the same richness and flexibility of an audible language. Languages are either visible or predominantly audible. Gesture-calls are often both.

Deception and lying. A great deal of research attention has been directed toward deception by primates, especially by chimpanzees. Chimps behave in ways that, at least to some human observers, look as though they are intended to deceive. When in the presence of others, chimps have been reported to avoid seeking food that they knew was available, presumably so they could wait for an opportunity to eat it alone. Jane Goodall described a young chimp who was having trouble getting all he wanted to eat at a feeding station. He walked off in a deliberate way that seemed to induce others to follow. When the others did follow, leaving the food behind, the young chimp circled back and managed to get more of it. A young adult female named Mel was digging a tuber—a difficult job. A juvenile named Paul watched her, but then let out an ear-splitting scream, and his mother came to the rescue. She attacked Mel, and Mel fled. Paul then ate the tuber. Such episodes remind us of behavior that we recognize all too clearly in ourselves, but deception is not the same as verbal lying. Human beings can feign with gesture-calls but language opens opportunities for outright lies to which even the most deceitful ape can never aspire.

With language we can speak truly or falsely and we can talk about things distant in time and space. Gesture-calls, both human and animal, are limited to the immediate situation. We can use language to talk about language but it is hard to imagine either animals or ourselves using gesture-calls to discuss gesture-calls. I know of no attempt to compare the number of human and primate gesture-calls, and the extensive grading of both would make any comparison difficult, but however hard it is to count the number of gesture-calls, we can be confident that the number of distinguishable words is many times greater. In one characteristic after another, in the subtlety with which gesture-calls communicate emotion, in their analog nature, in their relatively low degree of cultural variability, in their species-wide distribution, in their lack of productive syntax and their poor voluntary control, the gesture-calls of humans and animals are much more like each other than either is like language. It is the distinctive characteristics of language that cry out for evolutionary explanations.

A quarter of a century ago, a Dutch primatologist with a splendid string of middle initials, Jan A. R. A. M. van Hooff, wrote some wonderful articles that convinced me that human smiles and laughter are not only analogues but also homologues to well-known ape gesture-calls. This means that at least some human and ape gesture-calls have been inherited from the common ancestors that we share. The modern signals differ in detail, of course, both in the way they are formed and in the situations in which they are used, but they remain close enough to reveal their common origin.

Van Hooff proposed that the human smile is homologous to what primatologists have called the "silent bared teeth" display (SBT, for short), which is used by members of several primate species. For an SBT the lips are drawn back to bare the closed teeth, but the animal does not vocalize. The muscles that draw the lips back are homologous to those we use to smile. With a degree of tolerant generosity, we can even see a slightly grotesque smile in the silent bared-teeth display of a chimpanzee, although the bones and teeth that lie behind an ape's smile are shaped so differently from ours that the outward appearance of an SBT is rather different from a human smile. The SBT is not, it seems, an expression of joy. Rather, it is used a means of maintaining and repairing social relationships. Subordinate animals offer an SBT to express their submission to a higher-ranking member of their species, but high-ranking animals sometimes use a similar expression to re-assure a subordinate. Of course, we use smiles this way too. Instead of joy or amusement, many of our smiles express goodwill. Like apes, we use deferential smiles, and we smile to put others at their ease.

We think of laughter as closely related to smiling but, surprisingly, it seems to have evolved from a different primate gesture, one known as the "relaxed open-mouth display" The mouth is opened more widely for the relaxed open-mouth display than for an SBT, and the wide-spread jaw stretches the lips so that they hide the teeth. The relaxed open-mouth display is often accompanied by a sound that, with less than total precision, van Hooff describes as a "staccato ahah." While human beings do not find this sound to be much like laughter, it is produced with similar bursts of breath, and it is surely homologous with laughter. Young chimpanzees love to be tickled, and they react with the relaxed open-mouth display and staccato *ahah*s. Like human children, in other words, they laugh when tickled. This relaxed open-mouth display is often used by young chimps as an invitation to play, a situation that, among young human children, regularly calls for excited laughter. The SBT and the relaxed open-mouth display are usually distinct in other primates, but they have moved close enough in humans for us to think of a smile as a sort of reduced laugh. We may forget how often we smile when laughter would be inappropriate. A tense social situation that could be eased by a smile, might be badly aggravated by laughter. Both the enthusiasm of laughter and the courtesy of a smile belong securely to our primate heritage.

A third gesture used by young chimps is known as a "play face." This has a wide-open mouth but lacks the added breathiness of the open-mouth display. Young human children sometimes use an expression very much like the play face during enthusiastic playing and rough-housing, but it drops out of use among adults.

Bonobos may be even more like humans in their gesture-calls than are chimpanzees. Sue Savage-Rumbaugh described how easily she and the bonobos could understand each other when she was first getting acquainted with those caged at the Yerkes Regional Primate Research Center in Georgia.

Throughout this time, I was enchanted by the ready ability of the bonobos to interpret body language and facial expressions accurately. I had known common chimpanzees with similar skills, though only those raised by human caretakers. Chimpanzees raised in the wild, or by their mothers in large social groups, seemed to have difficulty recognizing laughter, smiles, frowns, and many other human facial expressions... Yet these wild-caught bonobos had no difficulty understanding the expression of these or other more complex emotions such as consternation, puzzlement, or gratitude, nor did I have difficulty seeing these emotions in their attitudes. We shared a language from the very beginning, albeit one that referenced mood and intent rather than specific objects.

Such ready understanding should banish any lingering doubt about the close phylogenetic relationship of human and bonobo gesture-calls.

Of course, some of our particular gesture-calls have unique features, but since every species has its own distinctive signals, that is only to be expected. We seem to have more mobile and expressive faces than other primates. By the standards of most mammals, ape and monkey faces are quite expressive, but human faces are more so. Even chimpanzees seem a bit dead-pan to us, though perhaps chimps can read the face of another chimp better than we can.

By comparison with language, the human gesture-calls are less variable cross-culturally, less easily subjected to conscious control, and more resistant to modification by experience. Nevertheless, they are not completely immune to learning or to cultural variation. We can read gesture-calls of people from a very different culture than our own, but we cannot do so with quite the same confidence as with someone from our own background. Different cultures do impose varied rules about when it is appropriate or obligatory to cry. We learn to control our laughter on some occasions, and a laugh does not mean precisely the same thing everywhere.

The cultural variability of human gesture-calls should not stop us from recognizing their homology to chimpanzee gesture-calls any more than the cultural variability of human eating and mating habits stops us from recognizing them as homologous with the eating and mating habits of every mammal and vertebrate. If the learned component of human gastronomy does not hide its homology with primate diet, then we should not let the learned component of our gesture-call system obscure its homology with primate communication. Unlike our own gesture-calls, language shows no hint of homology with any form of communication used by any other animal.

Nonhuman primates show their fear, subordination, aggression, and lust with their gesture-calls—and so do we. Primates can identify the sex and age of another animal by its cries and they can identify known individuals by their voices and appearance—and so can we. They are warned by another's behavior, both about that animal's own intentions and about dangers in the environment—and so are we. In a dozen ways, human gesture-calls resemble the communicative signals of other primates. If language had emerged by a gradual evolutionary modification from earlier gesture-calls, would we expect to find human gesture-calls still to be so much like those of primates? We will do better to look elsewhere for the beginnings of language.

More than our gesture-calls, more even than our upright posture, it is the human mind that has been most radically altered from its ancestral, prehuman, state. Our minds are as different from the minds of other primates as the wings of birds are different from the forelimbs of the dinosaurs, and a central contributor to the mind's transformation has been language. This implies no discontinuity between human minds and primate minds. Like the wings of birds, the human mind evolved, step by slow step, from something originally quite different. Language has exactly the kind of intimate entanglement with the other parts of the human mind that we should expect for a trait that had emerged as one component of an evolving mind. From our human perspective, the minds of apes show us a transitional stage between our own minds and the minds of more distantly related mammals. We can recognize qualities of mind that we share with apes but not with more distantly related mammals. By the kinds of measures that humans devise, apes are a lot smarter than most mammals. They solve our kinds of problems more easily. When we look at primate communication in the wild, it is hard to find features that move it, in any significant degree, away from the kinds of communication used by all mammals. We will learn more about the antecedents of language by studying primate minds than by studying primate communication.

I have put so much stress on the distinction between our language and animal gesture-calls because I want to be clear about the questions I will raise in the remainder of this book. It is the unique features of language that cry out for an evolutionary explanation. It is the referential power of language, its digital nature, its conventionality and learnability, its enormous vocabulary, its syntax and productivity that need to be considered if we are to begin to understand how our ability to use language evolved. How could an animal whose communication lacked all these features have evolved into an animal that has them?

It is these new features of language, the features that distinguish us from other primates, that we need to understand, and most of these new features are cognitive. How could they have emerged in an animal whose mind was quite like that of a chimpanzee, but very different from the mind of a modern human being? How might these features have been fostered by selection? The rest of this book is a search for answers to these questions.

4

The mind and language

The linguist, Kenneth Pike, used to enthrall an audience with a performance that he called the "monolingual demonstration." With as many as several hundred people in attendance, Pike would meet, for the first time, a speaker of a language that he had never heard before. Without using a single word of English, or any other language that both he and the speaker knew, Pike would spend an hour or two learning as much as he could about this unfamiliar language. He could keep the members of his audience on the edge of their chairs as he moved from single words to short phrases and then to sentences of increasing complexity. It was a startling demonstration of just how accessible a previously unknown language can be.

While never as skilled as Pike, I regularly did monolingual demonstrations for my introductory classes in linguistics, not only because they are fun to do and to watch, but because they demonstrate so clearly just how much we all know before we even start to learn a language. I would find someone who spoke a language I had never worked with, ideally a language very different from my own English and from the English spoken by the members of my class, and my instructions to my helper were minimal. I would simply tell her that I wanted to learn as much as I could about her language, that she should speak no English whatsoever, and that she need not prepare ahead of time in any way.

I always brought a few props to class—some stones, leaves, and small sticks, and perhaps a cup, a spoon, and some pens and paper. I also exploited whatever else was in the room, the desk and chairs, the door and windows, and even the members of the class. I needed to start at the simplest level, so I would hold up a stone or leaf and, looking quizzical, I would glance back and forth from the object to my helper. It never took more than a fraction of a minute before my helper realized that I wanted her to name the object. As soon as she said something that sounded like a word, I would imitate its sounds as best as I could, and then repeat it until she accepted my pronunciation. Her gestures and facial expressions were always enough to tell me whether she judged my pronunciation to be adequate. I then transcribed the word in phonetic characters on the blackboard, and hoped I would be able to remember it.

Having obtained the word for "stone" it was easy to obtain words for "leaf" and "stick." By holding up varied numbers of stones and sticks, sometimes with the aid of fingers held as if counting, the numbers came easily: "two sticks," "three stones," "four leaves," and sometimes a plural marker came along at the same time. With a stick and a stone I could elicit a phrase that meant "a stick and a stone" and I would usually have a way of saying "and" as well. Different-sized sticks or leaves, together with some helpful gesturing, elicited phrases such as "big stick" and "little leaf."

When I tired of sticks, stones, and leaves, I would move on to "eye," "nose," and "mouth." By pointing to my nose and then her nose, I could find out how she distinguished them, and then it would take only a fraction of a minute, often filled with amused giggles, to sort out the difference between "your" and "my." What she called "my nose" I had to call "your nose" and vice versa. That done, other noses in the classroom made "his nose," "our noses", and "their noses" easy to get.

By pointing to objects, I would find out how to say "shirt," "sweater," "blue," "red," "cup," "pencil," "desk." Then, with the help of some acting out, short descriptive sentences came easily: "the pencil is in the cup, "the cup is on the desk," "I put the pencil in the cup," "I open the door," "he walks from the door to the desk." It did not take long to get a feeling for the range of sounds in the language and for some rudimentary grammatical patterns. I would try to make sentences of my own, substituting new words in the patterns that I had found. Of course, I made mistakes. Sometimes I even made mistakes deliberately, hoping for a correction that would show me how the language really worked. More often my mistakes came naturally and with no special effort. The scowl on my helper's face told me clearly when I had said something wrong. When she said something along with her scowl, the context often made it easy to guess that I had heard a word meaning "no." I always looked for, and then seized, whatever words popped naturally from my helper's mouth, for the situation often suggested their meanings.

Starting with single words, it was possible, within a fifty-minute class period, to build up phrases, and then sentences of considerable complexity. Nouns, adjectives, verbs, conjunctions, negations, numbers, and prepositions fell into place, along with some of the prefixes and suffixes that decorate the words of many languages. I gained some feeling for the distinctive speech sounds of the language and for how these were grouped into syllables. Of course every language has thousands upon thousands of details and only a tiny fraction of them can be found in an hour, but enough can be discovered to give a class the sense that with more of the same kind of exploration, the entire language would gradually open up.

The demonstration is fun, but it also reveals with great clarity just how much we already know before we start to learn a language. I could assume that my helper and I would be able to understand each other's gestures and facial expressions—our gesture-calls. I could see the disapproval in her face when I said something wrong and her satisfaction showed just as clearly when I improved. I don't think I ever elicited "your" and "my," as I learned how to distinguish "your nose" from "my nose," without exchanging mutually satisfying grins as we both became aware of the problem of pronoun reference, and almost as quickly realized that we had solved it. We could smile to encourage one another and laugh to demonstrate solidarity. I knew that her language would have words, and I had a good idea of some of the things that her words would name. I could expect her to have distinct words for "eye," "nose," and "mouth" but I did not need to worry that she might have separate words for "left eye" and "right eye." All these words could be recognized and repeated. Props were essential. We could not even have started without the sticks and stones, the parts of the body, the shirts and sweaters, tables, chairs, and doors to which my helper and I pointed. Language is not a disembodied set of rules, and it is impossible to learn a language without relating it to things and events. For me, as for a child, strings of sounds became meaningful only by their association with the objects and events around us.

In addition to these very general background assumptions, I could assume that my helper and I could both use five specific cognitive tools, all of which were essential if I was to learn something about her language. They must have been just as essential when language first began.

First, I could assume that my helper and I shared a rich conceptual understanding of the world around us. I could assume that she made the same sorts of distinctions among objects, qualities, and events that I made and that she had an understanding of cause and effect. I knew that her understanding was close enough to mine to let us communicate. Her perceptions were very much like my own. She could see what I saw and hear what I heard. She had concepts for most of the same things that I did. I knew that she could describe the same things that I could. I knew that she knew an awful lot.

Second, I could assume that my helper and I could attend to the same objects and events. As the jargon has it: We could "achieve joint attention." Even more, I assumed that I could call her attention to something, and that, equally, she could call my attention. If I held up a stick and looked back and forth from the stick to her, she would know that I was thinking about the stick and that I wanted her to think about it too. We required not a single word to learn what the other one was attending to.

Third, I could assume an ability to imitate. I constantly imitated her sounds, her words, and the way she put her words together. She could recognize my efforts as attempts at imitation and she could judge their accuracy. Even when I imitated badly, she knew what I was trying to do, and she could, in a sense, imitate her own words by repeating them, so as to demonstrate what I ought to be imitating better.

Fourth, I could assume an ability to understand pointing gestures and gestures that resemble the objects that they refer to. When I looked for words meaning "big" and "small" I could hold up big sticks and small sticks, but to be certain that she knew what I was looking for, I could also stand tall and spread my arms and shoulders wide while holding the big stick. I could emphasize small size by making myself small, by hunching down, lowering my head, pulling in my arms, and even puckering my face.

Finally, I could assume that her language would be patterned in repetitive ways. I could search for these patterns and use them to predict what else she could say. If she said "stick big," with her word for "big" following her word for "stick," it was an excellent bet that she would accept "leaf little" from me, but not "little leaf." That was all I needed to extract a simple grammatical generalization. As I elicited longer phrases, I could recognize, and then use, more complex patterns of word order, and learn how words and affixes were joined to form larger words, phrases, and sentences.

We take these five assumptions so much for granted that we rarely even think about them, but all five are essential prerequisites for learning a language. They must have been just as essential when language was first getting started as they are now. Apes do better with these abilities than most mammals, but we do even better than apes. Before our ancestors could start to understand the behavior of others in language-like ways, they had to be better than the modern apes at all these skills. All of them need a closer look.

A rich conceptual system. Before we can give something a name, we need to have some sort of concept of that thing. We need to have some idea about a dog before we can learn to call it a "dog." This does not need to be any sophisticated sort of concept. Never mind how dogs differ from wolves or foxes, or even how they differ from cats, but even the earliest learner needs some sense that the furry thing that wanders around is different from his big sister, or from the rug or the table or the door or any of the other things are nearby and that can be seen and touched. Parroting the sound is not enough. The sound of "dog" has to be connected to some sort of idea of a dog.

Having an idea of a dog is, of course, no problem for a language learner. Well before they start to talk, children have all sorts of ideas about the important parts of their world. They distinguish objects from one another and expect them, or some of them, to endure through time. They have ideas about how all these things affect one another. They have at least a rudimentary sense of cause and effect. They know that some objects can move by themselves (they will eventually learn to call these "animals"), while others will move only when pushed or pulled by something else. They can recognize some objects as being the "same" as objects that they saw yesterday. Some objects are similar enough to count as the same sorts of things.

Nor do human beings hold a monopoly over concepts. Even dogs need to recognize some objects as more similar to each other than to other objects. They recognize some objects as dogs, others as cats, and still others as people, or bones, or trees, and they act differently toward members of each group. They could hardly behave appropriately toward them if they did not recognize some of them as similar and others as different. Dogs also act consistently toward individuals. They can recognize an unfamiliar furry animal as similar to others that humans call "cats," but a dog can also recognize the particular cat that lives in his own household, and treat him as much less threatening and much less deserving of attack than another cat that he has never seen before. The world for a dog, like the world for a human, is formed from recognizable objects that act on one another in coherent ways.

Chimpanzees are better at classifying than dogs. Viki, the chimpanzee raised in the home of Keith and Catherine Hayes and remembered primarily for her failure to articulate English words, triumphed when presented with other challenges. She liked to sort things. The Hayeses noticed that she sorted Tinker Toys into two piles: sticks into one, wheels into another. Later she stacked red blocks in one pile and blue blocks in another. Capitalizing on her interest, the Hayeses began to offer her objects to sort, and she needed no reward to demonstrate her skills. With very few errors, she was able to sort buttons from screws, spools of thread from safety pins, keys from joined nuts and bolts. She was able to sort two-inch nails from one-inch nails, small red balls from small red blocks, blue wooden diamonds from blue wooden triangles.

Toward the end of this evaluation, Viki entertained a party of callers with a sorting demonstration that seemed to delight her by its very magnitude. Given a pile of six varieties of assorted hardware—nuts, bolts, nails, screws, washers, and paper clips—she sorted the entire lot into six sections of a muffin pan without a single error. At this point, we decided it was not necessary to test her further on her *ability* to sort.

Most impressive of all, perhaps, was Viki's interest in sorting the same sets of objects according to differing criteria. She had a collection of buttons of eight types, including every combination of black and white, round and square, and large and small. On different occasions, but without prompting, she sorted these by color, by shape, and by size.

These performances have an intrinsic charm, but they also raise the interesting question of whether, and in what sense, Viki had concepts. Did she have a concept of a "key," of a "safety pin," of "red," "blue," "big," and "square?" That, of course, depends on how we define the word "concept." If we were to restrict concepts to ideas that have names, then Viki could not possibly have had concepts, but then deaf mutes who have never been exposed to sign language would also, by definition, lack concepts. Viki made decisions according to some sort of consistent criteria. She could hardly sort safety pins from other small bits of hardware without some idea of the distinctive properties of safety pins, washers, and screws. I find it churlish to deny her concepts.

All this insistence that language requires concepts and that concepts, or at least something very much like them, are found in other animals is needed because so many people have been tempted by a different view. Benjamin Lee Whorf famously wrote: "We dissect nature along lines laid down by our native languages...The world is presented as a kaleidoscopic flux of impressions which has to be organized by our minds—and this means largely by the linguistic systems in our minds." Generations of enthusiastic relativists, encouraged by Whorf, have given language much of the credit for the "way we see the world," thereby overlooking the absolute necessity of being able to see the world very clearly before language can even begin. We need to give Whorf his due. Perhaps language helps us to focus our perceptions more sharply, and to refine our categories. Having words for different breeds of dogs must help us to see the differences between a poodle, a beagle, and a dachshund, but such subtleties come only as fine-tuning of our conceptions, not as a prerequisite for them. Viki's enthusiasm for sorting hardware shows that, even without language, she had a firm grasp of at least some qualities of objects. She could even categorize objects that were never found in the jungle of her grand-parents. Far from being a world of "kaleidoscopic flux" a chimpanzee's world is filled with enduring objects and consistent qualities. I see no reason to imagine the world of either prelinguistic children or of our prelinguistic ancestors as any more of a kaleidoscopic flux than the world of a chimpanzee or a dog.

Primates need to deal not only with the concrete world of physical objects, but with a complex social world as well. Many fish swim in schools, but they do not need to recognize individual members of their schools. Even ungulates that travel in large herds probably do not recognize most herd members individually. Primates do recognize the individual members of their bands and they have intricately varied relationships with each of them. The complexity of their social life requires a corresponding conceptual complexity, and of course we share this complexity with other primates.

The ability to recognize similarities and differences among the phenomena of the world is as essential for a child who is just starting language, as it is for the monolingual demonstration. It was also essential for our ancestors when they stood at the brink of language. Even before they began to speak, they must have dealt with the world by means of a rich set of concepts. Names cannot be given to things and events unless the learner already has the ability to form concepts for those things and events.

Of the five psychological prerequisites for language that I have pointed to, it is concepts that seem best established among our primate kin. Their ability to achieve joint attention, to imitate, and to use pointing and imitative signs appears to be substantially better than that of most mammals, but still not equal to ours. Before they could start to talk, our hominin ancestors had to be better at all of these than modern apes are.

Joint attention. Willard Quine posed a question to which his fellow philosophers have given much thought: How can anyone learn a word simply by hearing it pronounced in the presence of the object to which it refers? Of the many objects that he can see, hear, or touch, how does a child know which one a word refers to? Perhaps it does not refer to a single object at all but only to a part of an object, or to its color or size, or perhaps to a whole collection of objects. As far as a child can know, the word "dog," pronounced in the presence of a furry four-legged animal, might mean "animal," "collie," "fur," "brown," "left hind-foot of a dog," "dog with a mournful expression," "the rug on which he lies," "the hand that points," "the rain beating on the window outside," or any number of other phenomena. The word might be either a proper name for this particular dog or a general name for any dog. How can a learner possibly know which of the infinitely many possibilities is the right one?

Somehow, the learner needs to know what the speaker is attending to. In doing the monolingual demonstration, I needed to know whether my helper was naming the stick or the leaf or my nose, and for this, we needed to pay attention to the same thing, to achieve joint attention. During the monolingual demonstration I guided my helper's attention, but language learners often need to adjust their own attention. Only by figuring out what a speaker is attending to, can a learner assign the right meaning to a word. This requires the learner to engage in a bit of mind-reading and then shift his own attention to correspond to that of the speaker. Even eighteen-month-old children are already adept at sharing attention with others.

Here is a place where young human beings are utterly different from young chimpanzees. Well before they start to talk, children delight in sharing attention with others. They look with interest at what others show them, and they eagerly hold up objects for others to see. They enjoy sharing their interests, and it soon becomes easy to attract a child's attention to something, simply by pointing to it. Children even recognize adult signs of satisfaction and dissatisfaction. When an adult experimenter tells a child that he is looking for a *blurg*, and then looks dissatisfied when inspecting one object, but pleased when inspecting another, the child will understand the second object to be the *blurg*. Young chimpanzees don't play these games. With noises or gestures they can call attention to themselves easily enough, but they do not hold objects up for others to inspect, and they do not have a human child's easy understanding of pointing. Even when searching eagerly for hidden food, a chimpanzee does not respond to explicit pointing that would be utterly obvious even to a very young human child.

Chimps can follow the direction of another's gaze. To a human being, it seems odd that a chimpanzee can follow something as subtle as a gaze while failing to understand a pointing arm or finger. Chimpanzees cannot help looking at things, however, and other chimps can profit from knowing where they are looking. Wild chimpanzees do not point and, except when they call attention to themselves, they appear never to make any deliberate attempt to direct the attention of another ape. An ape that lives in the wild has no reason to understand pointing, but he has excellent reasons for understanding direction of gaze.

Subordinate chimpanzees who would not dare to take food that a more dominant animal could see, have been observed, in laboratory experiments, to be less cautious when they understood that the dominant animal's view of the food was blocked. So chimpanzees can understand that a blocked view can leave another animal in ignorance, and this suggests that chimpanzees have at least the rudiments of a "theory of mind." One chimpanzee, in other words, can understand that another animal's knowledge can be different from his own. In their ability to follow another's gaze and in that way to gain some idea of what that animal is concerned with, and in their understanding that there are limits to another's knowledge, chimpanzees show some of the prerequisites needed for the ability to achieve joint attention, but humans are much better at it than chimps. We actively help each other to share attention. Chimpanzees do not.

Taken together, their rich conceptual understanding of the world and their easy ability to achieve joint attention allow children to solve Quine's problem, and to choose the right meaning for a word even when their world is so cluttered with things. In pragmatic fact, the child's choice is not much more difficult than mine was when I did a monolingual demonstration. Like adults, children come equipped with firm expectations about what sorts of things are most likely to attract attention and to receive names. A word has little chance of meaning "dog with a mournful expression" or "left hind-foot of a dog" instead of simply "dog." That is knowledge that children bring to the task of language learning. Of course, children are not immune to mistakes. A good many children who learn the word "dog" in the presence of a dog, go on to use it for any four-legged animal. This is a mistake, though a reasonable one, and it is a mistake that will be corrected as soon as the child learns that cats, horses, and cows all have their own names.

Two people find it so easy to focus their minds on the same thing, that a learner can usually pick out a reasonably correct referent of a word. Chimpanzees lack our easy ability to gain joint attention, but if they have at least a rudimentary theory of mind, they are closer to us than most mammals are, even if they are not close enough to let them learn words in the easy human way.

Words are highly efficient tools for achieving joint attention. When I use a word, I show you what I am thinking about and you can then turn your attention to the same thing. The referent of the word, the thing to which it refers, does not need to be present. When I use a word I am really drawing attention to a concept, not necessarily to an object, and since I can have concepts for parts of objects, for collections of objects, and for the characteristics and actions of objects, I can as easily draw your attention to one of these as to a whole object. I can just as easily draw your attention to phenomena that have never even existed except in the worlds of our imagination.

Imitation. A word could not spread to an entire community, or be passed from one generation to the next, without skillful imitation. Every time we repeat a new word in order to convey a new meaning we are imitating. Indeed, every time we use any word at all, we need to imitate something that we first heard from someone else. Even on those rare occasions when someone makes up a new word, he almost always uses familiar, imitated elements. We are much better imitators than apes.

Imitation is a cognitive skill. An imitator needs to perceive a similarity between his own actions and those of the person, animal, or object that he wants to imitate, but imitation comes so easily to us that we rarely stop to think about just what a remarkable skill it is. A child who imitates a word can, at least, hear his own imitation and presumably he can check his pronunciation against the original, but small babies mimic facial expressions without being able to see what happens to their own faces. Just how they manage this is still not certain, but for present purposes it is enough to recognize that the ability to imitate is a specialized skill and that human beings are very good at it. Well before they use words babies eagerly mimic the sounds of speech. Their genetic birthright gives children the extraordinary ability to imitate the idiosyncratic sounds, words, and grammatical patterns that are used in their community.

Human beings are not the only animals to imitate. Many birds learn the details of their songs by duplicating the songs of conspecifics in their neighborhood. Imitation is less common among mammals, but some whales and dolphins copy one another's vocalizations. Monkeys and apes are often supposed to be skillful imitators, but this turns out to be far from obvious, and anyone who imagines that imitation is a simple matter must be astonished by the amount of controversy generated by the question of whether apes, let alone monkeys, show any ability to imitate at all. Some primatologists, particularly those who have studied apes in captivity, have found it difficult to find any experimental evidence for imitation. Others, including some who have observed apes in their natural habitat, have been more accepting.

Part of the disagreement is nothing more than a difference in the meaning given to the word "imitation." Everyone seems to agree that apes mimic. In other words, they copy another's behavior. However, a skeptical observer does not count this as imitation if it merely reproduces the movements or sounds of another animal without using these movements to achieve a parallel goal. By this definition, we should say that a baby who reproduces a facial expression is mimicking but not imitating.

Apes do seek goals that they have seen others achieve. Having watched another ape crack nuts and eat the meat, a chimp may try to find a way to get some nut meat for herself. If she has been attracted by broken nuts, she may find the stone that others have used to crack them and then, without any help from imitation, reinvent a way to crack the nuts for herself. The skeptical observer will not count it as imitation unless she also mimics the specific procedures of another chimp. Only when mimicry is coupled with pursuit of a goal is the skeptic willing to count the behavior as imitation, and it has been difficult to catch a chimpanzee in such an unequivocally imitative act.

If this seems excessively restrictive, consider what we mean when we say that children use imitation to learn a language. A babbling child reproduces the syllables of his doting parents. Certainly the child mimics, but even while recognizing this as preparation for language, we don't count it as real language because it is not directed to the goals for which we use language. Parents recognize their children's first words as something quite different. They certainly mimic the words, but now they are doing so for a purpose—to express an idea that others have expressed with the same word. Since they now have a goal, their word counts as imitation. Defined in this way, a parrot that can do no more than mimic falls short of imitation. Mimicry is necessary for language learning, but not enough.

Among the field primatologists who have looked with more favor on imitation are Anne Russon and Birute Galdikas, who worked with orangutans that were living in reasonably naturalistic conditions on the island of Kalimantan in Indonesia. They describe animals that watched a human throwing a log across a stream in order to cross. The orangs immediately maneuvered their own logs across the stream and were then able to use them as bridges. An orangutan that was familiar with hammocks and that had watched them being hung from trees, was able to wrap the hammock ropes around trees well enough to let the hammock briefly support her own weight, although she did not manage to tie a firm knot. The same animal was seen sloshing water out of a dugout canoe by rocking it back and forth in the way that she had seen people empty water from canoes. Russon and Galdikas argue that the laboratories where captive apes have been observed impose unfavorable conditions that make imitation difficult to detect. Christophe Boesch and Hedwige Boesch-Achermann even describe a chimpanzee mother who appeared to demonstrate deliberately just how to hold a wooden hammer in order to crack nuts. Her daughter seemed to imitate her mother's way of holding the hammer, and her cracking improved. This is a nearly unique observation of teaching, however, and not everyone is convinced.

Apart from observing imitation in action, we might infer it from behavior that differs from one group to another, as long as neither environmental nor genetic differences seem to be the likely explanation. Language differs from one human community to another, and it is this that convinces us that language is not fully built in. It is the variability between populations of birds and whales that also convinces us that their singing needs more learning than the barks or growls of dogs. Birds and whales are good at learning from each other, and it seems fair to describe them as capable of imitating. A good deal of effort has gone into searching for similar kinds of behavioral variability in primates, but it has been easier to find variation in other kinds of behavior than in communication. Andrew Whiten and other field primatologists find considerable variability among local groups of chimpanzees in the details of tool use and manipulation of objects. The members of some groups use a leaf napkin to clean their bodies, but others do not. Some wipe ants off a stick with their fingers, while others use their mouths. Only in some groups are probes used to extract fluids. Only in some do the animals knock with their knuckles to attract attention. This variability is difficult to explain by either environmental or genetic differences, and this leaves learning as the most likely reason for the behavioral differences. Specific techniques seem to spread when one chimpanzee learns from another. Local populations converge on shared behavior. Whiten and his colleagues write with increasing confidence of "cultural" variation among chimpanzees and it is difficult to imagine any way that this kind of variation could develop or be maintained except by imitation.

We even have a few hints of vocal imitation among primates. When male chimpanzees from different backgrounds have been brought together in captivity, they appear to converge on similar styles of pant-hoots, one of the characteristic calls of male chimpanzees. One chimpanzee in the wild was observed to take over the distinctive pant-hoot of another chimp who had disappeared. Rhesus monkeys of different maternally related kinship groups are reported to use different vocalizations. Reports like these suggest that chimpanzees, and even some monkeys, do have a degree of vocal adaptability and even some ability to imitate. Chimpanzees do not, however, have as much control over their vocal tract as we do, so they cannot possibly imitate sounds in the way we can. Even human beings, of course, do not find it easy to perform good vocal imitations of anything except language. We are no more likely to fool chimpanzees by our imitation of a pant-hoot or a long call than they are to fool us by their efforts at speech.

The last word on incipient imitation in apes has yet to be written, but it does seem safe to conclude that apes come closer to us than most mammals in their ability to imitate, as well as in their ability to achieve joint attention. At the very least, they can mimic, and the suggestions that they can imitate details of tool use and methods of eating need to be taken seriously. Abilities similar to those still found among chimpanzees could have started us along the path to the more skillful imitation that was needed to learn a language.

Motivated signs: icons and indices. The philosopher Charles Sanders Peirce famously classified signs into "icons," "indices," and "symbols." An icon, by Peirce's definition, is a sign that resembles the thing that it stands for. Pictures and diagrams are icons, as are onomatopoetic words. Indices are signs that point to their referent or that have some logical or physical association with the referent. Smoke is an index of a fire. My pointing hand is an index of the object to which it points. A symbol, finally, is a sign in which the relation between the meaning and the form is entirely arbitrary, purely a matter of convention. Most of the words of spoken languages are symbols because each word's pronunciation is utterly unlike the thing it stands for. Neither icons nor indices are arbitrary. In order not to keep repeating "icons and indices," I need a word to cover both kinds of non-arbitrary signs, and I will use the term "motivated signs." Unlike most of the words in our spoken languages, motivated signs are related to their referent by more than just an arbitrary convention.

Human beings have no trouble producing and understanding many kinds of motivated signs, from points, pictures, and wiring diagrams, to onomatopoeic names for birds, and the many iconic and indexical signs of the manual languages of the deaf. Members of other species rarely use either icons or indices, but a few bonobos, chimpanzees, and gorillas have demonstrated a modest ability with them. Even the ability to recognize their own reflection in a mirror sets these primates apart from other animals, and chimpanzees are also able to recognize objects, people, and animals in two-dimensional photographs, an iconic capacity that is well beyond the ability of most animals.

Several captive chimpanzees have gestured spontaneously in iconic or indexical ways to show their human companions what they want. Viki was inventive with iconic gestures.

At times her gestures became very explicit. Watching bread being kneaded, she begged for a sample of dough by going through the kneading motions for a while, and then holding out her hand, palm up, moving her fingers in the gesture which means "give me" to both her species and ours. A similar incident occurred during the weekly ironing as she grew impatient for her turn to do the napkins. She stood on a nearby table, moving one clenched fist slowly back and forth above the ironing board while her other hand tried to take the iron away from "mamma."

More recently, iconic gesturing has been observed in an adult male gorilla named Kubie who was living among other gorillas in reasonably naturalistic conditions in the San Francisco zoo. Kubie interacted frequently with a female named Zura, and he used iconic gestures to show her what he wanted her to do. By moving his hand downward, either while touching Zura's body or simply by moving it where she could see it, he indicated that he wanted Zura to move downward, like his hand. Kubie also patted his own chest in a gesture that seemed to call attention to himself. He, and to a lesser extent Zura, used many other gestures in what appears to have been a rather subtle form of communication. All of these gestures were spontaneous, not taught by humans.

Savage-Rumbaugh gives a striking example of the ability of a chimpanzee named Booee to read a novel iconic gesture of a human being.

[Booee] hung by his hands from the top of the cage and did a 360° turn while we were playing. I laughed and, wanting to see that again, held up my hand and spun my index finger around in a 360° arc and pointed to the top of the cage. Booee at once grasped my intent and proceeded to repeat his flip for my benefit. This gesture was not one of Booee's signs. In fact no one had ever made that sort of gesture or request to him before ... Yet he was immediately able to comprehend the meaning of my gesture—repeat that flip you did up there.

When he was a year and a half old, Kanzi, the bonobo whose ability to understand spoken English was described in the first chapter, began to extend his arm, though not his index finger, to indicate the direction in which he wanted to travel. When riding on Savage-Rumbaugh's shoulders he would sometimes lean his whole body in the desired direction or even forcefully turn Savage-Rumbaugh's head to show the direction he wanted to go. "[Kanzi made] a twisting motion with one hand while pointing to the jar to be opened with the other one. When he wanted nuts cracked, he made hitting motions in the direction of the desired nuts. And if he wanted an object given to him, he gestured first at the person and then at the object, as human infants do." Even more striking, perhaps, because no human participants are involved, bonobos use iconic hand and arm gestures to indicate the positions they desire their partner to assume for copulation.

None of these animals would make iconic or indexical gestures deliberately if others did not already have the ability to interpret them, but even gestures that are made without deliberate intention might be useful for others. The hand positions by which things are held and manipulated predict the activities that follow. Postures predict movements. Animals would profit from knowing what to expect from the positions and postures of others. The better they understand iconic and indexical actions, the greater are the opportunities for one animal to exploit another's understanding by performing these actions deliberately.

Little is known about the use of motivated signs by apes in the wild but it is difficult to imagine that the iconic gestures used by Kubie when communicating with Zura, or those used by bonobos during copulation, would be possible unless they reflected behavior that is also used in the wild. We don't really know how, or to what degree, the use of motivated signs by captive apes reflects the behavior of apes in their natural habitat, and it must be ferociously difficult to study motivated signs among wild apes. So far as I am aware, no one has tried very hard to find them.

Since gesture-calls first develop by the ritualization of instrumental behavior, they begin with the inherent iconicity of all instrumental actions. With the passage of enough evolutionary time, communicative signals tend to become increasingly stereotyped and even to lose their initial motivation, but until stereotypy takes over completely, signals retain some of their original iconicity or indexicality. When a dog curls his lip as if to bite, it can be interpreted as an icon of a bite. What is missing from most animal signaling is the kind of productive iconicity that lets human beings so easily use sounds, gestures, and pictures to produce new likenesses of objects, but even the modestly iconic signaling observed in apes is very different from their own gesture-calls and from the gesture-calls of other mammals.

Although apes can use gestural icons, I have never seen any hint that vocal iconicity might be possible for a nonhuman primate. They probably do not even have sufficient voluntary control over their vocal organs to produce vocal icons. Still, once our ancestors began to gain better control of their vocal tract, the cognitive abilities needed to recognize and to produce visible iconic signs must have been available for audible signs as well. We do use a few onomatopoetic words, after all, and we can produce all sorts of onomatopoetic noises that we do not count as words. Perhaps onomatopoetic noises and words were more important for our early ancestors than they are for us.

Most of the examples I have given here have concerned the production of motivated signs, but recognition had to develop before deliberate production could be useful. Every dog that ever picked up a scent has recognized an index of the animal that left it. Any behavior which we would be tempted to call "intelligent" must recognize similarities and differences. Survival depends on such understanding. The production of indices and icons is much less common than their recognition. Language began with comprehension.

In the next chapter, I will argue that icons and indices played a greater role during the earliest stages of language than they do in the spoken languages we use today, but even modern spoken languages have more iconicity than we sometimes recognize. At the early stages of any conventional form of communication, iconicity and indexicality are the most obvious principles to exploit.

Pattern finding. Human beings cannot resist finding patterns in the objects and events of their experience. We recognize regularities in such ordinary matters as the seasonal sequence of blooming flowers, the behavior of our friends, and the special eagerness of mosquitoes to bite us in the evening. To enjoy music we need to appreciate its many levels of patterning. All of science is a search for the regular patterns that lurk behind superficial appearances. Before we can understand a language, we must discover an enormous number of patterns.

To learn a language, children need to find the complicated patterned relationships between sounds and meanings. They need to discover the conditions when *dog* is appropriate and the contrasting conditions that make *cat* a better choice, and later they need to learn the differences among thousands of other words. Children also need to gain control over the grammatical patterns of their community. The ability to learn a language is the endowment of every reasonably normal child. We can give a name to that ability and call it a "language acquisition device" or "universal grammar," but that is only the starting point. Every child must use his innate ability to learn all the details by which his particular language differs from other languages. Learning these details requires a formidable ability to find patterns in the language that a child hears.

Very young children can recognize patterns in recordings of synthesized speech. The psychologist Jenny Saffran and her colleagues gave eight-month-old infants the joy of listening to a repetitious stream of syllables such as: *tibudopabikudaropigolatupabikutibudogolatudaropidaropitibudopabikugolatu*. After being subjected to this for a mere two minutes the infants had somehow taken account of the four three-syllable "words" from which this stream is composed. Nothing in the recording marks the breaks between these "words," but when *tabidu, pabiku, daropi*, and *golaku* were played to the children separately, but now interspersed with new and unfamiliar trisyllables, the infants reacted differently to the new words than to those made familiar by their two minutes of listening. The infants had found repetitive patterns.

In another experiment, the psychologist Gary Marcus and his colleagues asked seven-month-old infants to advance the cause of science by listening to short sequences of syllables. In one version of the experiment, the infants spent two minutes listening to strings such as *ga-na-na, li-na-na, li-ti-ti, li-la-la, ni-gi-gi, ni-na-na, ta-la-la*, and *ta-ti-ti*. These have a very restricted set of consonants and vowels, they all have exactly three syllables, and the second and third syllables are always identical. After two minutes of habituation, the infants were given new examples, now composed of three unfamiliar syllables. In some of these new examples the odd syllable came first, as in the habituation examples, but in others the odd syllable came last. In other words, some examples had the familiar ABB pattern, while others had AAB. All sixteen of the infants tested, showed more interest (as measured by the length of time they attended) in the examples with the unfamiliar sequence. The children had learned an abstract pattern and they could recognize it in new examples.

Being able to distinguish ABB from AAB sequences looks like the kind of ability that would be useful in language learning, but lest one jump to the conclusion that this skill is a specific adaptation for language, Marc Hauser and his colleagues tried the same experiment with cotton-top tamarins, a species of New World monkey. Tamarins were able to perform much as human infants did. Once habituated to ABB sequences, they reacted with more interest to AAB sequences. Those first habituated to AAB sequences reacted more strongly to ABB.

Where do pattern-finding skills like these come from? Both people and animals must adapt to the regularities of nature, and to the behavior of other individuals. Being able to learn patterns well enough to have reliable expectations ought to be a valuable skill, and in spite of the tamarins, it is tempting to guess that, once we know just what to look for, human beings will turn out to be much better than other animals at finding patterns. Studies of pattern finding among animals are in their infancy, however, and we do not even know very much about how human beings find the more complex patterns that they need in order to use a language. ABB and AAB hardly scratch the surface. At present the best we can do is to recognize the crucial importance of pattern finding for language learning, guess that pattern finding is better developed in humans than in any other animals, and wait for more research.

The five prerequisites for language that I have identified here are all cognitive. This seems obviously true for a rich conceptual system, joint attention, and pattern finding, but it is true also of imitation and the use of motivated signs. Icons and imitation both require us to recognize similarities among things that are far from identical. To imitate, you must understand how your own behavior resembles whatever you are imitating. Any animal that can understand or produce an icon or index must be able to perceive similarities among disparate phenomena: between an object and the gestured approximation of its shape; between a bird and an imitation of its call; between a pointing hand and the thing it points to. Motivated signs like these became possible only with a growing ability to puzzle out interrelations among the phenomena of the world. Most animals show little sign of any of these cognitive prerequisites but apes have moved part-way in our direction. All had to develop further before language could begin.

The great apes are better than most mammals, even monkeys, at joint attention, imitation, and motivated signs, but their skills are not sufficient to let them learn the kind of languages that modern human beings learn so easily. If our own early ancestors had abilities that were similar to those of modern chimpanzees and bonobos, then we ought to wonder what selective pressures could have fostered those cognitive skills, and brought them to the point where language could begin. Once a bit of language was in place, it could itself have become an object of selection. Those who were better at understanding and speaking would have been favored for survival and reproduction. Before language could even begin, however, something other than language had to bring better joint attention, imitation, and pattern finding, and more skill in the use of motivated signs. The best candidate for early adaptive pressure for these abilities is the increasingly diverse environment into which early humans moved, and the advantages that behavioral flexibility would have brought to a species that had to keep adapting to new environments.

At the start of the hominin experiment, commitment to life on the ground brought about the split between our own ancestral line and the line that led to the chimps and bonobos. Even apes spend much of their time on the ground. They can walk upright, carry objects in their arms, and use tools. Reciprocally, people can climb trees, and a few muscular folks can even brachiate. The similarities in our locomotion and manipulation are obvious, but we do walk better on our hind-legs than chimps do, while the apes win hands down at tree climbing and brachiation. Although they are by no means exclusively arboreal, both safety and the need for food require chimpanzees and bonobos to clamber around in trees. Since they must be adapted for skillful clambering, they cannot be ideally adapted for life on the ground. Once the trees became a clear second choice for the earliest hominins, however, all adaptive pressures favored the best possible bodies for living and moving about on the ground. Tree climbing suffered.

Standing upright and walking on two legs are the most obvious adaptations to life on the ground, but the liberation of the hands from locomotion may have been almost as important. Upright posture allowed both the forelimbs and the hind-limbs to become more specialized, each for their different tasks. The legs took on almost all the responsibility for locomotion, so they became bigger and more muscular, but also less good at manipulation than the hands and arms. Our block-like feet with their immobile big toes work better for walking long distances than feet that are equipped with thumbs, but foot-thumbs must be wonderful in the trees. Being no longer needed for the heavy work of either brachiation or knuckle walking, hominin upper limbs could become adapted for more delicate work. As legs became better for walking, the hands and arms become better at carrying weapons, food, and babies. Tools could be more skillfully produced and used. When our ancestors made a commitment to the ground, manipulation could blossom along with bipedal locomotion.

As taking refuge in the trees grew more difficult, predators became a more serious danger, and even the earliest of the ground-living hominins must have taken great comfort in a simple club. An ape who can crack nuts with a rock and twiddle out termites with a bit of grass, should not have had much trouble learning to brandish a club, and even an unworked stick might have tipped the balance when facing a hungry lion. With a bash on the head and a bit of luck, a hominin might stand a fighting chance of persuading the lion to run off without leaving behind so much as a scratch.

In the longer run, the selection for the ability to use a club was just one part of selection for better manual skills. The manufacture, carrying, and use of objects must all have improved along with upright posture and better manual control. Food could be carried instead of being eaten on the spot. Mothers whose arms were no longer needed for locomotion could take more responsibility for holding their babies, so babies could be born at increasingly helpless stages of immaturity. Always there were trade-offs, of course. The better designed the hands and arms were for the relatively delicate activities of carrying babies and manipulating tools, the worse they would be for heavy-duty locomotion.

When our ancestors first left the other apes behind for the risky adventure of living on the ground, they radically changed their environment, first by adapting to life on the ground and then by emerging from the forest and learning to cope with open country. Within a few million years of standing up and leaving the trees, Homo erectus had become sufficiently adaptable to wander over large parts of the old world. Emerging almost two million years ago, erectus traveled across and lived in a wide variety of environments, and these must have required quite varied adaptations. The almost complete loss from the archeological record of everything except stone tools leaves us ignorant of the variability of Paleolithic material culture, but anyone who is capable of shaping recalcitrant stones into tools must also have been capable of working much more malleable wood, grass, leaves, and mud into all sorts of other useful objects. Homo erectus passed too quickly from one environment to another for specific adaptations to have been built in by natural selection. Instead, selection must have favored the ability to learn, and no method of learning would have been more immediately helpful than imitation. Exploiting imitation as a short cut to learning would have had an enormous selective advantage in a population whose environment kept changing. Imitation requires no language and no deliberate instruction, but the better our ancestors could imitate, the more easily the most promising experiments could have spread throughout the community, whether these were new ways for coping with the cold or new ways of catching a previously unknown kind of fish. The individuals who could most easily imitate the new techniques would be those most likely to survive and leave children.

In a population of early hominins that was adapting to rapidly changing environmental conditions, and among whom social relationships were growing more complex, individuals would find it advantageous to infer as much as possible about what is going on in another's mind. Anyone who wants not only to mimic but also to achieve a goal, must grasp what others are trying to accomplish. Selection would then have favored those who best understood where another's attention was directed. Even where no communication had been intended, an imitator would have benefited by an ability to understand the instrumental gestures of others, to understand their goals, and to infer iconic and indexical meaning from instrumental gestures or vocalizations. It was the learner, not the producer, who would benefit by understanding the other's focus of attention, goals, and motivated acts. It was the learner who would benefit by imitation. As always, the onus was on the receiver, not the producer.

Those who could use increasingly skillful mimicry to achieve observed goals would have been favored by selection. With wide enough imitation, learned behavior could be shared by a whole community and passed down from one generation to the next. Imitation was a crucial preadaptation for language, but long before it was ever used for language, it could have been used as a means for learning many other sorts of adaptive behavior in new environments. Imitation would have allowed instrumental acts to be shared among neighbors without the thousands of generations that natural selection would need to build them in.

As hominins became better at figuring out the direction of another's attention, better at understanding the iconicity and indexicality of instrumental signs, and better at imitation, the time would finally come when one individual might benefit by helping another to understand. A pointing gesture might have been among the earliest ways of helping. No great gulf separates an animal that can follow another's gaze from one that can recognize that reaching for an object also suggests attention to it. A considerably greater challenge faces the animal that wants to call another's attention to something, and skilled comprehension must have been possible before deliberate production could begin. A producer needs to know that her own gestures can be understood by others, and she must be willing to help them. Perhaps she can learn that others can interpret her outstretched arm and she may then find it worthwhile to try to help. Once that step had been taken, some modest conventionalization and stylization was all that would be needed to turn such a reach into a point.

When a signal can be learned by imitation, an individual who first understands it can later produce the same signal. As more individuals imitate one another's signals, conventions spread through a community. At the same time, different communities can develop differing conventions, so distinct cultural traditions can be established and then perpetuated. Gesture-calls that are set by common inheritance cannot lead to varying cultural traditions, but imitated signals can. It is imitation that allows different communities to settle on different signals, and it is imitation that makes differing dialects and languages possible.

Imitation, motivated signs, joint attention, and the ability to find patterns are all prerequisites for language, but they do not explain how or why language actually began. Several launching mechanisms have been proposed, most of which I find difficult to take seriously, but since every one of them has been taken seriously by someone, they need to be considered, if only to dispose of them. In the end, selection is the most obvious of all mechanisms, and I find it the best, but I will tick the others off first.

An invention. First, could language have been an invention, like agriculture or the wheel or even like written language or printing?

The mind and language

These inventions all originated at a particular time and place and then, as people found them useful, they gradually spread to wider communities. Perhaps language began when some prehistoric genius had a brilliant idea that he taught to his family and friends, and that was then copied by others. What makes this implausible is the universality of language. Inventions are irregularly distributed. Not everyone writes or grows crops, and even the wheel was unknown in some parts of the world until the last century. Language is not distributed in this irregular way. Barring catastrophic biological or social pathology, people simply cannot be stopped from learning a language. Even in a community where the only common language is a chaotic pidgin of the sort I will describe briefly in Chapter 8, a fully flexible language always emerges among the maturing children. When deaf children who have no language at all are brought together, they create a new sign language. Children who lack experience with wheels or writing cannot be counted on to invent them because children are not adapted for wheels or writing in the way they are adapted for language. We need to learn a vast number of details of our particular language, but we bring specifically designed equipment to the task. The ability to learn a language was built into us during the course of evolution and the building took many long generations. Language was no more invented than was walking on two legs.

A byproduct. Instead of being an invention, perhaps language developed as a byproduct of something else. Perhaps natural selection favored general intelligence, and once we got smart enough, language just followed along. Noam Chomsky suggested that language might be the result of "emergent physical properties of a brain that reaches a certain level of complexity..." but this is nothing more than hand waving. Language is far too complex, and far too specifically designed for communication, to let us imagine that it simply "emerged." Chomsky has done more than anyone else to persuade us not only that language is highly complex but also that much of its complexity is built in to us by our biological inheritance. I find it paradoxical that he so casually dismisses natural selection from any role in language origins. Language is much too complex and too well adapted to communication to have come about as a byproduct of something else.

A mutation. A surprising number of linguists have found it so difficult to imagine how a language could have evolved gradually,

89

that they have resorted to a transforming mutation as the only possible explanation. Most prominently, Derek Bickerton once argued that a single macro-mutation carried language from a stage that he called "proto-language" to the full syntactic language that we use today. This failure to imagine how syntax could develop gradually is an eerie echo of William Paley's inability, two centuries ago, to imagine how such a beautifully designed organ as an eye, could have originated except as the creation of an intentional designer. To attribute language to a single mutation tells us no more than to attribute it to an act of a divine creator. Or, as Steven Pinker has said, to imagine that a language could be put together by a single mutation makes about as much sense as to suppose that a jumbo jet could be assembled by a hurricane.

Discovery. If language could not have been invented, could it have been discovered? However foolish this sounds, it strikes me as a considerably more plausible way to think about the rise of language than invention. Of course, language could not have been discovered fully formed where nothing had existed before, but as listeners struggled to interpret the instrumental behavior of others, they could have discovered bits and pieces of behavior whose meaning could be inferred even when the producer had no intention at all to communicate. The more listeners discovered, the more producers would find it worthwhile to exploit the listener's ability to understand.

Selection. I think we can put inventions, byproducts, and magical mutations behind us, and discovery cannot explain how linguistic capacity was built in. This leaves selection as the only plausible means for bringing language into existence. This is the only reasonable mechanism for creating a complex adaptive system like language. We must still ask just what it was adapted for, however, and there are two candidates. The most obvious is communication, but another possibility is that it began as a way of improving thought, and then later came to be exploited as a means of communication. Language so persistently floats through our minds that we often feel that we think in language. We may wonder how a prelinguistic child, or even a deaf mute who has never had a chance to learn signed language, could possibly think. We know that such people do think, however, for deaf mutes who have learned a language only in adulthood are able to look back and describe their mental lives during the period before they had a language.

Language certainly had to conform to, and be adapted to, the conceptual system that we already had. Our ancestors could give names to things only because they could already form concepts for those things. We can form an infinite number of sentences only because we can think of an infinite number of propositions. Thought, however, does not require phonetics and phonology. Nor does it need the intricate morphology and syntax that help a listener to figure out how the words are constructed and how they are related each other. Anyone who has had a word on the tip of his tongue but failed to dredge its pronunciation from memory knows that it is possible to think of a concept without having an accessible word for it. We do not need all this apparatus in order to think.

I am, myself, guilty of having once argued that language first developed as a tool for thought and that it was only later exploited as a tool for communication. I now think that this was the wrong way to describe what happened, but it was my way of addressing a conviction that something important had to be in the mind before minds could start to communicate with each other. I would no longer use the word "language" for whatever we had in our heads before we began to exchange ideas, and it now seems better to describe whatever was in the mind first as a conceptual system, rather than as language. Later, as linguistic communication improved, language may have had an influence back on the mind. Perhaps language now helps us to handle some complex concepts more easily than we could without it, but language did not need these conceptual refinements in order to get started. The specific features of language, its words, its phonology, and its syntax, were all selected to let us communicate, not as a way to help us think.

In the end, then, we arrive at the almost banal conclusion that the reason for language is, and always has been, communication. Selection for better communication brought language into existence and fostered its development. The characteristics of language that have been built into us, and the characteristics of whatever particular language we happen to learn, need to be understood as adaptations for communication. I still find it reasonable to say that language evolved as one part of an evolving mind but, from the start, linguistic ability was selected to help one mind communicate with another, not to help us with our private thoughts.

5

Signs and symbols

At least since the time of Ferdinand de Saussure, early in the twentieth century, linguists have insisted that the relationship between the form and the meaning of linguistic signs is entirely arbitrary. Whether we call the place we live a *house, maison,* or *casa* matters not at all as long as everyone in the speech community agrees on some consistent convention. To be sure, a few onomatopoetic words, like *whoosh* and *whippoorwill,* echo the sound of wind or the twittering of birds, but these have generally been looked on as minor exceptions to the more usual arbitrary coupling of meaning with sound.

The arbitrariness of our languages places a terrible burden on our memory, so anyone setting out to design a language from scratch would be tempted to use motivated, rather than arbitrary, signs wherever they were possible. Icons that resemble the thing named and indices that point would be much easier to invent, and much easier to learn than totally arbitrary symbols. This means that when language began it was probably much more dependent on motivated signs than our modern spoken languages are. Signs that are conventional and arbitrary have competing advantages, however, and with time, these advantages came to outweigh those of iconic or indexical motivation.

I need to prepare the ground now by giving a fuller description of several types of human communication that I mentioned briefly in Chapter 2, for these demonstrate how extensively we still rely on motivated signs—on icons and indices. In the next chapter, I will trace the steps by which an early form of language with extensive motivation could have become increasingly conventionalized and, in the end, largely arbitrary.

C. S. Peirce's typology of signs was a bit more complex than the three-way division into "icons," "indices," and "symbols" that I described in the previous chapter, for he further divided icons into three subtypes: "images," "metaphors," and "diagrams." Of the three, it is images that have the closest physical resemblance to their referents. Pictures that look like their referents, and onomatopoetic words that sound like them, both count as images. We can create an image by such a simple gesture as wiggling two fingers while pointing them downward in imitation of walking legs. Metaphors relate to their referent in a more abstract way than images do. When talking about a plan of action, I might hold my hands with their palms facing each other, just as I would when insisting on the size of a fish that got away. When describing a plan, my hands would not suggest the plan's absolute size, but they would reveal my sense that this plan has some similarity to a bounded object. It has a beginning and an end. My hands would not form a picture of a plan so they would not shape an image, but they could reveal, metaphorically, something about the nature of a plan, or at least of this particular plan. Finally, diagrams show the relationships among the parts of the object, but nothing about a diagram needs to resemble either the whole object or its parts. A wiring diagram shows how the parts of a circuit are connected, but neither the overall shape of the diagram nor the representations of its individual parts needs to resemble the physical circuit. Illustration 4 shows Peirce's typology of

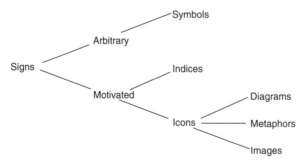

Illustration 4. Peirce's Classification of Signs

signs, except that I have added the level of "motivated" and "arbitrary," which Peirce did not make explicit.

Iconicity is found in many parts of our languages. A linguist finds it easy to overlook the rampant iconicity of the gesticulations that we use with speech, because gesticulation is not usually considered to be a part of language at all. Since it is the the most unambiguously iconic component of human communication it is important to understand how it works. Syntactic iconicity is more extensive than some linguistis have recognized, and intonation, including the patterns of rhythm, pitch, and volume of our speech, is strongly iconic. Taken together, these show just how pervasive iconicity is, and they suggest that it may have been just as important when language began.

Gesticulation. All of us, now and then, mold our hands and wave our arms as we speak. These movements reflect the meaning of our words and sentences so closely that they form a sort of counterpoint to speech. It is these hand and arm gestures to which the word "gesticulation" most specifically refers, but we often bob our heads and even hunch our shoulders in cooperation with our moving arms and hands, and the bobbing and hunching belong with gesticulation in a broader sense.

Due in no small part to the careful work of David McNeill, as reported in his book *Hand and Mind,* the motivation of gesticulation is as well understood as the motivation of any other form of our communication. McNeill uses the word "gesture" for what I, following Kendon and others, prefer to call "gesticulation." I will follow McNeill's analysis, but I will substitute "gesticulation" for his "gesture" in hopes of avoiding confusion with either quotable gestures, such as a head shake, or with the hand and facial gestures of the gesture-call system.

Linguists rarely think of gesticulation as belonging to language. Since it is visible rather than audible, it is simply not a part of what linguists pay attention to. Gesticulations, moreover, are graded rather than discrete, so they are analog, not digital, signals. Even if linguists became interested in gesticulation, they might find it hard to describe its graded signals with their usual analytical tools, but McNeill's work shows that, despite its very different structure, gesticulation is intim- ately tied to vocal language. Whether it is considered to be a part of language or to form a separate set of signs that accompanies language is no more than a matter of definition, of course. What matters, is what it does and how it relates to (the rest of) language.

McNeill finds several distinct kinds of gesticulation. First, what Peirce called "images," McNeill calls "iconics." These imitate the shape or movement of something that the speaker is talking about. We may move our hand upward when talking about someone who is climbing. We hold our hands wide when talking about something big. We may pinch our faces together for something small or trivial. We outline the shape of almost anything with our hands.

McNeill's "metaphorics" correspond to Peirce's metaphors. They are similar to iconics, but they represent more abstract ideas. We may direct our palm first up and then down to show that there are two sides to some issue. We often move our hand back and forth several times when talking about something repetitious, thereby referring to something that occurs in time by the movement of our hand in space. Although not pictures of physical objects, metaphorics often augment the information that we simultaneously express with our words.

McNeill's "deictics" are pointing gestures, so they would be included among Peirce's indices. We may point to people or physical objects when we talk about them. We may also point more abstractly, as when we point first in one direction and then in another to refer to two absent people, to two different events, or even to two opposing viewpoints.

What McNeill calls "beats" mark the points in our sentences that we find most important. Beats can be small movements of the finger or hand, or they can be bobs of the head. Of all our gesticulations, beats are generally the least conspicuous, but they are also the most tightly bound to language. Say *I ábsolútely will nót dó it* very forcefully, by placing a firm spoken stress on *áb-, -lút-, nót*, and *dó*. You can probably nod your head downward so easily with each stressed syllable that you hardly notice you are doing it. Try, instead, to lift your head up just a bit on the stressed syllables. Then try nodding your head downward on unstressed syllables, such as *-so-* and *-ly*, instead of on the stressed ones. You will quickly discover how tightly you are constrained in where you can put a gesticulated beat. Beats almost always coincide with stressed syllables, and they point to the important parts of our discourse.

Gesticulations augment the meaning conveyed by our words. If a man describes fumbling for a pen and simultaneously gesticulates toward his shirt pocket, listeners may remember him as saying that he looked for the pen in his pocket. Linguists sometimes recognize the close relation of gesticulation to language by including it, along with tone of voice, as part of "paralanguage."

Gesticulations are analog signals, but they are much less stereotyped than our analog gesture-calls. Gesticulations are usually well motivated, but unlike the iconicity of onomatopoeia, sound symbolism, or even of syntax, the iconicity of gesticulation is highly productive. Far from limiting ourselves to a fixed repertoire of conventional gesticulations, we continually invent new ones. We may be no more than vaguely aware of what we are doing as we move our hands, but we constantly mold them to display new icons and to reflect, metaphorically, our abstract ideas. The productive iconicity of gesticulation is one of many examples of our ability to perceive similarities among objects, pictures, shapes, gestures, activities, and sounds. The metaphors that we create with language exploit the same ability.

We often suppose that gesticulation is quite varied from one culture to another. Southern Europeans, especially Italians, are sometimes said to wave their arms more vigorously than inhibited northerners. We have little systematic knowledge of gesticulation in other cultures, however, and some of the apparent variation may be due to differing quotable gestures rather than to differing gesticulation. The research that would show the extent of cultural variation in gesticulation remains to be done, but we can be confident that people of all cultures gesticulate.

Sound symbolism. Speech sounds have their own symbolism. The clearest examples are found in words meaning "little" and "large." The vowels used in these words are often icons of the words' meanings. Words that mean "little" often have vowels that have the tongue pushed up and to the front of the mouth. The vowels of *itsy bitsy* are obvious examples. Words meaning "large" more often have vowels with the tongue lower and pulled further back. Much of the appeal of *humongous* lies in the sound symbolism of its vowels. Its vowels sound big, just as the vowels of *teeny weeny polka dot bikini* sound small. The small vowels of *teeny* are formed by a small opening of the vocal articulators.

A larger opening is needed for the large vowels of *humongous*. It is true that *big* and *small* violate this generalization, since *big* has a vowel with the tongue high and front in the mouth, while for the vowel of *small* the tongue is both lower and further back. Nevertheless, so many examples from so many languages fit the generalization, that the relationship is convincing in spite of some exceptions.

Syntactic iconicity. Iconicity has been no more than a minor theme in the study of syntax, but it is not hard to find once it is looked for. Iconicity is particularly clear in word order, and in the order of morphemes within words, and it is seen most clearly of all in the tendency for word order to reflect the temporal sequence of the events being described. A logician might argue that *I went inside and ate* reveals nothing about where I did my eating. The rest of us will normally understand this sentence to mean that the eating took place after going in, so it must have taken place inside. Someone who says *I ate and went inside* is more likely to be understood to have eaten outside. We understand *Veni, vidi, vici* to mean that Caesar's first accomplishment was to come. After that he saw. Still later he conquered. Of course, language gives us ways to say things out of chronological order, but this usually comes at the cost of more intricate syntax. If Caesar had been willing to sacrifice grace, he could have said the Latin equivalent of *Before I conquered, I saw and before that I came*. Compare that to *I came, I saw, I conquered* and you will understand why Caesar chose *Veni, vidi, vici*.

A less obvious form of syntactic iconicity is shown by the order of words in an English noun phrase. The order of the words in *the old red iron steam engine* cannot be easily changed. It is not quite impossible to say *the red old iron steam engine* or even *the old red steam iron engine* but neither of these comes easily. Why do we prefer *the old red iron steam engine* over any alternative order? Is this simply an arbitrary order that we have to learn in order to speak English?

Far from being arbitrary, the order turns out to elegantly diagram the relationship among the concepts that the words stand for. The modifiers that stand closest to the noun are also closest to its meaning. Other than *steam engine*, *steam* is used as a modifier in only a handful of noun compounds: *steam boiler, steamroller, steamship, steam whistle, steam shovel*. These are so few and so distinctive that dictionaries list them as separate entries. *Iron* can modify many more words than *steam*, among them *nail, hinge,* and *key,* but only rarely and metaphorically would *iron* be used to modify a word that refers to something soft. *Red,* on the other hand, can be used as easily with soft things like *shirts* and *cheeks* as with hard things like *nails* or *engines.* The meaning of *old* is even more general, for unlike *steam, iron,* or *red,* it can easily be used with words for abstractions, as in *old problem, old question,* or *old argument.* Finally, *the* is the most general modifier of all, for it can be used with any common noun in the language (i.e. a noun that is not a "proper" noun). The pattern is consistent: Modifiers whose meanings are most specific to the meaning of the noun are placed closest to it. The most general modifiers are furthest away.

If word order were consistently motivated, we might expect all languages to use the same order. Why don't they? In some cases different orders seem to have little difference in motivation. Whether a modifier comes before or after its noun, for example, seems to make little difference. In other cases, historical processes of various sorts probably drag languages away from perfect motivation. We might expect that if languages lose too much motivation, pressures would build until they are pushed back to a more motivated state. As I will point out in the next chapter, it is clear that children learn motivated constructions more easily than constructions that violate motivation. If children use motivated forms often enough these forms could gradually seem less and less like mistakes. After a sufficient number of generations have passed, the motivated form might replace the older unmotivated form. At that point, the language would be pushed back to a form that is more clearly motivated.

Intonation. "Intonation" refers to the melody of speech, first of all to the rises and falls of pitch that accompany our words and sentences, but more generally, to the rhythm and volume as well. The pitch, volume, and speed of language can vary over continuous ranges, so that instead of being contrastive and digital, intonation is graded and analog, just as gesticulation is.

Because intonation is produced with the voice rather than with the hands, and because we hear it right along with the vowels and consonants, it needs to be closely coordinated with the contrastive part of the phonology. This is why linguists generally regard intonation, but not gesticulation, as belonging to language. Nevertheless, gesticulation is also coordinated with the audible component of language, and it is the similarities between intonation and gesticulation, and their shared differences from the rest of language, with which I am now concerned. Intonation, like gesticulation, supplements and supports the contrastive parts of phonology, and like gesticulation it is markedly iconic, though in a quite different way. Gesticulations can be used to form visible images and metaphors. The iconicity of intonation is entirely metaphoric.

To start with, high pitch is associated with high tension, arousal, excitement, eagerness, activity, lack of finality; low pitch goes with low tension, relaxation, completion. As the linguist Dwight Bolinger said: "In the course of an action we are up and moving; at the end, we sit or lie down to rest. In a discourse this translates to higher pitches while [an] utterance is in progress and a fall at the end." Mothers soothe their infants with low-pitched reassuring sounds. High-pitched enthusiasm is stimulating. We raise our voices in fear, anger, excitement, or intense interest. Our voices drop with boredom and fatigue. We hold the floor with a rising intonation. We yield to another speaker with a fall.

Rises and falls of pitch modulate the meaning of the words with which they are used. The end of a statement most often has a fall in pitch, sometimes gradual, sometimes quite abrupt. In English, as in most languages, questions that call for a *yes* or *no* answer, usually end with a terminal rise (*Is he hére?*), but it is misleading to consider this rise as simply a "question intonation." Questions do not always rise, and rises can be found in other places than questions. *Where is he?* does not usually rise on its last word. On the other hand, subordinate clauses typically do rise: *If I had some ríce, I'd eat it.* Rises are more accurately described as indicating a lack of completion. Like subordinate clauses, questions show that something else is expected, but they invite the listener to supply the rest. Statements that end with a terminal rise often suggest uncertainty on the part of the speaker: *I'd like to try that mustárd*, with a rise at the end, leaves room for doubt. Perhaps the speaker is not quite sure he wants it, or not quite sure that it is proper to ask for it. A falling pitch would show more certainty.

The movements of gesticulation and the melody of intonation occasionally escape their usual association with language. We can form our hands into images even without words, of course. We lean our bodies or thrust our shoulders indexically to show a direction. Our hand shapes often reflect the manipulation of real objects in the world. We use our voices iconically whenever we imitate a noise. We can even hum an intonation in the absence of words. In a sufficiently unambiguous context we can answer a question simply by humming the tune of *I don't know*. Even without any vowels or consonants, the intonational contour sounds enough like the sentence to convey its meaning. Try it.

Emphatic stress. Most literally, "stress" refers to the volume with which a word or syllable is spoken, but stressed English syllables are usually also higher in pitch than unstressed ones, and they may be longer. The strength of stress tends to be proportional to the strength of the speaker's emotions. *His name is John* can be said with hardly any perceptible emphasis on *John*. As *John* acquires progressively more volume and higher pitch, the assertion becomes increasingly forceful until it finally becomes a scream. The beats of gesticulation are always closely coordinated with the points of stress, so it seems a bit misleading to insist that stress and intonation belong to language while gesticulation does not. Since extra stress comes at important points of the discourse, often the points where new information is introduced, it reflects the pragmatic flow of information, just as the beats of gesticulation do.

The rises, falls, and discontinuities of the melodic line mark the syntactic divisions of sentences. Each phrase is likely to have one particularly important point marked with especially prominent stress, and this helps to set off the phrase from its neighbors. The melody helps the hearer to untangle the structure of sentences.

Tone of voice. At the periphery of language we find what most people call "tone of voice" and what linguists sometimes group with gesticulation as a part of "paralanguage"—near to language but not quite a part of it. The different voice qualities of men and women count as paralanguage, as do the qualities of children's and adults' voices and the qualities that let us recognize particular individuals, but tone of voice conveys more than just personal identity.

A high-pitched tone of voice suggests small size. It can also suggest the related characteristics of weakness, helplessness, submission, courtesy, or a lack of confidence. A low or falling pitch suggests large size, assertiveness, authority, aggression, confidence, self-sufficiency, and threat. The iconicity is obvious. We expect high pitches from small people and small musical instruments—children, women, and violins. Large people and large musical instruments—men and bull fiddles—are pitched lower. Even among animals, high pitch is associated with submission. A dog's submissive whine is pitched higher than its threatening growl, just as an infant's pleading whimper is high while a sergeant's forceful command is low.

We project an image by the way we speak. Hoping to sound more authoritative than we feel, we may try to mask our nervousness by lowering our voice. In many languages, a rise in pitch is used for polite speech. Women are said to use hesitant and deferential rising intonation more often than men. We can hope to get our way either by submissively raising the pitch of our voice or by forcefully lowering it, but a careful assessment of one's relative social position is needed before deciding which is more likely to be successful. Too forceful a command to a person in authority is not likely to help your cause, but you can easily undermine your own authority by high-pitched whining to a subordinate. We easily recognize the meaning of these pitch differences when others talk, and we assess people's character by the degree of deference or authority shown in their voices. We reveal ourselves with the volume and pitch of our delivery, sometimes more clearly than we intend.

Both by our tone of voice and our gesticulations we convey our emotions and our attitudes toward what we are saying. We can hear the echoes of laughter or sobs in the words of our companions. The emotions themselves are much older than language, and we easily recognize some of our emotions in other mammals—anger and fear, for example, and even the joy shown by frolicking puppies. Our prelinguistic hominin ancestors certainly had mammalian emotions, and they must have used their voices, at least as clearly as apes do, to express them. From the time when vocalizations were first used in word-like ways, the tone of voice probably carried enough information to suggest something about the emotions and attitudes of the speaker. Like the first words of children, the first words in prehistory must have expressed emotions along with their referential meanings. This means that even the very first word-like utterances were, in a limited sense, combinatorial. Adding tone of voice to words did not yield syntax, but it would have helped even a very restricted vocabulary to convey a good deal of information.

Our voices show others how friendly, angry, fearful, joyous, tired, excited, or grief-stricken we are, and we can gesticulate happily or angrily, hesitantly or forcefully, ingratiatingly or in a domineering way. These are the attitudes and emotions that we convey with our gesture-calls, and both gesticulation and tone of voice can be understood, in part, as a contribution of the gesture-call system to language. Gesticulation and tone of voice are used with language, but they remain distinct from its phonological and syntactic core. We do without the communicative contribution of gesticulation every time that we talk in the dark. We strip away the tone of voice when we write. If we want to write well, we must learn how to compensate for its absence.

Poets use the term "prosody" to refer to the metrical structure of poetry, to its rhythms and rhyming patterns. Linguists use the word in a related sense to refer to the pitch, volume, tempo, and rhythm of ordinary spoken language. At the heart of prosody is intonation, but prosody extends in one direction toward the core of language and in the other direction toward our gesture-calls. In Chapter 2, I showed just how different our human gesture-calls still are from language. Nevertheless, we ought not to be surprised if our two communication systems sometimes get tangled up with one another, and nowhere do they get more tangled than with prosody. If we had nothing but the contrastive phonology of vowels and consonants at one extreme, and tone of voice at the other, they would be easy to distinguish. Contrastive phonology, with its discrete units, its high degree of cultural variability, its conventionality, and the ease with which it can be used to construct a large vocabulary, belongs securely to language. Tone of voice, with its graded signals, its relative immunity to cultural variability, and the subtlety with which it signals emotions, belongs just as securely with our gesture-calls.

The difficulty is that we use pitch and volume in several other ways that seem to straddle the differences between contrastive phonology and tone of voice, and it is these for which the term "prosody" is most properly used. Closest to segmental phonology are tones. In a typical tone language like Chinese, each syllable is characterized by a distinctive tone just as each syllable in every language is characterized by distinctive consonants and vowels. Tones may differ in the level or contour of their pitch, so they may be high, low, rising, or falling, and they contrast with one another as clearly as vowels and consonants do. Like vowels and consonants, the function of tones is to keep words distinct from one another. They are clearly a part of contrastive phonology. If tones count as part of prosody they are the most linguistic part. Indeed tones behave so much like vowels and consonants that it might be better to exclude them from prosody altogether, but since they are distinguished by pitch, they need to be taken into account.

Contrastive stress, which distinguishes such pairs of words as *cóntent* "that which is contained," and *contént* "satisfied," is a bit less tightly bound to segmental phonology than tones are. Contrastive stress, in English at least, is less pervasive than the tones of a typical tone language. Fewer pairs of words are distinguished by stress alone than are usually distinguished by tone. Most English word pairs that are distinguished primarily by stress are also related in meaning, but belong to different parts of speech: *cóntrast* as a noun and *contrást* as a verb; *cómplex* as a noun and *compléx* as an adjective.

Even further from contrastive phonology, is emphatic stress. We use emphatic stress to highlight important words, as in *Where were yóu? Í was wórking!* We can use stress to give a word any desired degree of emphasis, so emphatic stress is graded, not contrastive.

Intonation, like emphatic stress, is graded and it is even further than stress from the contrastive system of vowels and consonants. The rises and falls of intonation, as it sets off subordinate clauses and marks questions, do need to be integrated with the more central parts of language, but they do not form a part of the core phonology. The rises and falls of intonation are nothing like the rises and falls of a tone language.

Finally, we come to the tone of voice and its expression of emotion. This is furthest from the linguistic system of vowels and consonants and closest to our gesture-calls.

Sometimes a distinction is made between "linguistic prosody" covering one end of the continuum, and "emotional prosody" covering the other. If forced to draw a dividing line, I would put it between contrastive and emphatic stress. Tones and contrastive stress are digital and would fall under linguistic prosody, while emphatic stress, intonation, and tone of voice are all analog signals and belong to emotional prosody. Imposing a sharp division seems a bit artificial, however. We might even wonder if prosody could have served as an evolutionary bridge connecting the ancient gesture-call system to more recent language. Could language have evolved from gesture-calls via this prosodic bridge? The flaw with such a proposal is that it is difficult to imagine how linguistic prosody could have come before the other aspects of language. Linguistic prosody could not have existed independently of the words and syntax of language. I find it more revealing to look on language as fundamentally distinct from gesture-calls, but to recognize that when two communicative systems are used by the same animal, they are bound to get entangled with one another. Nowhere are the entanglements greater than with prosody. I see prosody as an area where some features of the gesture-call system have invaded language. We hear the echoes of gesture-calls in the prosody of our friends.

Motivated signs and motivated constructions remain important in contemporary languages. Our icons reflect the way we conceive of the world around us. From the beginning of language, the stress and pitch of words probably conveyed the attitudes of the speaker. The earliest humans who grouped words into bunches were probably pushed by their way of thinking to favor some word orders over others. Listeners who were able to exploit these patterns to help them understand would have been able to win the competition with their less well-endowed contemporaries. While motivated signs have an obvious utility, however, arbitrariness and conventionality are more characteristic of modern languages than motivation. The next step is to ask how conventionalization could have undermined the greater motivation that probably characterized the earlier stages of language.

6

Icons gained and icons lost

Students of animal communication use the word "ritualization" for the evolutionary process by which signals, such as a dog's retracted lip, are built in as stereotyped hereditary traits. Ritualization takes a long time and it leads to a signal that requires little learning. A much faster way for a signal to become established is by conventionalization. This is a social agreement that some action will have a particular meaning. As the differences among human languages show so clearly, human beings are ferocious conventionalizers. More modest conventionalizing can be found in apes.

Michael Tomasello and his colleagues studied the communication of young chimpanzees growing up in a semi-naturalistic situation at the Yerkes Primate Center Field Station in the state of Georgia. These young chimps devise and conventionalize gestures in order to communicate, both with each other and with adults. My favorite example is that of the idiosyncratic ways by which infants let their mothers know that they want to nurse. These gestures begin instrumentally. A baby simply shoves his mother's arm aside so that he can reach her nipple. It doesn't take long for the mother to recognize this instrumental act, and once she does, she can cooperate by moving her arm when the baby starts to poke. It is not when the baby first pokes, but only when the mother recognizes the baby's act, that it becomes communicative. At that point the baby can simplify and standardize his poke until he needs only to touch his mother in some characteristic way to let her know what he wants. The interesting thing about these nursing pokes is that they are quite idiosyncratic. Mother–child pairs settle on varied spots where the baby pokes, and on varied ways to poke. Since each infant uses his gesture only with his own mother, each pair is free to conventionalize its own poke.

Young chimps invent other idiosyncratic gestures that they use with each other. Some slap the ground, as an invitation to play. Some stamp their feet or throw sand instead. Infants direct an adult's hand or point to the side of their bodies when they want to be tickled. They present their backs when they would like to be groomed. Adults never make these gestures to an immature chimp, so the gestures cannot be learned by imitation. Nevertheless, they vary from one individual to another, and they are less stereotyped than a dog's retracted lip or the chimpanzee's own pant-hoot. Nursing pokes and requests to be tickled are conventionalized by each young chimp as part of growing up.

The human arms-up gesture is conventionalized in the same way. Unlike a baby's first smiles, the arms-up gesture needs conventionalization, but unlike most conventional and quotable gestures, such as the bye-bye wave, it is learned neither by imitation nor by deliberate instruction. It is, instead, an adjustment to the actions of other people. It is conventionalized from an instrumental gesture but it turns into a deliberate communicative signal.

We share one conventionalized signal with chimpanzees: the begging gesture, made with the hand extended, the palm upward, and the fingers held tightly together. The begging gesture is learned in much the same way as the arms-up gesture. The infant, either human or chimpanzee, learns to use his extended hand to receive objects from an older individual, and the gesture gradually becomes conventionalized as a request. The begging gesture requires more learning by each infant than do the inherited gesture-calls, but since both species use this gesture it probably has deep roots. Our ancestors may have been learning to use it for all the thousands of generations and millions of years since we and the chimps went our separate ways. It would be surprising, after so much time, if natural selection had not built in some facility for learning the gesture.

Audible conventionalized signals are used by some deaf mutes. I was surprised by the vocalizations of several deaf people whom I met in rural India. These people were living with their families and isolated from other deaf people, but each of them used a characteristic vocalization to attract the attention of other members of their families. I presume that they were unable to hear their own voices, but they must have been able to sense their vocalization in other ways. Probably they could feel its vibration. Each deaf person must have accidentally stumbled on a useful signal, and each had his or her own idiosyncratic vocalization. The signal I remember best was a young deaf woman's wavering moan, and it was a highly effective way to call attention or solicit help. These deaf people had conventionalized their signals as they interacted with their family members. If deaf people in the west do not make such vocalizations, it is probably because they have been taught not to. Hearing people may find the noises embarrassing, but by training our deaf children to be quiet, we deprive them of an exceedingly useful way to communicate.

The process by which instrumental acts are conventionalized into communicative signals has sometimes been called "ontogenetic ritualization." To call it "ritualization" is to recognize how much it resembles the ritualization of animal signals, such as the dog's retracted lip. Both kinds of ritualization result in stylized communicative signals, but "ontogenetic" ritualization takes place during maturation and does not have to wait for natural selection to do the job. Signals like the dog's curled lip, that might take hundreds of thousands of years to be built in, are said to result from "phylogenetic ritualization," which is to say that it happens over the long course of evolution rather than in the childhood of each individual. In the hope of preventing the jargon from getting totally out of control, I will use "conventionalization," which seems much easier than "ontogenetic ritualization," but whatever it is called, it must be distinguished from the much slower kind of ritualization that is phylogenetic. Chimpanzees are capable of some conventionalization. Human beings conventionalize so easily that we hardly notice it happening.

Table 2 summarizes the most salient characteristics of conventionalized instrumental acts, and compares them to other types of animal and human signals. Examples from both humans and animals are listed at the left of the Table and some of their properties are shown at the right. The examples in the top half of the chart are gesture-calls that have been built into each individual by the long phylogenetic process of ritualization. Like the gesture-calls of other mammals,

Table 2. Human and Animal Signs

	Phylogenetic Ritualization	Ontogenetic Conventional-ization	Imita-tion	Analog vs. Discrete-Digital
Mammalian gesture-calls				
Vervet alarms	x			D
Dog's snarl, growl, bark, tail wag	x			A/D
Most ape calls	x			A
Ape play face	x			A
Angry and submissive postures	x			A
Human gesture-calls				
Laughs, cries, sighs, etc.	x			A
Facial expressions: joy, fear, anger, sorrow, etc.	x			A
Angry and submissive postures	x			A
Conventionalized instrumental acts				
Arms-up, begging		x		D
Chimpanzee nursing pokes		x		D
Quotable gestures and vocalizations				
Thumbs up, head screw, etc.			x	D
Oh-oh, tsk-tsk, etc.			x	D
Words of spoken languages			x	D
Signs of signed languages			x	D

those of human beings come to us as part of our genetic birthright. At most, they need no more than a bit of triggering by the experiences that come to each of us in the normal course of maturation. They are narrowly constrained by our genetic inheritance.

At the bottom of the chart are examples of the most language-like parts of human communication, including not only spoken and signed language, but also our quotable gestures, and quotable vocalizations such as *oh-oh* and *tsk-tsk*. Between the upper extreme of gesture-calls and the lower extreme of language, are conventionalized instrumental acts. These look like the first hints of the abilities that eventually led to language. Sharing some characteristics of words, but differing sharply from words in other ways, the conventionalized instrumental acts show us what is still needed for anything that we would want to call a "word."

The signs shown in Table 2 differ most sharply in the way they are acquired. Both gesture-calls and conventionalized gestures begin as instrumental acts, but gesture-calls become communicative by being ritualized through the long process of natural selection. Nursing pokes and the arms-up gesture have to be learned by each individual in the course of growing up, just as language does, but unlike language, these gestures are not learned by imitation. Only imitation allows languages and the quotables to be perpetuated as a part of a community's cultural tradition.

In addition to being learned, the conventionalized gestures resemble words in being discrete. No halfway point can be found between two conventionalized gestures any more than a halfway point can be found between two contrasting words. The nursing poke does not grade into anything else. Unlike a laugh, it does not occur along a range of slightly varied forms with slightly varied meanings. An arms-up gesture is unambiguously a request to be picked up. No intermediate gestures connect it to anything else. As discrete as human quotable gestures, the conventionalized gestures are decisively more language-like than are the gesture-calls of either apes or human beings.

On the other hand, conventionalized instrumental acts are less arbitrary in form than most words, for they reflect their instrumental origins. In spite of their conventionalization, for example, the arms-up and begging gestures retain a good deal of the iconicity of their instrumental starting points. The upward pointing arms mean "I want up." The begging hand is positioned to hold something. Most nursing pokes are made somewhere in the vicinity of the mother's breast. The conventionalized gestures differ from words, but the learning needed for nursing pokes and the arms-up gesture distinguishes them, also, from human or animal gesture-calls. They suggest a starting point from which increasingly language-like signals could have developed.

The arms-up gesture and nursing pokes are imperatives, used to call attention or to ask for help, and they are used asymmetrically. Chimpanzee mothers do not ask their infants for the nipple, and human adults do not hold up their arms to ask a baby to pick them up. Since these gestures are never directed to an infant or child, they cannot be learned by imitation. A parent who uses the arms-up gesture does so in playful imitation of the child, not as a serious request. It is the parent, not the child, who is the imitator.

When conventions began to be imitated, a new world opened up. Imitation allowed signals to spread, first to a few intimates, and then to an entire community. This was nothing less than the birth of culture, for imitation must have encouraged a certain degree of standardization. Private signals that are confined to a single pair of animals can easily vary from one pair to another. Once signals start to be imitated, some limits on variation are needed. If everyone needs to understand everyone else, then all the members of a community need to converge on a shared convention. At the same time, conventionalization within a community implies the possibility of differences between communities. Imitation even allows the distinctive conventions of each community to be passed down from one generation to the next. Traditions became possible.

Human beings are both master conventionalizers and master imitators. We copy every conventional detail of our languages, and each community converges on its own set of shared conventions. These conventions can change as the years pass, but even the changes are a demonstration of our skill at imitation. We need to keep imitating, just to keep tuned to our neighbors. The same adaptability that lets each community converge on its own conventions also lets us adapt to changing styles of clothing, music, language, and much else. The result is a world that is filled with wonderful variation, including thousands of mutually unintelligible languages.

Signals that are both conventionalized and shared are not common in other species, but songbirds and some whales show us that they are not unique to human beings. The learning needed for the songs of birds and whales, allows local populations to converge on conventionalized communicative patterns, just as learning allows the conventionalization of human languages. It is right to call the localized signals of birds and whales "dialects," for like our own dialects they are made possible by imitation. Just as the dialects of language change through time, so do the local dialects of birds and whales. These animals are exceptions, however, for most mammals have little or no ability to imitate conventionalized signals. With careful guidance by humans, a few nonhuman primates have shown some ability to learn conventional signals, but only the human primate learns them easily.

A conventionalized linguistic signal, such as a word, has a superficial resemblance to a ritualized signal such as the retracted lip of a snarl. Both have meaning, both are stereotyped, and both can be understood by another animal. A dog's retracted lip, however, is the product of a long evolutionary history. Only slowly did it develop into a stereotyped threat. The process of ritualization by which natural selection builds in communicative signals can take thousands of generations and hundreds of thousands of years. A word can be conventionalized in a single minute. All it takes is for two people to agree to use a particular sequence of sounds to convey a particular meaning. Languages like ours would be impossible without both easy imitation and easy conventionalization.

No records were left to tell us how conventionalization began in spoken language, but we know a good deal about how it began in writing and in deaf signing. In both, iconicity was important at the earliest stages, but the iconicity gradually yielded to more and more arbitrary forms. Modern spoken languages are better known for their arbitrariness than for their motivation. It seems paradoxical to suggest that these systems of arbitrary signs developed from more extensively iconic ones, but that is the direction taken by both writing and deaf signing, and it's a plausible guess that spoken language followed the same path. Since icons and indices are easier to learn than arbitrary signs, we need to look for compensating advantages that allowed arbitrary signs to win in the end.

Writing. All the earliest forms of writing that we know about were much more iconic than the writing we use today. Ancient Egyptian, the earliest Chinese writing, and Sumerian, the first well-developed written language of Mesopotamia, all relied on pictographs. These offered an easy, though only partial, solution to the problem of representing, on clay or papyrus, the huge number of words in a spoken language, and even in the earliest surviving examples of writing, the pictographs were quite stylized. Illustration 5 shows several cuneiform signs at various stages of their development, with the oldest and most iconic Sumerian forms on the left. The iconicity of these early signs is obvious. The earliest form of the word meaning "water," for example, was formed from two wavy but generally horizontal lines, easily understood as representing waves. Later, for unknown reasons, this sign, along with all the rest of Sumerian writing, was rotated by 90 degrees, and the wavy lines were henceforth written vertically. At once, the sign for water, along with many others, lost much of its former iconicity. Then, with the development of a stylus that made triangular impressions in clay, one wavy line was replaced by a long vertical stroke while the other was replaced by two shorter strokes, one above

an dingir	"heaven" "god"					
ka dug	"mouth" "speak"					
sal munus	"pudendum" "woman"					
kur	"mountain"					
geme	"slave girl"					
ninda	"food"					
ku	"eat"					
a	"water"					
nag	"drink"					

Illustration 5. Origin and Development of Cuneiform Symbols from about 3000 BC to 600 BC. (Reprinted with permission from Samuel Noah Kramer, *The Sumerians*, © 1963. University of Chicago Press, Chicago. pp. 304–5.)

112

the other. By then, the sign had lost any hint of its original iconicity. The gradual loss of iconicity of several other signs can be seen in Illustration 5.

The earliest surviving Chinese characters, a few of which are shown in Illustration 6, were also far more iconic than those used today. A trace of iconicity can still be seen in a handful of modern characters, but most have become completely arbitrary symbols that represent the syllables of the spoken language.

No written language used today has much help from iconic or indexical symbols. At the same time, the last few decades have seen the development of a whole new world of written icons that are used for traffic signs and for instructions on how to assemble or use manufactured objects. Traffic signs and instructions need to be understood

ancient graph	modern character	modern pronunciation	meaning
	象	xiàng	"elephant"
	口	kǒu	"opening, orifice, mouth"
	目	mù	"eye"
	月	yuè	"moon, month"
	田	tián	"(cultivated) field"
	女	nǔ	"(kneeling) woman"
	其	qi	"(winnowing) basket"
	天	tiān	"overhead" > "sky, heaven"
	羊	yáng	"sheep, ram"
	馬	mǎ	"horse"

Illustration 6. Oracle Bone Characters and their Modern Chinese Descendants. (Reprinted with permission from William Boltz "Early Chinese writing," *World Archaeology* 17: 420–35, © 1986.)

by people who speak many different languages. When it is impractical to provide instructions in every language, we resort, again, to pictures.

Sign language. People who have no knowledge of American Sign Language (ASL) find almost all of its signs to be entirely obscure. They cannot be understood without an explanation. Nevertheless, as was pointed out in Chapter 2, many signs are much more clearly motivated than are most words of spoken languages. Signers name things by pointing at them, and form their hands into many iconic shapes. Many ASL signs whose meanings would be difficult to guess without an explanation have enough motivation to be clear once they are explained. Although conventionalized, these signs have not lost all motivation.

Signers who lack a name for something, find it easy to invent one, and their newly invented signs are often clearly iconic. Edward Klima and Ursula Bellugi describe a sign for "cinnamon roll" that was invented by a three-year-old child. She held one hand in a cupped position, and just above it, she made a circle with the index finger of her other hand. She sketched the swirls, the most salient feature of the rolls. Klima and Bellugi also describe a sign made by deaf researchers who needed to talk about a videotape recorder. The machine they needed to name had two reels that spun together as the tape moved from one to the other. The sign invented by the researchers called for the index fingers of the two hands to trace circles, in imitation of the turning reels. Gestures like these are not very different from the gesticulations that a hearing person might make while saying "cinnamon roll" or "videotape recorder," except that, from the start, the signs needed to carry the full burden of communication.

Unlike gesticulations, the signs invented by deaf people tend quickly to become conventionalized. The sign for the videotape recorder began with both fingers circling in the same direction, in realistic imitation of the spools. Soon, however, the signers began to circle their fingers in opposite, complimentary directions. At the cost of reduced iconicity, this not only made the sign easier to form (try it both ways!), but also brought it closer to the style of established ASL, where signs are often formed by the two hands working in mirror-image symmetry. The history of many ASL signs parallels that for the videotape recorder.

Many signs began as clear iconic representations of the objects or actions they referred to, but then became adapted to the established patterns of the language.

With enough time, the original iconicity of a sign may be completely lost. ASL grew from a form of signing that was brought from France to the United States, early in the nineteenth century. Its history in America is relatively short, and many of the changes that it has undergone are well known. One example is the sign for "home." Home is the place where you eat and sleep and its sign began as a compound formed from the sign for "eat" followed by the sign for "sleep." "Eat" is made by a gesture that suggests bringing food to the mouth. For "sleep" the palm of the hand is placed beside the head, as if sleeping. Both signs are transparently iconic, and when they were joined by being formed in rapid succession, their meanings were also joined to express the sense of "home." With time, however, the two parts of the compound merged until it now consists of no more than two taps of the extended fingers on the cheek. The hand shape of "eat" has been retained, but it is now made in approximately the location of the sign for "sleep." The revised sign is quicker to form than the original, but it has lost all trace of the earlier iconicity of its parts. It has become as arbitrary as the English word "home."

Even now, ASL has far more iconic and indexical signs than any spoken language does. In part, this may be due to the relatively short history of the language. When signs are first needed, iconicity makes them easy to invent and easy to learn. Perhaps ASL simply has not yet had enough time to lose the motivation with which it began. More likely, the three spatial dimensions within which signs are produced invite a degree of both iconicity and indexicality that is impossible in the single dimension of time to which spoken languages are confined. Signing offers an opportunity, lacking in spoken language, and the opportunity is richly exploited. The hands can easily form pictures of hundreds of visible objects. Since most of these objects are silent, we cannot possibly imitate them with our voices. Still, sign languages are by no means entirely iconic. They are nothing like pantomime. All their signs are conventionalized and many are as arbitrary as any spoken word.

Signs of deaf children. Centuries were needed to squeeze the iconicity out of writing, but a few generations have been enough to bring considerable conventionalization to American Sign Language. We can watch conventionalization happening even more quickly as every child learns to talk. With her study of deaf children of hearing parents, Susan Goldin-Meadow has given us a compelling example. The children with whom Goldin-Meadow worked had no contact with an established sign language, and their deafness cut them off from the spoken language of their homes. In spite of the absence of linguistic input, these deaf children devised elaborate gestural systems by which to communicate with other members of their families. The signs they used were all iconic or indexical, and at first, they were not so different from the gesticulations of their hearing parents. The children pointed to things as a way of naming them, and they formed shapes with their hands, just as hearing people sometimes do. The gestures of these deaf children had to stand alone, however, and they quickly became conventionalized into something more like words than like gesticulations. Each deaf child created what amounted to a simple language.

All the deaf children used their gestures to convey information about past, current, and future events, and to cope with the world around them. Like children who learn conventional languages, the deaf children requested objects and assistance from others, but they could do so only with their gestures. For example, one child used a point at a book, followed by a "give" gesture, and then a point at her own chest to ask her mother to give her the book. A "hit" gesture followed by pointing at mother asked the mother to hit a tower of blocks. Like children learning conventional languages, the deaf children commented on the actions of objects, other people, and themselves. A point at Lisa was followed by an "eat" gesture along with a head shake, and this was followed, in turn, by a point at the child himself and another "eat," this time with a nod. This string of signs said that Lisa would not eat lunch but that the young gesturer would. Gestures could also be used to recount events that had happened some time in the past. One child used gestures meaning "away," "drive," "beard," "moustache," and "sleep" to comment that the family had driven away to the airport to bring home his uncle (who had a beard and a moustache) so that he could spend the night.

The signs invented by the deaf children differed from the gesticulations of hearing people in two ways. First, they were segmented into a much clearer linear sequence than our more fluid gesticulations. Second, they became sufficiently standardized to contrast with one another. The signs of the deaf children had a more consistent form than the gestures returned by the hearing members of their families. For those who could hear, the gestures stayed closer to ordinary gesticulations, but even the children's signs never become so conventionalized as to be totally arbitrary. They always retained some of the motivation with which they started. An isolated deaf child who is trying to make his or her needs known to people who lack fluency in the sign system is limited to signs that are sufficiently motivated for others to understand. Goldin-Meadow suggests that at least two language users may be needed before arbitrariness can be introduced into a communication system. Two users may find it helpful to agree on arbitrary conventions.

Starting in the late 1970s, a natural experiment took place in Nicaragua that demonstrated the ability of a community of deaf children to develop a full language of signs where none had existed before. Before this time, most Nicaraguan deaf children had been isolated in their families, with no chance to learn a sign language from other deaf people, but when the Sandinistas came to power, they established special schools that brought the deaf children together. Here, in a community of young deaf people, who had as much to talk about as any of their hearing contemporaries, a full language of conventionalized signs emerged. This was a genuinely new language. It could not have been invented by a single person, but when enough people who want to talk are gathered together they always find a way to do so. Within a very few decades, a language developed with the same kinds of grammatical complexities and rich communicative power as any other language. A full language cannot be invented by a single person, but it is impossible to stop a community from inventing one.

The invention of Nicaraguan sign language is an example of what is known as "creolization." When people with no common language but an urgent desire to talk are thrown together, they first invent a "pidgin." Pidgin languages typically have a limited vocabulary and simple, even chaotic, grammar. People just use whatever works, generally stripping the words down to their bare essentials, and each speaker's pronunciation is likely reflect his own linguistic background.

When children grow up in a community where the only common language is a pidgin, they may have no full and conventional language on which to model their own first language. Nevertheless, as they talk to adults and, even more, as they talk to each other, children gain a fluency that their parents may never have managed. Collectively, the children invent a new language that is far richer than the pidgin of their parents, but also very different from any earlier native language. Imitating each other, children conventionalize thousands of details of the new language. A creole of this kind is the invention of a community of maturing children. They soon develop it into a language that is as rich and expressive, and every bit as conventionalized, as any other language. Nicaraguan sign language and spoken creoles show us how quickly a language can be invented. If a community does not already have a language, it takes only a single generation to develop a new one. One person cannot do it, but a community can.

Hearing children. Even among children who grow up in a community that already has a well-developed spoken language, early motivation gradually gives way to increasing conventionalization. The psycholinguist Dan Slobin gives examples from many languages where the "incorrect" word order of small children is more iconic than the "correct" order of the adult language. Logically, for example, most negatives negate the entire sentence in which they appear. It would be diagrammatically iconic to negate *The train will come on time* as *Not–the train will come on time*. Placing the negation outside the rest of the sentence would show that it is not the meaning of just of one of its parts that has been negated, but the meaning of the entire sentence. In ordinary English, we tuck the negation inside the sentence and say *The train won't come on time*, but this loses diagrammatic iconicity. As they begin to learn English, small children often place the negative outside the rest of the sentence: *No sit there, No the sun shining, No fall, No play that*. This violates adult rules of grammar, but it diagrams the meaning of the sentences more accurately than does the grammar of mature speakers. Iconicity comes naturally.

Conventionalization is ubiquitous in human communication. All the written and signed communication systems whose origin we know something about began by relying heavily on motivated signs, but as each system became established, its signs became more and more conventionalized. Finally, having lost all the motivation with which they began, signs reach the point of arbitrariness. On the face of it, this seems odd. The transparency of motivated signs would seem to give them a clear advantage over those that are arbitrary, but conventionalization and arbitrariness have so regularly won out that they must have important advantages that compensate for the loss of motivation. What are they?

In part, conventionalization and arbitrariness represent the victory of the producer (the speaker, signer, or writer) over the receiver (the listener to speech, the viewer of signs, or the reader of words). The receiver might like signals that are clear, explicit, and carefully produced, but the producer's quest for ease and efficiency will lead him to simplify the signals by speaking quickly and even carelessly. Even more, the triumph of conventionalization represents the victory of skilled and experienced users over learners. Motivated signals are much easier to learn than arbitrary ones, so learners should have a clear preference for extensive motivation. Unfortunately for learners, their power to influence the form of a communication system is limited. Generally, they have no choice but to take the signals as they find them. Experienced producers have more control over the language, and they find it advantageous to cut corners, to make a diagram instead of a picture, a stylized hand movement instead of a pantomime, a conventionalized sequence of sounds instead of a realistic imitation of a noise.

The power of vested linguistic interests shows clearly in the ghastly spelling of modern English. Schoolchildren could learn to read and write far more easily if we had a less archaic and irregular spelling system, but by the time those children become writers, editors, and teachers themselves, they will have acquired a stake in the conventional spelling, and they would find little benefit in a more transparent system. Throughout history, and through long stretches of prehistory, language learners have had no more power over their society's forms of communication than our own schoolchildren have over the irrationalities of English spelling. Learners have always had to adapt to the abbreviations and conventionalizations that producers find convenient and that skilled receivers have learned to understand. Learners probably do have more influence over some other aspects of language. When noniconic word order yields to more iconic order, the change is probably helped along by the choices of learners. Children can't do much about our spelling except knuckle under.

Conventionalization speeds up communication and makes the job of the producer easier, but conventionalization has other advantages as well. As signs become standardized they also become less ambiguous. In a highly iconic system, we might expect the signs for "cat," "tiger," and "leopard" to be quite similar, but these are exactly the kinds of things that it is important not to confuse. For practical communication, it is important to keep similar objects distinct. It is much more dangerous to confuse a domestic cat with a leopard than with the kind of tractor that is also sometimes called a "cat." The context will generally suggest whether any given instance of the word refers to an animal or to a tractor. The context is less likely to help us decide between cat and leopard. Too much iconicity invites dangerous ambiguity.

As words became more frequent, conventionalization and arbitrariness would have an additional advantage. People who are clever enough to agree to keep their words in a consistent order should be able to communicate more successfully than those who jumble their words at random. If modifiers are always kept on the same side of the word they modify, listeners will understand them more easily, simply because they will know which word is the modifier and which is the modified. Even this modest degree of conventionalization implies the beginning of syntax and of rudimentary parts of speech.

The rather diverse examples given in this chapter imply something of a paradox. When communication systems begin, motivated signs have a great advantage over arbitrary ones. From the curled lip of a dog to the pictograms of early writing and the iconicity of sign language, all communication systems about whose origins we have any knowledge began with highly motivated signs. In all cases, the sign systems then became increasingly arbitrary until the motivation with which they began was undermined or lost. Animal signals become ritualized. Human signs become conventionalized.

Of course, we do not know about the earliest form of spoken language. We cannot know for certain whether modern human language grew out of communication that had more audible or visible iconicity than we find today. Language has been so heavily conventionalized that linguists have taken arbitrariness to be the norm, but a good deal of motivation can still be seen lurking behind the arbitrariness. This motivation may represent the last fossilized remnant of a much more motivated early form of language.

7

From a few sounds to many words

We need to grapple with a question that is easy to pose but hard to answer: Why did audible languages become dominant over visible languages? People who, because of deafness, cannot use a spoken language are able to develop sign languages that appear to be every bit as rich and as flexible as the spoken languages of the majority. Spoken languages and signed languages each have their own special advantages, but both can be used for the same purposes. Animals, too, communicate with both visible gestures and with audible calls and cries. Yet in spite of their apparent equivalence, hearing people always choose spoken words in preference to gestured signs. How was audible language able to beat out the competition?

Our anatomy suggests that spoken language has been around for a long time, for the human vocal tract has been modified in ways that distinguish it from the vocal tracts of apes, and that adapt it specifically for language. Most importantly, we have much more direct and precise voluntary control over our vocal tracts than apes have. To be sure, we can also use our hands with more precision than apes can, but the hands and arms are not specialized for signed language in the way the vocal tract is specialized for speech. For all their subtlety, sign languages give the impression of being substitutes for the audible languages that most of us use. They are highly effective substitutes, but substitutes nonetheless. Most of us do not need a sign language and most of us will never learn one. If we are interested in the evolution of the ability to learn a language, we must be interested, first of all, in the ability to learn a spoken language.

Thus it is puzzling that, when speculating about the earliest forms of language, it is so much easier to propose stories about visible signs than about audible ones. The fact that chimpanzees have considerably better control over their hands than over their vocal tracts makes it seem easier to begin with gesturing than with the voice. Just as important, iconic and indexical signs are much easier to produce with the hands than with the vocal tract, even for people who are fluent in a vocal language. We might not gesticulate so much if we could point and make shapes with our voices. In searching for iconic and indexical signs in this chapter, I will often find it easier to suggest convincing manual examples than convincing vocal examples.

The ease of making iconic and indexical manual signs has encouraged an enthusiastic minority of scholars to argue that language must have begun with visible gestures rather than with audible vocalizations. Apes can be taught to form manual signs much more easily than they can be taught to articulate words. The sign languages of the deaf are splendid tools for communication, and it is relatively easy to devise iconic manual signs that look enough like the thing they represent to ease the learning of these signs. It is not surprising that gestural theories of language origins have been so popular. Nevertheless, the gestural theory has one nearly fatal flaw. Its sticking point has always been the switch that would have been needed to move from a visual language to an audible one.

Once a visible language had become established, it is difficult to imagine any way that it would yield to a language that is audible. Opportunistic natural selection would have been more likely to build further on what was already in place than to start fresh with a new medium. A new and initially clumsy vocal language would have offered poor competition for an established system of gestures. If at any point in our own ancestry incipient visible language was significantly better than an audible counterpart, no form of audible communication would have had much chance of catching up and becoming dominant. It is not enough to point out, as Armstrong, Stokoe, and Wilcox did, that vocalizations are produced by articulatory "gestures" (by which they mean movements of the vocal organs), and then imply that the switch from manual gestures to vocal gestures would be unproblematic. The gestures of the vocal tract are largely invisible and we perceive them with our ears, not with our eyes. In no way is this a trivial switch that can be hidden behind the common use of the word "gesture." The unanswered puzzle about the switch to speech can be rephrased but not disposed of: Once a language of visible manual gestures had been launched, what could have induced a switch to audible vocal gestures?

One partial answer to this puzzle is to recognize that the earliest adaptations and preadaptations for language were all cognitive. The understanding of both visible and audible signs should have benefited from better joint attention, better imitation, and a more skillful ability with motivated signs. As cognitive abilities improved, our ancestors should have become better at understanding both vocalizations and visible gestures. A second partial answer is to presume that, even if communication by visible gestures was important at first, vocal communication began very quickly and managed to become dominant before visible gesturing had forged irreversibly into the lead.

I am left dissatisfied by these answers and I see a genuine and serious problem. Iconicity and indexicality, which we know to have been important at the inauguration of both writing and deaf signing, together with better voluntary control over the hands than over the vocal tract, should have given an early advantage to visible language, but once visible language had begun, how could audible language ever have competed? A speculative answer, but an answer that we should probably take seriously, is to propose that voluntary control over the vocal tract came first as an adaptation to something other than language. The obvious candidate would be some sort of wordless singing or chanting.

The musical theory for language origins has a mixed history. In his book *The Descent of Man and Selection in Relation to Sex*, none other than Charles Darwin suggested that music helped to get language started:

We must suppose that the rhythms and cadences of oratory are derived from previously developed musical powers...We may go even further than this, and...believe that musical sounds afforded one of the bases for the development of language.

Fifty years later, Otto Jespersen proposed something similar. The modern reader is likely to be taken aback by Jespersen's insistence on the "primitive" nature of the languages that he supposed were still spoken by the "savages" of his day, but perhaps we should not dismiss him too casually when he says "[Love] inspired many of the first songs, and through them was instrumental in bringing about human language."

For most students of language origins, even during the last three decades when the topic has regained a degree of respectability, the idea that music could have preceded language and contributed to its development has been ignored or, if thought about at all, dismissed as silly. The latter part of the nineteenth century saw several much-ridiculed theories for the origin of language. These came to be known as the "bow-wow" theory (that language began with imitations of animal cries), the "pooh-pooh" theory (that it began with emotional interjections), and the "yo-heave-ho" theory (that it began as a means of coordinating labor). These and the "tra-la-la" theory, which offered music as a way to get language started, have rarely been mentioned except in ridicule. We do not find it easy to imagine an ancestor who could chant but not talk. On the other hand, music and language have so much in common that we are unlikely ever to understand the evolution of one without taking the other into account. The evolution of music, and even the relation of music to language, has recently attracted serious attention, and linguists and musicologists who care about evolution should be able to give one another some help. We should, for a change, take music seriously.

Some animal vocalizations that are particularly complex or that human beings find particularly lovely, have been referred to as "songs." We all talk of "bird songs," and both the extraordinary long-distance vocalizations of humpback whales and the elaborate calls of gibbons have also been called "songs." Gibbon songs have a special fascination because gibbons are so close to us phylogenetically. I have heard the calls of wild gibbons ringing through the forest in north-eastern India, and the first time I heard them, they sounded so human that I wondered, just for a moment, if they came from high-spirited young people. Gibbon song bouts are very loud. Typically, they last from ten to thirty minutes, but Thomas Geissmann reports that he once recorded a song bout that kept going for eighty-six minutes. Males produce distinctive short phrases that gradually increase in complexity and, at intervals, the female inserts her own distinctive phrases. It is easy to believe that birds and gibbons find their songs as beautiful as we do.

Learning has little or no part in gibbon duetting, but it has a large part in the songs of some birds and whales. Something about communication seems to invite imitation. Humpback whales, to say nothing of birds, are too distant from us phylogenetically for either their singing or their imitation to be directly related to ours, but the analogies are intriguing. If birds and whales can imitate audible signals, then human vocal imitation is not unique.

What animal singing lacks is the regular metronomic beat of human music. We don't usually call something "music" unless it has has very evenly timed beats that let us synchronize both the production of the music itself and the dancing that so often goes with it. We can tap a foot to music, but not to ordinary prose language nor to the vocalizations of any non-human mammal. Among mammals, as far as we know, only human music and poetry have a metronomic beat. A few birds have repetitious songs that come close, but birds do not synchronize their behavior with the help of their songs. To find metronomically synchronized behavior among any species but humans we need to look as far away as the chorusing of frogs, the chirps of some kinds of insects, and most beautifully, the synchronous flashing of some species of tropical fireflies.

Much poetry, of course, is metrical, but does language that is not overtly poetic have a regular rhythm? Language has sometimes been said to have a regular beat. Certainly English stresses can occur with sufficient regularity to give it a rhythmic feel, and short stretches of English can have stresses that are evenly enough spaced to count as rhythmical if not quite metrical. If I say *I dó nót wánt bróccoli* with enough vehemence, I can space the stresses on four successive words as evenly as the beats of metrical poetry or music.

A regular beat allows us to anticipate the beats of others so that we can coordinate our behavior with great precision. We can clap in unison because we can predict the instant when others will clap. We can dance, and the vast majority of men who are recruited or drafted into the world's armies can be persuaded to march in step. We coordinate our speech so closely with our conversational partners that it can have a rhythmical feel. We could not do such things if we could not predict the timing of our partner's behavior. No other mammal will do such things. Not even teams of circus horses can be trained to walk or run in step. Unlike music, poetry, marching, or dancing, however, prose language does not have a sustained metronomic beat. We can find bits of prose with four or five evenly spaced stresses but we rarely find more. If you attempt to recite ordinary prose while spacing the stresses as evenly as the beats of music or metrical poetry, you will quickly discover that it is impossible to make your language sound remotely like normal speech.

Does this have anything to do with the origin of language? If we are not afraid to speculate, we can imagine an early hominin with a single type of vocalization that was ancestral to both music and language. It would have lacked the precise and continuous beat of music but it might still have allowed close coordination among the participants. Like the duetting of gibbons, perhaps, it could have allowed pairs or groups to sing or chant, either together or in turn, but it would have been more voluntary and more dependent on learning than a gibbon duet. It would also have been more variable among individuals and groups than gibbon vocalizing. Like both our music and our language it would have been subject to conventionalization. If we push the analogy with birds and whales, we might wonder if early human vocalizations could have been used to mark local bands—to distinguish "us" from "them." Perhaps it was used for display. Perhaps it was a way to attract mates. If the men and women of the Paleolithic found each other's vocalizations attractive, sexual selection could have fostered a rapid increase in vocal skills.

Another possibility could have been the use of vocalization for what has been called "motherese," the special style that many people, not only mothers, use with small children. Motherese is typically higher in pitch and uses longer vowels than most speech, and it may have a more rhythmical quality. While most of today's motherese comes with the syntax and segmental phonology of ordinary language, its distinctive prosodic features could have been used to sooth or stimulate a child long before either words or syntax existed. Vocalization would have communicated something, as all vocalizations do, but with what mixture of emotional and cognitive messages it is hard even to guess.

After a united initial phase, vocalization would have had to split into two parts. The part carrying the more emotional messages would have developed a more regular beat and become music. The part that carried the more cognitive messages would have turned into language. This scenario would account for the deep parallels that are still found in music and language, and a period of common vocal development would have given the time needed to bring the vocal tract under voluntary control. If sexual selection contributed to the development of both vocal song and vocal language, that would suggest an even closer relationship between music and language.

The proposal for a common period of prelinguistic and premusical vocalizations is nothing if not speculative, but it does suggest one way by which the need to switch from visible to audible communication might have been avoided. We can imagine the vocal tract coming under good voluntary control before anything we would want to call "language" had even begun. If the voice was being used to soothe infants, to signal affiliation to a local group, or to attract a mate, it might then have been co-opted for more language-like communication. The scenario is too speculative to be regarded as a "solution" to the problem of just how audible language became dominant, so in the rest of this chapter I will have to finesse the problem. I will write as if the very first stages of language profited from the ease of recognizing and making visible motivated signs, but assume that the later stages were primarily vocal. This is considerably less than satisfactory, but is the best that seems possible just now.

Gaining the ability to use words may have been the single most important step in the evolution of language. Without words, neither syntax nor phonology would have had any reason to exist, but single words would be useful all by themselves. The words we now use fit into specific syntactic roles, but as long as single words were never used in combinations, but only alone, they could have had no syntax.

A word relates a particular form (either a vocalization or a manual gesture) to a concept. I write "concept," here, rather than "thing" or "meaning," because concepts always mediate between words and things. Some of our concepts relate to objects and qualities of our world, but we also have concepts for all sorts of things that do not exist in reality, from griffins and elves to flying saucers and imaginary numbers. We give names to these concepts of our imagination as easily as we give names to our concepts of palpable and visible material objects.

To an observant animal that was good at recognizing another's focus of attention and good at motivated signs, all sorts of instrumental gestures and vocalizations would take on meaning. In this way, observers and listeners would pick up hints about the intentions and behavior of others. If proto-musical vocalizations were being used to coordinate behavior or to entertain, they could have been one source for incipient words. In an observer's mind, another individual's actions would become associated with the actor, with particular places where the action took place, or with associated objects, desires, or emotions. Reaching would indicate the focus of attention as clearly as the direction of gaze, and the manner of reaching would give hints about what was wanted. We should imagine a community where individuals were recognizing scores or hundreds of such signs before anyone was imitating them or trying deliberately to communicate with them. Learning to interpret all these signs amounts to a considerable expansion of the kinds of understanding that we find in apes, but no sharp break.

Cooperation, of the kind that can be coordinated by nursing pokes and the arms-up gesture, could have increased even without imitation, but as learning and conventionalization became easier, imitation would allow several individuals, and then whole communities, to share the same signs. An ever wider range of instrumental vocalizations and gestures could turn into shared signs. The shape and movements of the hands used for holding and peeling a banana, the posture needed for picking up a baby, or the chant used to entice a lover might be conventionalized and copied. Iconic and indexical signs should have been particularly easy to recognize, and once understood, these too could have been imitated and gradually turned into conventional symbols that an entire family or band could share.

The first signs to spread through a community by imitation could hardly have had all the characteristics of the typical words we use today. Since there was no syntax, the first words could not have fallen into syntactic classes. There could have been no nouns, verbs, or adjectives, although there could have been gestures and vocalizations that called attention to objects, actions, or qualities. Nor was contrastive phonology ready and waiting for language to begin. Rather the first words, whether audible or visible, were probably as holistic as *tsk-tsk* and *unh-unh* in sound, and perhaps they were like our exclamations in meaning: *hey you!, damn!, hello, wow!, yes, no.* Many of the first words could have been used to persuade another individual to do something: *come here, go away, follow me, groom me here, give it to me.* Perhaps they were used to agree and refuse, to question and answer, to scold and praise, to tease, warn, greet, and take one's leave. Such words need no larger syntactic context, and hominin ears, as acute as those of an ape, could surely have distinguished several dozen spoken holistic vocalizations. Even before they used words, social animals needed to greet one another, call attention, seek cooperation, tell someone to go away, and accept or refuse one another's blandishments. An increasing ability to recognize and interpret the gestures and vocalizations that others used in all these situations would have allowed the signalers to conventionalize their cries and movements, and in that way, make them more explicit.

The first word-like signals may have been as limited as vervet alarm calls to specific situations. Without syntactic support from neighboring words, they could only have been interpreted with the help of the nonverbal context. But however restricted the first words were in sound and meaning, they still differed from all earlier forms of primate communication in being both learned and conventional. Almost surely, something like prosody and tone of voice came along with even the earliest proto-words. The pitch, rhythm, tempo, and volume of spoken signs, or the vigor, size, and speed of gestured signs, would have conveyed a great deal about the emotions and intentions of the producer.

What was missing was the ability to use each word in a wide variety of situations, but even if the earliest conventional proto-words were used with narrow meanings and in limited situations, observers and listeners would always have profited by interpreting beyond what producers intended. It is easy to imagine possible scenarios, but difficult to go beyond speculation. Conventional vocalizations might be used to call other people, each vocalization being used for just one individual and only for the single purpose of calling. Such calls would be useful but they would not yet be personal names. If A's call to B was overheard by C, however, C would be reminded of B. C could then use that information for his own purposes, so for C, its meaning would be widened from a mere call for attention to a sign for an individual. Once listeners were associating distinctive vocalizations with particular individuals there would be no great jump for A to call C's attention to B deliberately, but understanding had to come first.

In a species where imitation, iconicity, indexicality, and joint attention were all improving, individuals would become increasingly adept at finding meaning in the behavior of their fellows. After the shape of a hand used for holding a club began to be associated with a club, the hand shape could be used deliberately to remind someone of a club even when no club was close by. If proto-music had brought the vocal tract under voluntary control, and if vocal displays were a way to gain status and attract mates, distinctive vocalizations could have collected meanings as easily as gestures.

Even if the earliest learned and conventional signs were more social than referential—greetings, commands, warnings, threats, requests, refusals—listeners would always profit from inferring more than their comrades intended. Random events could lead people to associate noises or gestures with places, things, events, or actions. Once speakers could exploit their listeners' abilities, and deliberately use signs or vocalizations to call attention to objects or events in the world, names would be born.

None of this needed to happen suddenly. No magic moment marked the birth of the first word. Thousands of generations could be used for a glacially slow growth in the ability to bestow meaning on instrumental gestures and sounds. There must have been an equally slow expansion in the range of situations in which individual signs could be used. We will never know the details by which meanings expanded, but we know the outcome: The ability to understand, imitate, conventionalize, and use an enormous number of words with all their intricate and varied meanings.

I doubt if words were ever built from older animal cries and calls. Pant-hoots, long calls, warnings of snakes and hawks, and all the rest of the primate call repertory, like our own sobs and laughter, are too narrowly constrained by biology to have been converted into learned and conventionalized signals. Rather, it is signs that can be learned and shared among small groups that can be turned into words. It was these that could be conventionalized and imitated. These were also the signs whose meanings could be stretched.

With words becoming less limited to specific situations, something recognizable as language had begun. No animal in its native habitat uses anything like words, though the apes that have learned from humans show us minds that are on the brink of linguistic ability. All of phonology and syntax remained, but with words, the first major step had been taken. Even single words in isolation would have given skillful users and understanders the means to build more complicated social systems and to maneuver within them.

Can we say anything about the sequence by which words of various meanings were added to the lexicon? We can find hints from two related kinds of change that we can still observe and that could go back to the very beginning of language. First, words with abstract meanings are generally derived, gradually but persistently, from words with more concrete meanings. Second, what linguists call "function words" are generally derived from "content words."

The most concrete of all words are the names we use for our concepts of objects, qualities, and actions. These are concepts of things that we can perceive and point to in the world around us: *dog, house, moon, red, hot, run, cry, sleep.* Even these concrete words force us to classify. We need to be able to recognize that some objects or actions are enough alike to let us call them by the same name, while other objects or actions are different enough to need different names. We could not talk at all without classifying, but the boundaries of our classes are rarely precise. *Dog* means, first of all, the familiar domestic canine, but we extend the word easily to foxes and wolves. All of them, in an extended sense, can be called *dogs.* With only a bit more difficulty, we use *dog* for a person who acts in ways that we associate with dogs. We persistently stretch the meaning of words, push their borders to use them in ways that, although metaphoric at first, come with time to be accepted as an ordinary part of the meaning of a word.

Red refers, most literally to a color, but it can also stand for left-wing political ideas, and when we *see red*, we are angry. Machines cannot walk but they can *run*. When older machines *ran*, wheels turned or pistons moved back and forth, even if they did not *run* across the room. Now, computers can *run* with no perceptible movement at all. Concrete names for body parts can be used for abstract spatial relations. Americans describe something as *in back of us* and then *in back of the house*, or even *in back of the tree*, as if a tree could have a front and a back. Words whose most literal meaning is spatial, such as *at*, *on*, and *in*, are pressed into service to describe time. We can not only shop *at* a department store *on* Fifth Avenue *in* New York, but we may arrive *at* 9:30 *on* a Monday *in* March. Temporal terms like *since*, in turn, can take on a causative meaning in a sentence such as *Mary has come here since she was unhappy at home.*

Perhaps the earliest vocabulary grew in the same way that vocabulary still grows. The first names were probably used to call attention to concrete objects, qualities, and actions (*baby, wet, walk*), etc. Perhaps the first humans to have words did not even have the intellect for more abstract concepts. Except for proper names, which refer to a single object, even the earliest words would have had to be used for a variety of similar but less than identical objects or events. Such words imply an ability to classify. Some things, but not others, were within the range of a word's meaning, but there would probably always have been a tendency to push the limits. Listeners would infer more than speakers intended, and then speakers could exploit their listeners' broader understanding. Gradually, words with more abstract meanings (*enemy, weird, allow*) would become possible. Words and phrases like *unicorn, phlogiston,* and *the perfect triangle* show us how easily we can name ideas that have no reality beyond our imagination. Other words became specialized for grammatical use, to show how the content words are related to each other. It is difficult to say much more about the paths by which vocabulary grew.

The most astonishing thing about the modern lexicon is its sheer bulk. Incomparably larger than the stock of signals of any animal species, it has to rank as one of the most spectacular characteristics of human language. Language-trained apes have learned more signs than any other animals, but they cannot rival humans in the numbers of their words. It has been difficult to find much relationship between brain size and either vocabulary size or general intelligence in modern humans, but the vast size of the human brain must have something to do with the need for a vast amount of storage to hold that vast vocabulary. By some unknown combination of bulk and better circuitry, our brains have been selected to let us learn and use an awful lot of words.

If skill at word learning gave some individuals an advantage over others, we have an obvious place for an evolutionary arms race. Until some physical limitation made a puffed-up brain too much of a burden, either during birth or simply as an expense to maintain, it is hard to imagine any limit beyond which a larger vocabulary would cease to give an advantage. The ability to learn and to use a large vocabulary could have developed slowly but relentlessly over a very long period. As vocabulary expanded, the beginnings of phonology and syntax would have been useful, but they could have developed as gradually as the vocabulary.

As always, comprehension must have guided production. Like us, our ancestors must always have understood more words than they could use. Even in communities where, by our standards, the language was rudimentary, the members of a small family or a group of friends may have been able to agree on private words, just as a mother and an infant chimpanzee still agree on one form of a nursing poke, and just as modern human families delight in their own idiosyncratic and private words. Some words could have spread through the community while others remained limited to a few speakers, but even a small community would offer enough words to let an exceptionally gifted word learner know more than her average neighbor.

It has been known for several decades that the spoken vowels of our languages are characterized by bands of dominant frequencies that are known as "formants." We distinguish vowels by their differing formants, but it is the relationship among the formants, rather than their absolute frequency, that makes each vowel distinctive. This is a good thing, because the absolute frequencies vary with the pitch of the speakers' voices. Somehow our brains normalize the vowels so well that we hear the speech sounds of different speakers as if they were the same. We hear a high-pitched child's *hat* as if it has the same vowel as the *hat* of a deep-voiced man. Listeners even use the formants to help identify the consonants that surround the vowel.

The use and recognition of formants was once regarded as a uniquely human skill, but it is now known that other mammals also produce and recognize formant patterns. Macaques seem to perceive formants as acutely as we do. They can identify individuals by their voices, and they can judge the size of another animal by the characteristics of its formants. Even mammals that are phylogenetically remote from us can be trained to discriminate human speech sounds. Kanzi's ability to learn to understand a large number of English words shows us that his ears were ready for the sounds of our language, but the bonobo ability to distinguish human speech sounds is not due to any special adaptation of bonobo ears. Rather, bonobos can discriminate the sounds of human speech because our human vocal tract was designed to be used with our own primate ears, and bonobo ears are very much like ours. We have no evidence that humans have any specific abilities in speech perception that we do not share with other primates. Our hearing abilities go back a long way in phylogeny, and to whatever extent the vocal tract has become adapted for language, it was an adaptation to the primate ears that we already had. Our tools for comprehension came before our tools for production.

The human vocal tract shows more adaptations to language than our ears do, but the significance of the vocal tract changes has been a topic of considerable controversy, even acrimony. The human vocal tract is bent at a sharper angle than that of chimpanzees, and the larynx is placed lower in the throat. The bending may be, in part, an incidental result of upright posture. As humans stood up to walk, the face had to tip downward in relation to the body so it could still look forward at the world. The resulting bending of the vocal tract may have prepared it for a more diversified range of vowels than chimps could manage even if they had better voluntary control over the machinery. Upright posture developed several million years ago, however, and Philip Lieberman and his associates once contended that the critical changes in the vocal tract were much more recent evolutionary developments. Lieberman believed that only the most modern humans are able to talk and that even people as recent as Neanderthals who lived less that a hundred thousand years ago were incapable of making the vowels required for articulate speech.

This argument has some other serious problems. Even if early languages had to manage with fewer or slightly different vowels than we have, this may imply no more than that their vowels would sound a bit odd to the modern ear. The reconstructions of battered fossil skulls may give a poor indication of the angle of the vocal tract. Even with the best-preserved skulls it is difficult to judge the position of the larynx, and perhaps it was lower in early humans than the reconstructions have implied. More recently, moreover, W. Techumseh Fitch has shown that humans are not the only mammals with low larynges. Even where its resting position is high, the individuals of some species lower their larynges during vocalization. I am not persuaded that our vocal anatomy was so late to develop or is so different from that of early humans that it gives evidence for the late development of language. To the extent that our vocal tract has been adapted for speech, moreover, it must have adapted to language that was already in use. Once language had started, some tinkering could have improved the vocal tract, but the tinkering had to follow, rather than precede, the beginning of language.

Gaining voluntary control over the movements of the vocal tract was probably more important than any refinement in its shape. If vocal chanting or some other nonlinguistic use of the voice had come first, that would have eased the beginning of vocal language, but whenever it happened, voluntary control must have come about gradually. When vocal signals became useful, anyone with better than average voluntary control would have had an advantage. Each improvement would have increased vocal versatility and, at the same time, raised the stakes. Perhaps when we remember how much variability is still found in voluntary control over the muscles that wiggle the ears and scalp, raise one corner of the upper lip into a sneer, and curl the tongue or turn it over, we should not be surprised that the members of an earlier population could have varied in their control over the lips, tongue, velum, and larynx.

Nor must we forget that the ease with which deaf people develop rich manual languages shows us that the most crucial adaptations for language were cognitive. By comparison with the changes that came to the brain and the mind, the changes in the input and output machinery seem almost trivial.

The earliest word-like vocalizations surely lacked the organized and contrastive phonology of modern languages. Vocalizations must have been more like *shh!* or *tsk- tsk* than like most of the words we now use. Our modern quotable vocalizations are not constructed with ordinary vowels and consonants, but even quotable vocalizations have recognizable syllables, and the ubiquity of syllables suggests that they are phylogenetically ancient. Typical syllables are made when the vocal tract closes to make a consonant and then opens again for a vowel. Every child's first babbled *ga-ga-ga-ga* is syllabic, and the appearance of syllables sometime in prehistory could have marked the first step toward the kind of sound patterns we still use. Syllables probably developed from the repetitive oscillations of the mouth and jaw that all mammals use when they chew and swallow, and that primates also use for the gestures and noises known as "lip smacks," "tongue smacks," and "teeth chatters." During all these gestures, the jaw oscillates up and down so that a relatively closed mouth alternates with a relatively open mouth, much as it still does when we articulate a sequence of syllables. Once the vocal cords added their vibrations to the oscillation of the jaw and mouth, something recognizable as a sequence of vocal syllables would have become possible, although at both the open and closed phases of the syllables, distinctive vowels and distinctive consonants still needed to be differentiated.

Audible holistic words, such as *tsk-tsk* or *unh-unh*, are few in number. A few dozen might be as many as we could easily distinguish, though perhaps we could manage more if the vowels and consonants of our conventional phonology were not so conveniently available. As the number of words expanded, some way was needed to keep them all distinct from one another, and this was achieved by means of a phonological code. "Phonology" refers to the sound system of a language, and most specifically, to the manner in which speech sounds are organized into an inventory of contrasting phonemes. The phonemes are the units of sound, such as the sounds of *p, b, t,* and *s,* that would be represented by distinctive letters in a spelling system that was more regular than that of English. English spelling obscures the phonemes of the language by using different letters for the same phoneme (e.g. *c* and *s*) or the same letters for different phonemes (e.g. the differing *th*'s in *thy* and *thigh*). Students of sign language have borrowed the word "phonology" to describe the analogous system of discrete hand shapes, positions, orientations, and trajectories that deaf signers use to distinguish the many words of their languages. The analogy is reasonable because many words of signed languages, like virtually all the words of spoken languages, are constructed from sets of meaningless, but contrastive, components. Spoken words are formed from a sequence of distinctive sounds; signed words can be formed from a cluster of distinctive manual features.

Why do natural human languages, whether spoken or signed, always use a phonological code? Because, as Wilhelm von Humbolt famously said, a code is the only way to make "infinite use of finite means." A finite number of spoken phonemes or of manual shapes, positions, and movements can be organized into an infinite number of spoken words or manual signs. Those of us who have normal hearing and who use an audible language can keep tens of thousands of words distinct by shuffling a few dozen contrasting phonemes into varying combinations. Deaf signers can do the same with contrasting shapes, orientations, and movements of the hands, although they supplement these compositional signs with others that are holistic and iconic. Nature has provided other codes that exploit the ability to make "infinite use of finite means." The atoms of about one hundred elements can be arranged into a potentially infinite number of chemical compounds. A mere four nucleotides of DNA can be shuffled around in ways that define the twenty amino acids, and these in turn can be built into an unlimited number of proteins. Atoms, nucleic acids, and phonemes, all sharply restricted in number, can be combined to yield an unlimited number of chemical compounds, proteins, and words.

As the number of holistic words of an early audible language increased, hearers had to attend to ever finer phonetic distinctions, and the time would come when two words were kept distinct by no more than a single phonetic feature. A feature that could distinguish one pair of words must then have been easy to extend to a second pair. Once *ohoh* was safely different from *ahah*, a listener probably would also be able to attend to the difference between *okok* and *akak*. Using the same phonetic distinction for many pairs of words would be a quick and easy way to increase the number of words that could be kept distinct. Distinctions could be added until a whole system of contrastive phonology was available that could keep an unlimited number of words distinct. Of course neither the hearer nor the speaker did any of this with deliberate intent but, as the vocabulary grew, there would have been insistent pressure to exploit whatever distinctions had already been mastered.

With the development of repetitive but meaningless phonological distinctions, a new level of structure found its way into language. Phonetic features, produced by such varied articulations as the position of the tongue, the shape of the lips, and the vibration of the vocal cords, could be combined to form consonants and vowels of the kind that are used in all modern spoken languages. While meaningless in themselves, the phonemes could be combined in endless ways to form the meaningful morphemes and words of a language. As this system became established, language developed two distinct structural levels, the level of meaningless sounds that could be combined to form words, and the level of meaningful words that could be combined to form phrases and sentences. The result is the kind of combinatorial phonological system that is now found in all natural languages. Phonology was separated from syntax. We describe this by saying that language is characterized by "duality of patterning."

By comparing the difficulty of speech sounds, we can make a guess about the sequence in which they found their way into language. The vowels and consonants that children most often learn first are those that are also found in the most languages. Children who grow up with English, for example, usually learn *m* and *d* before they learn *r* and *th*. The sounds of *m* and *d* are also much more widespread in the world than are sounds like English *r* or *th*. The parallels between children's learning and wide distribution suggest that people really do find some sounds easier than others to distinguish and to articulate. The easy ones would be good candidates for early appearance in phylogeny as well as in ontogeny. We can guess that consonants such as *p, t, k, m*, and *n* and maximally distinct vowels, such as those in *heat, father,* and *boot*, would have come early. Since all languages have open syllables (syllables that lack a final consonant) but some languages lack closed syllables (those with a consonant after the vowel), and since infant babbling begins with open syllables, it tempting to guess that, like a child's babbling, the earliest syllables were also open.

The phonology of our modern languages is so pervasively combinatorial that it can be hard even to imagine a phonology that is only partially combinatorial. *Tsk-tsk* and the other holistic and quotable vocalizations are so few in number that we are likely to dismiss them as irrelevant. We don't even think of them as part of our language. We need look no further than the sign languages of the deaf, however, to find languages whose phonology is incompletely combinatorial. American Sign Language has shapes, positions, movements, and orientations of the hand that are as meaningless and repetitive as the phonemes of spoken languages. These can be used to construct signs whose forms are just as arbitrary as the pronunciation of any spoken word. At the same time, ASL also uses many holistic signs that cannot be so easily analyzed into meaningless parts. The revolving finger that a child used when she invented a sign for "cinnamon roll" was iconic and holistic, not built from a fixed inventory of meaningless hand motions. Many other holistic but conventional signs are used even in mature ASL. Perhaps this is because ASL is a relatively young language that has not yet had time to develop a fully combinatorial system. More likely, ASL simply exploits the potential of its visible medium for iconic and holistic signs. In any case, ASL shows us that a partially combinatorial language is possible. The combinatorial phonology of spoken language could have begun modestly and developed gradually. At first, conventional but meaningless phonetic distinctions would be used for only a few words, but as the vocabulary grew, the combinatorial system spread to embrace almost the entire language until nothing was left behind except for handful of linguistic fossils such as *tsk-tsk*.

As the ability of our ancestors to use words grew, combinatorial phonology provided an elegant solution to the problem of keeping huge numbers of words distinct. Combinatorial phonology allowed the vocabulary that each of us controls to reach huge numbers. None of the elaborate phonology that we find in modern languages has any reason to exist except to keep our words distinct. It does its job extremely well.

Even conservative estimates credit every mature speaker of a language with tens of thousands of words. The currently popular but nonconservative estimate is 60,000. Children seem to learn their words without strain, but as everyone who has ever tried to learn a second language as an adult knows, gaining control over enough words to give fluency is a huge investment of time and effort. Constructing the storage capacity that our brains need in order to hold all those words could have taken millions of years of natural selection, and every growing human being needs a decade and a half of almost full-time effort to stuff words into that storage capacity. To use our words, we need to know not only their distinctive sequences of vowels and consonants, but also the intricacies of their meanings and the range of syntactic constructions in which they can be used. Every bit of this mass of information has to be squeezed somewhere into the brain. No one should be surprised that two or three years of high-school or college French fails to give full fluency. The centrality of the lexicon becomes clear when we realize that the only reason we need contrastive phonology is to give us a code with which to keep all our thousands of words distinct, and the only reason we need syntax is to let us join our words so as to communicate complex meanings with efficiency. Under duress, we can communicate a great deal with very little syntax and with badly mangled phonology. Without words we are reduced to pantomime. Words must have come first in the course of evolution just as they still come first in everyone's childhood.

Much thought and effort has been expended in asking what changes had to come to the ape-like brain of our ancestors in order to use the kind of syntax that we find in modern languages. The changes to the brain that allow us to learn, store, and then retrieve all those words have attracted less attention, but they are every bit as important. For each of the tens of thousands of words that every one of us knows, we have had to learn a pronunciation, a meaning, and a set of grammatical patterns into which it can fit. Just the meaning of a single word requires a substantial amount of storage. This storage space must have expanded gradually. All the millions of years that the human brain has been expanding from an ape-like size must have been needed in order to build the storage capacity, but however it happened, natural selection has given us a brain with an awesome ability to absorb words, and an equally awesome ability to find exactly the words we need at the instant when we need them. We fetch our words from their huge memory bank with split-second efficiency.

Here is a thought experiment: I have no difficulty imagining a species that is very much like Homo sapiens except for having a much higher proportion of its language hard-wired by inheritance. For this species of my imagination, most of language would not need to be learned at all, but like the barks, growls, howls, and whines of dogs, or like our own laughs, screams, and scowls, the language would simply mature. If such a species were to have the flexibility to adapt to new situations, it would have to be able to add new words to its language now and then. No language could be totally hard-wired without crippling the adaptability of its speakers, but I see no reason, in principle, why a species similar to us might not have all of its syntax and phonology and a large part of its vocabulary fixed by its genes and firmly hard-wired into its nervous system. The individuals of such a species would even have some clear advantages over existing Homo sapiens. Maturation would not have to be delayed by the need to learn so many linguistic details, and interpreters would be needed only to translate whatever small fraction of the vocabulary varied from one community to another due to changing circumstances.

I have invented this species as a way of expressing my qualms about too much insistence on the built-in nature of language. Our biological inheritance has certainly equipped us with the ability to learn a language. I have no doubt that many specific biological adaptations are needed to make this learning possible. I am equally certain that an enormous amount remains to be learned. All the many ways in which each language differs from all the others can only be acquired by learning. Since syntax is variable, we can be confident that a good deal of syntax also has to be learned. Anyone who can imagine a species that has more of its language specified by heredity than we do should wonder why our inheritance does not do even more for us. The linguistics of the last half century has so strongly emphasized the built-in nature of language that it is worth asking why even more has not been built in. Why do we still need to learn so much?

Once posed, one answer to the question is probably obvious. Building in even half the number of words that are found in Japanese or English, or in any other language, would have required many times the five million years since we split from the chimpanzees. We know almost nothing about how words are actually stored in the brain, but surely the DNA recipe for empty storage space is vastly simpler than a DNA recipe for tens of thousands of specific words could be. Like the repetitive structure of a computer's memory chips, the empty storage capacity of the brain may even have a rather repetitive structure. The design and construction of memory chips is far simpler than building the detailed circuitry of more specialized chips, and it must have been very much simpler for natural selection to increase the capacity for learning new words than to hard-wire the (conservatively estimated) hundreds of thousands of phonological, semantic, and syntactic details that everyone needs to know in order to use the tens of thousands of words of a language. The few million years since our hominin ancestors left the chimps and the trees behind was simply not enough time to build in all the lexical details that a language requires. And once we grasp the need for learning so many lexical details, it should not be hard to admit the need to learn a large number of syntactic details as well. Even if we can be fairly credited with a "language instinct," a huge amount waits to be learned.

An even more fundamental problem stands in the way of the species of my imagination. Our twenty-three pairs of chromosomes have been estimated to encode something on the order of 30,000 genes. As many as a half of these genes may have some influence on the growth and structure of the brain, but not even all the DNA of all of our twenty-three pairs of chromosomes could begin to hold all the phonological, semantic, and syntactic information needed to specify the pronunciation, meaning, and syntactic properties of every item in our mental lexicon. The only conceivable way, within a few million years, that we could have been given the ability to use the many hundreds of constructions and the tens of thousands of words that every language needs was to build an enormous but empty storehouse and then assign many years of everyone's life to filling that storehouse. However important the built-in component of language may be, the learned component is every bit as essential.

8

Syntax: wired and learned

Ever since 1957 when Noam Chomsky shook linguistics with his first book, *Syntactic Structures*, syntax has occupied a central spot in the thinking of a large number of linguists. Linguistic syntax has a kind of magnificent intricacy that appeals to some kinds of minds, and it has come to be seen as so unbelievably complex as to defy full understanding. All the attention lavished on its interrelated complexities has led some linguists to conclude that its parts are so interdependent on one another that none could exist without all the others, and this has encouraged the idea that full syntactic language could only have arisen all at once, as some kind of linguistic big bang, even as a single mutation. The idea that syntax was born suddenly has, in turn, often been linked with the idea that it appeared quite late in human evolution. If syntax is central to language, then language itself must have came quite late and quite suddenly.

I have never found the arguments for the late and sudden appearance of syntax persuasive. One reason for my skepticism is the memory of listening to my own children pass through successive stages of increasingly complex syntax. We don't have to believe that children follow the same course as the species did when language first evolved, but the years that children need to master syntax ought to persuade us that some sort of step-by-step development of syntax would have been possible in evolution too. Even Bickerton, once the most passionate advocate of a catastrophic mutation, has now backed off, but the idea that language came relatively late and relatively suddenly, even if not as a single mutation, lingers on. The reasons for the popularity of this idea need to be taken seriously, if only to cast doubt on them.

For linguists, the most important support for the sudden appearance of language has probably been the authority of Noam Chomsky. Although Chomsky has said little about evolution, even his most casual pronouncements are taken seriously. He has not denied that the capacity for language evolved, but since we have no direct evidence of its earlier stages, he has tended to dismiss speculation about it as useless. In a rather offhand way, he has suggested that language may not have arisen as a specific adaptation at all, but come instead as a byproduct of a brain that evolved for some other reason. That would mean that our language capacity would never have been the object of selection at all.

Steven Pinker and Paul Bloom disposed effectively of this rather strange idea when they argued, with surgical care, that language is simply too complex to have come about in any way except as an adaptation brought about by selection. This is the only mechanism we know by which complex biological systems, such as the eye or language, can arise. Imagining that language was made possible by a brain that managed to expand for some other reason, amounts to attributing it to chance, and language is simply too complex and too well adapted to our communicative needs to suppose that it was all a lucky accident.

Those attracted by the idea of a sudden development of language have also appealed to the authority of the paleontologist Steven J. Gould and to his arguments in favor of what he called "punctuated equilibrium." We generally think of evolution as a slow and protracted process, but the paleontological record often shows long periods with little change interrupted by shorter periods when changes come more rapidly. It is the shorter periods of relatively rapid change that Gould called "punctuations." Punctuated equilibrium has been interpreted by some of Gould's readers as permitting abrupt evolutionary lurches. Some writers have even suggested that a single mutation or chromosomal reorganization might suddenly give rise to a new species. This interpretation of Gould's position has encouraged the idea that a single mutation might have been responsible for language. Unfortunately for those inspired by Gould, he rejected this extreme interpretation of punctuated equilibrium himself, when he proposed that a punctuation might take as long as 100,000 years to reach completion and could then be followed by a ten-million-year period of stasis. On a geological timescale, anything that happens in a mere 100,000 years counts as "sudden," but such changes result from thousands of generations of selection, not just a single mutation. Punctuated equilibrium is not a doctrine capable of supporting a belief in the abrupt appearance of language.

The third strand of the argument for the rapid and recent appearance of language rests on the evidence of mitochondrial DNA. Most of the DNA in our cells is contained in the nucleus and inherited in almost equal amounts from each parent. In addition to this nuclear DNA, our cells contain small cellular bodies known as "mitochondria" that contain shorter bits of DNA. Unlike nuclear DNA, the mitochondrial DNA is inherited exclusively from one's mother, but like all DNA, that of the mitochondria is subject to mutation and selection. Mutations are relatively rare events, so each of us ordinarily has exactly the same mitochondrial DNA as our mother, our siblings, and our sister's children. Except for an occasional mutation, women but not men have the same mitochondrial DNA as their children. A single mutation results in DNA that is still very similar to the older form, but as mutations accumulate over many generations the DNA slowly diverges. The degree of difference separating the mitochondrial DNA of two people can be taken as a measure of the time since they shared a common ancestor in the female line. This allows researchers to arrange humanity into matrilines, groups of people who are related exclusively through women and descended through long lines of women from the same ancestral "grandmother."

Estimates can be made of the rate at which DNA mutates, so we can calculate approximately how much time has passed since any two matrilines diverged. Similar matrilines will be judged to have diverged relatively recently, while less similar matrilines must have diverged earlier. By comparing the most divergent mitochondrial DNA found anywhere in a species, we can estimate how long it has been since the time of a single female who was the ancestor, through females only, of every individual alive today. Many varied estimates have been made for the date of our mitochondrial "Eve," as she has inevitably been called, but most are between 100,000 and 200,000 years ago. These are surprisingly recent dates, and they have been used to support the argument that fully modern Homo sapiens developed very late. The dates have even been taken to imply that it was language that burst into existence with mitochondrial Eve and that allowed her, and her children and grandchildren, to reproduce so successfully and to conquer the planet.

This argument is not without problems. The method itself guarantees that *some* date will be found for a common female ancestor. That is no more than a deduction from the amount of variability found in the mitochondrial DNA of the modern species. The method, moreover, does not imply that mitochondrial Eve was the only woman of her era to leave descendants. Any number of her female contemporaries could be among our ancestors, but like our paternal grandmother, and like every single one of our ancestors except for the women in the direct maternal line, they would be ancestors whose genes reached us only after passing through one or more men. It is a logical certainty that, at some point in prehistory, a single female must have been the ancestor, in the female line, of every single one of us who lives today, but we have no evidence whatever that would implicate this woman in the earliest use of language.

A good deal of excitement has been generated recently by the discovery of a gene, known by the snappy name "FOXP2." When FOXP2 goes wrong, it causes a specific impairment in language, which effects about half the members of a large extended British family. These people suffer from difficulties with articulation, and they have trouble producing and understanding word inflections and complex syntactic structures. The gene responsible for this disability, and even the precise spot on the DNA where the gene sits, is known. This is the first gene to be located that is so clearly involved with language, and it is startling to find such a specific impairment connected with such a specific bit of DNA. The discovery of FOXP2 holds out the hope that we will soon be able to understand genetic mechanisms in far more detail than has so far been possible.

FOXP2 should not be considered a "language gene," however. Several thousand other genes are believed to contribute to building the human brain, and a large proportion of these could contribute, in one way or another, to our ability to use language. Any one of them might interfere with language if it were to mutate in a destructive way. Nor is the influence of FOXP2 confined to language or even to the brain, for it is known to play a role in the embryological development of lung, heart, and intestinal tissues. Mice have a gene called, not by coincidence, Foxp2. The protein encoded by the mouse Foxp2 differs from the human protein in only three amino acids out of more than seven hundred, and the mouse and human versions of this gene play very similar roles in maintaining neural circuitry. Obviously FOXP2 is not a recent addition to the human genome, although the precise modern form of the human gene does seem to have spread through the population only within the last 200,000 years or so. Whether recent changes in the FOXP2 gene had anything at all to do with helping to fine-tune the most recent stages of our language ability is not known. Even if it did, it is certainly only one of many factors that contributed. FOXP2 tells us nothing about when language began.

The claim that all humans older than modern Homo sapiens lacked a vocal tract that would have allowed language is a fifth argument that has been used to support the late and sudden development of language. I gave the reasons for my skepticism about this argument in the previous chapter.

One argument remains. I have left it until last because it strikes me as a good deal more persuasive than any of the others. The period of the Upper Paleolithic brought important changes to human life. Perhaps as early as 40,000 years ago, people were able, for the first time, to cross the water and to reach Australia. A bit later, other people moved into the difficult environment of Siberia and then on to the Americas. In Europe, the Upper Paleolithic that began about 35,000 years ago, marks the beginning of the era when, in both physique and culture, the people seem hardly different from the hunters and gatherers who have lived in our own time. The human fossils from the European Upper Paleolithic were left by people whose bodies were hardly distinguishable from ours. Dress them and clip their hair in a modern style and they would attract no stares in a modern crowd. The artifacts that survive from the period, most famously the cave paintings of western Europe, but also new and different tool assemblages, show us a technology and aesthetics that seem well within the range of twenty-first-century humanity.

Some archeologists see the Upper Paleolithic as representing a sharp break with everything that came before. In western Europe, the Upper Paleolithic has sometimes been interpreted as abruptly different, even from the immediately preceding Middle Paleolithic of the Neanderthals. If the human bones and technology of the Upper Paleolithic show such a sharp break from their predecessors, archeologists need to search for a cause, and one possible explanation is that it was language that made the difference. Both the human bones and the surviving artifacts from Upper Paleolithic Europe look so much like those of recent people that is hard to imagine them without the kind of languages that recent people have used. It is easier to imagine everyone who lived earlier without language.

Here, too, however, we find disagreement. The break with earlier periods was by no means complete. The Middle Paleolithic shared a good deal with the Upper Paleolithic that followed, and some archeologists read the record to show more continuity than abrupt change. As Illustration 7 shows, moreover, the brain had begun its expansion long before the final cultural burst of the Upper Paleolithic. The apparent acceleration of brain growth would look even less impressive if the data were graphed on a logarithmic scale that showed the percentage of growth per unit of time rather than absolute growth. Changes in technology are hard to detect throughout much of the earlier Paleolithic. Through hundreds of thousands of years, stone artifacts such as the Acheulean hand axes showed little change, but the brain must have been enlarging for something. If selection was directed less toward fostering technical skills than toward social skills such as language, the results of selection might not be visible in the archeological record. We must wait for a better consensus among the archeologists before basing confident conclusions about language origins on the evidence of surviving artifacts.

In the meantime I find it more in harmony with the usual course of evolution, and more in harmony with the two-million-year expansion of the brain, to suppose that there was a long step-by-step development of all aspects of language, including syntax. My own guess is that the beginnings of the special human adaptation for language reach all the

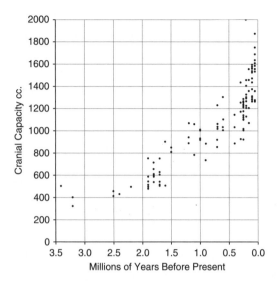

Illustration 7. Cranial capacity of Australopithecus and Homo specimens. (Data for most specimens since two million years ago from Sung-Hee Lee and Milford H. Wolpoff, "The pattern of evolution in Pleistocene human brain size", *Paleobiology* 29 (2003): 186–96. Data for earlier specimens: courtesy of Milford H. Wolpoff.)

way back to the first expansion of the human brain that carried it beyond the size of a chimpanzee brain. That could be as early as the Australopithecines, as much as three or four million years ago, although more serious brain enlargement came only with early Homo erectus about two million years before the present. This does not seem to be too much time to build in the capacity to learn a language of the kind we speak today. The earliest Homo would not have been capable of language like ours, of course, and we might not even want to give the name "language" to whatever it was they had. Still, they could have begun to move beyond the communicative skills of chimpanzees and bonobos, and so started our ancestors along the path that eventually led to language. The widespread consensus in favor of a late development of language looks to me like a case of everyone looking over everyone else's shoulder. Each person concludes that if the experts in another field than his or her own believe language was late, then it must be so.

We should try not to polarize positions, however, and we can agree that an early start for language does not deny the likelihood of some late fine-tuning. Even if the first steps in the direction of language date back to the Australopethecines, development may have picked up with the more rapid increase in brain size that came with the genus Homo. The even more rapid brain growth of the later Paleolithic could imply that late refinements in linguistic skill gave the people of the upper Paleolithic an edge over their predecessors and competitors. Still, it defies our understanding of the way evolution works to suppose that most of the complexities of language could have come as an explosion from a single mutation, or even from a small and relatively sudden cluster of mutations. The real mistake, I believe, is to suppose that it is even possible to assign a date to the beginning of language. It is more likely that some features came early and others late. To point to one particular feature of language as forming the all-important Rubicon that needed to be crossed, distorts the gradualism that we should expect in evolution. Even Gould's punctuations need many thousands of generations.

Creationists have always argued that organisms are so complex and have so many interdependent parts that they could not have been built gradually by natural selection. The only alternative they can see is divine creation. The only sensible response by an evolutionist to this creationist argument is to propose simpler, but still useful, structures that could bridge the gap between nothing at all and the modern organism. Some linguists have supposed that language is so complex and has so many interdependent parts that it could not have been built gradually by natural selection. The only alternatives they can see are a single mutation or the emergence of language as a byproduct of something else. The only sensible response by an evolutionist to these nearly creationist arguments is to propose simpler, but still useful, forms of behavior that could bridge the gap between no language at all and the language we know today. That is what this book is all about.

Arguments among scholars too often become polarized, and no argument has been more starkly polarized than the one over whether syntax grows in us spontaneously as we mature or, instead, depends almost entirely on learning. Chomsky, leading the side that emphasizes spontaneous maturation, has always insisted that language is simply too complex to be acquired by any generalized learning mechanism. The examples of language available to a learner, he says, are too fragmentary, too broken, and too incomplete, to serve as a model for the construction of an adequate grammar. All of us know things about our language that we could never have learned from the fragmentary evidence that we heard as children. This is the "poverty of stimulus" argument, the doctrine that the evidence available to a child is simply too thin. The only alternative, Chomsky tells us, is that each of us comes to the task of language learning with great deal of knowledge of how language works already built in to us by our genes. This built-in knowledge was once called the "language acquisition device," but it has been renamed "universal grammar," usually capitalized and abbreviated to "UG" to make sure that nobody misses the deep significance of the concept. "Universal Grammar" suggests, even more strongly than "language acquisition device," that what is really interesting about language is what is built in. What comes from the outside can come to seem relatively unimportant.

This idea has an enormous appeal. With it, Chomsky almost single-handedly destroyed the hegemony of behavioral psychology. It is no longer possible to think of the infant mind as a *tabula rasa* that waits, unspoiled, adaptable virtually without limits, and able to learn all that is needed with nothing but simple stimulus–response learning mechanisms. In place of a *tabula rasa*, Chomsky offered us a dedicated linguistic capacity, able to learn only because it already knows so much. Far from being empty, the infant mind is a complex machine. Its universal grammar allows it to acquire a language, and whatever is found in any human language, can be there only because the ability to acquire it has been built into every human learner. Since language is so central to the human mind, this doctrine implies that when we discover something about language we also discover something about the nature of the human mind.

In one rather weak sense, no one should doubt that human beings have some sort of built-in capacity for language. It is this capacity, more than any other, that distinguishes us from other animals. Every human being who has any claim to normality acquires a language as a part of growing up. Children do not even seem to find the task particularly difficult, and caretakers must engage in truly pathological behavior to prevent any reasonably normal child from acquiring a language. No animal, not even a carefully nurtured chimpanzee or bonobo, comes close to any ordinary human child in the ability to acquire a language. Clearly, we have a special capacity. We can give a name such as the "language acquisition device" or "universal grammar" to whatever it is that lets us acquire a language, but defined in this general way, the concept doesn't get us very far.

Linguists, of course, usually mean something more by "universal grammar" than the bland assertion that humans are different from other animals, but it is not always easy to know exactly what any particular linguist has in mind. Sometimes, it seems almost to be implied that we have specialized language genes, lengths of DNA that provide a detailed blueprint for the neural circuitry that lets us talk. Even the term "organ" which Chomsky has used to describe the human language capacity can sound as if it points to some physical object, rather like the gall bladder or a kidney, something that not only has a specific function, but that is physically recognizable as a distinct object. I doubt if anyone has ever put the claim as strongly as this, and to do so, of course, would be absurd. While some parts of the brain seem more directly involved with language than others, no part is totally specialized for language, and language processing appears to go on throughout much of the brain. To call the aspects of the brain that allow us to learn and use language an "organ" is, at best, a metaphor by which a widely distributed network is likened to a physical object. The network gives us the capacity for language, but it does so in ways that we have hardly begun to understand. Nevertheless, if the language "organ" is not a physical object, what is it? If the word "organ" is nothing more than a way of asserting that we have a capacity that other animals lack, it is not very illuminating. We have known that all along.

In the face of the insistence on how much is built in, we must not forget that a huge amount needs to be absorbed from the environment before a growing child can fully control a language. Languages do, after all, differ. All those tens of thousands of words can differ from one language to another, and if we need to learn so many words, we ought to be able to learn quite a bit of syntax as well. To nonlinguists, assertions about how much is built in can seem like wild exaggerations. To imply that the details of neural circuitry can be attributed to a blueprint laid down by the genes seems outrageous to anyone who knows more about brain and less about language than most linguists do, and it can evoke a sort of equal and opposite reaction. Perhaps we can learn language by "general learning mechanisms" or by some rearrangement of processes that were already there, though exactly what these mechanisms and processes are is not always clear. Perhaps the difference between us and animals is simply that we can do it faster and that we have more storage capacity, so we can hang on better to whatever we learn. Perhaps the same machinery that lets other animals learn to crack nuts lets us learn language.

I have caricatured these two positions, but not by much, and surely the truth must lie somewhere between the extremes. Something certainly distinguishes our brains from those of the apes, even if DNA sequences do not provide a detailed blueprint for our neural circuitry. At the same time a great deal of language, including all of its vocabulary, has to be learned. Language would not exist without lots of learning as well as lots of heredity. Such a banal conclusion is less exciting than staking out an extreme position from one side or the other, but it is more likely to lead us to sensible questions and plausible answers. Instead of setting up nature and nurture as if they are in conflict, we would do better to ask what part each plays. The undramatic truth is that, like everything else that we are and do, our language results from the way our genetic potential makes use of our experience. We could not learn language if we did not start with the right equipment. Nor could we learn a language without massive amounts of exposure to that language. Posed too simply, the argument about learning and innateness becomes silly.

In my own judgement we do not yet know enough about how the brain works to make it profitable to argue about exactly which bits of language must be credited to the genes and which bits to learning. In any real brain, nature and nurture are so thoroughly scrambled as to defeat any present attempt to sort them out, and I admit to finding some of the claims made about heredity and environment rather pointless. In the rest of this chapter, and in the next, therefore, I will be little concerned about exactly what is genetic and what is learned.

Instead, I want to explore the processes by which the capacity to learn increasingly complex syntax could have evolved.

We should ask, more often than we do, just why our languages have such complex syntax. Languages with much simpler syntax are possible, as we know from pidgin languages. These are ways of talking that are devised by people who lack fluency in any common language. The classic pidgins developed on colonial plantations where slaves or indentured servants from many language groups were thrown together with no shared language, and where they had to develop some rough and ready way to talk to each other.

One modern pidgin has blossomed in a quite different situation. At least twenty mutually unintelligible languages are spoken in the little mountainous state of Nagaland that lies along India's far northeast border with Myanmar. Before the colonial period, whose full force was felt only in the twentieth century, the Naga people had little need to speak with anyone except their immediate neighbors, but their world has radically changed. Roads, schools, and a government bureaucracy now require the Nagas to speak with people from all over the state. They cannot expect to learn twenty languages, so they speak with each other in what they call "Nagamese." Most of the words of Nagamese are taken from the Assamese language that is spoken in the low country west of Nagaland, but when speaking Nagamese, people don't bother with the noun and verb suffixes of conventional Assamese. Nor do they make much attempt to conform to Assamese pronunciation, but are generally content with the phonology of their own native languages. Elaborate syntactic constructions are avoided. Sentences are usually fairly simple, and the range of vocabulary may be restricted. Until very recently, children have hardly ever learned Nagamese as their first language, so everyone who speaks it uses it as a second language, and no one feels any loyalty toward it. In fact, people see it as a broken language, a ridiculous way to speak, but in spite of such scorn, its very simplicity and lack of standardization make Nagamese easy to learn. It provides a remarkably effective way to communicate.

Why are most of us not content with a syntactically simple pidgin like Nagamese? Or, better, why wasn't something like a pidgin enough for our hunting and gathering forefathers and foremothers? One answer to this question will be given in Chapter 10, where ornate syntax, like ornate vocabulary, will be seen as a social asset that helps the most skillful speakers to gain both power and desirable spouses. This would give fancy language direct selective advantages. Now, I am concerned with the more prosaic uses of syntax, with the help it gives us in joining our words in clear and efficent ways. These are ways that can be called "functional"—efficient for achieving the purposes of communication. Pidgins can be used to get one's meaning across, but they don't really work as smoothly as other languages.

Like phonology, syntax serves the lexicon. If we had no words, we would have no more need for syntax than we would for our elaborate phonology. It is words that carry the greatest part of our meaning, but syntax lets us combine our words with crisp efficiency and creativity. By showing the relationship among words, syntax shows the relationship among the ideas that the words stand for. Syntax speeds up communication and helps us to avoid ambiguity.

Think about pronouns, for example. A language ought to be able to manage without pronouns. Instead of saying *he* or *she*, we could simply repeat the description of the person or object to which we want to refer. In telling a story about *the cute little girl I saw yesterday* I could repeat the whole phrase every time I needed to refer to *the cute little girl I saw yesterday*. I could even use my own name when referring to myself, and your name when referring to you. Rather than being essential, pronouns are a bit of a luxury. They give us a few extra words to learn and a bit of extra syntax, but they are useful because they let us speed things up by avoiding repetition. Adding pronouns to a language boosts its efficiency, but it does so at the price of a sliver of extra complexity. All languages have pronouns, and we are all able to learn to use them. That capacity must be a part of our universal grammar, and we can probably agree that the advantages of speed that pronouns give us outweigh the disadvantages of this bit of grammatical complexity.

Pronouns are only the tip of the syntactic iceberg. Other aspects of syntax also promote clarity, efficiency, and functionality, and they do so in more complex ways. Rigid word order and obligatory suffixes tell the listener how the words are related—which word is the modifier and which the modified; which is the subject and which the object; what happened first and what happened later. Complex forms of subordination show how one clause is related to another. Syntax, in other words, is not just a decorative nuisance. It has a serious job to do. The problem facing the evolutionist is to figure out how our minds could have evolved to make them capable of learning such useful complexities.

The most obvious explanation for the development of syntax is to suppose that individuals who were fortunate enough to have the right genes would be able to understand and speak better, in some sense, than their fellows. At the cost of more complex syntax, their genes would make their language more efficient. If efficiency with language led to success in reproduction, the "good language genes" would spread. Just as genes that build long necks help a giraffe to eat, thrive, and reproduce, so genes that allow efficient language should help people to talk, thrive, and reproduce. Language, however, requires both a listener and a speaker and this makes selection for language much more complex than selection for long necks.

Listeners will understand most easily if they can count on others to produce consistent forms. If all languages used case markers on nouns, for example, and if verbs always came at the ends of sentences, language understanding and language learning would be eased if the understander and learner had a built-in expectation for case markers and late verbs. As long as languages vary in case markers and verb position, however, learners need to be flexible enough to learn to understand whatever happens to be in vogue in their community. Given the variation found in the world's languages, children with a syntax that leads them to expect case markers and late verbs would be hopelessly handicapped if they had to grow up in a place where case markers are rare or verbs early. If language was more chaotic in its early days than it is now, it would be absolutely essential for listeners to remain flexible, but as long as listeners are flexible, speakers have no reason to be rigid. If neither speakers nor listeners can profit from more rigid syntax, it is hard to see how natural selection could move a species in that direction. How did the syntactic particularities that seem to be built into the languages we use today emerge in a species where listeners had to be flexible and where speakers had no incentive not to be flexible? Part of the explanation is that human beings are not the only phenomena that undergo selection. Forms of language are selected as well. To understand how this happens, we have to consider how a language passes from one generation to the next.

Every adult who has learned a language can be said to have a version of that language lodged in his mind. Linguists sometimes call this "internal language" often abbreviated as "I-language." This internal language gives adult speakers the ability to understand the utterances of others and to form their own utterances. Internal language is not the same as universal grammar. The child starts with universal grammar, and it is this universal grammar that gives him the means to acquire internal language. The internal language is the mature system.

Once they are spoken, utterances escape the confines of an individual's mind, and pass through what the linguists Simon Kirby and James Hurford have called "the arena of use." Such utterances are no longer internal language, but "external" or "E-language." This is the language that can be heard as it passes from speaker to listener, and it is the language that we can record on paper or tape. Children who are learning the language apply their universal grammar to examples of external language that reach them through the arena of use, so their developing internal language depends crucially on both their inborn capacity, as bestowed by the universal grammar, and on their experience with the external language that is supplied by other people. No more than any other behavior can internal language develop without both hereditary potential and environmental experience. I find it reasonable to think of our universal grammar as a "language instinct" but we have lots to learn before we can talk, so we have to think of universal grammar as an "instinct for learning a language" not as an "instinct for talking." The rather misnamed universal grammar is the means by which we learn, not a collection of the specific grammatical forms that are found in every language. Only as the universal grammar guides children to build their internal language, can they start to produce their own new examples of external language.

As the generations pass, we see an alternation between internal language and external language. Internal language is a mechanism by which an individual can construct utterances in external language.

159

Syntax: wired and learned

External language, in turn, provides the examples which allow a child to construct a new internal language. Each makes the other possible. The reproduction of language from generation to generation is accurate enough to let children communicate with their parents and their grandparents, but no more than genetic heredity is linguistic heredity perfect. With each generation, small changes are introduced into the language and as the generations pass, these changes accumulate. After fifteen or twenty generations, the accumulated changes are likely to be so great that, if we could bring the earlier and later stages together, we would judge them to be different languages. Most of the changes that come about as language passes from one generation to the next are probably neutral in the sense that they make the language neither better nor worse, neither more nor less functional. Every language is in constant flux, but most changes do not accumulate to produce any significantly new type of language.

By using their internal languages, the members of the community fill the external language with every sort of construction. Children must base their new internal language on the external language that swirls around them in the arena of use, but they will not find all the available examples equally useful. In particular, those examples whose parts are easy for the child to sort out, and to that degree more functional (more precisely: those examples that are easiest to parse), will be understood before more difficult examples. In this way, the sentences that are easiest to untangle will serve as the earliest and, quite likely, most important models for learners. Children can be expected to base their new internal language on a sample of the external language that has greater than average functionality. With each passing generation, the new internal language of children should shift just a bit toward increasing functionality. Children's slightly more functional internal languages would then be used to construct increasingly functional examples of external language as well. This lets us tease out a third kind of language change to add to the very long-term cumulative changes brought about by natural selection, and to the random and noncumulative short-term cultural changes that bring constant flux but move in no consistent direction. This third kind of change is "linguistic selection." It does not depend on biological changes, but can nevertheless bring cumulative changes to the

160

language. Once again, we see the crucial role of the listener. Natural selection should favor those who can understand most skillfully, but the listeners and learners will also change the language as they give preference to those examples that are easiest to understand.

Although this kind of linguistic selection should work much more rapidly than natural selection, it is still too slow for us to detect in recent history. If we can detect no differences in the degree of functionality in the natural languages we know, it may be because they have been undergoing linguistic selection for such a long time that they have all arrived at an equivalent degree of functionality. Notice that if linguistic selection consistently favors functional forms, the universality of a functional trait is no guarantee that it is built into our genes. It may have found its way into every language simply because it is so universally useful that learners have selected it everywhere. The end result of linguistic selection is that languages can have the appearance of good design, but some of that design comes from linguistic selection rather than from natural selection. Genes cannot claim all the credit for good design.

This scenario has one problem. It is generally assumed that many generations are needed for linguistic selection to bring significant changes. Each generation may tug the language in the direction of greater functionality, but the tug is gentle. The language of the children differs modestly, not radically, from the language of the parents. Creole languages, however, are said to blossom within a single generation. When children grow up in a community where the only common language is a pidgin, they gain a degree of fluency that escaped their own parents. A community of children, who draw on the pidgin of their parents, but who quickly conventionalize forms as they talk with each other, soon develops a language that is as rich and complex as any other language. Haitian French began as a creole that grew from an earlier pidgin French, but it appears to have the same degree of complexity and flexibility as any other language. Even Nicaraguan sign language needed only a very few decades to develop into a fully flexible language. Children who can invent a language in a single generation would seem to have more built into them than learners who make only slight advances toward functionality in each generation.

To reconcile the slow changes implied by linguistic selection with the much more rapid changes that we find in creolization, we need to look back to earlier stages of language when learners were much less proficient than our own children. Even then, linguistic selection could have slowly guided language in the direction of greater functionality. Linguistic selection can bring changes to language much more rapidly than natural selection, and it should have encouraged better design. Gradually, the functional forms themselves must have become a part of the environment in which natural selection took place. This would have given an advantage to whoever was best at learning the more functional linguistic forms that had come into use. Over a sufficiently long period of time, natural selection would have adapted the species to the kind of language that had already come into existence by linguistic selection. Instead of biology needing to change in order for functional language to become possible, therefore, functional language could have come first as a result of linguistic selection, and then became a part of the environment within which natural selection worked.

This is an example of what is known as the "Baldwin effect" in which innovative behavior comes first, but then provides a changed environment for natural selection. A particularly clear example of the Baldwin effect was the spread of lactose tolerance in human populations that use the milk of animals. Where, as in eastern Asia, milk has not been a traditional part of the adult diet, a relatively high proportion of the population usually has a poor tolerance for lactose. Where milk is not used, lactose intolerance has no disadvantage. When animal milk first began to be used as human food, some people must have been better than others at digesting its lactose. The best digesters benefited most from the new food so they were able to survive and reproduce at a higher rate than their less fortunate and less tolerant contemporaries. Gradually the proportion of lactose-tolerant individuals rose, until now, wherever animal milk is widely used, lactose intolerance has become a relatively unusual affliction. In this case, the behavior came first, and genetic adaptation followed. This is the Baldwin effect.

Just as natural selection favored those who could tolerate lactose, so it should always have favored those who were best at learning and understanding the linguistic forms that were already found in the external language of their environment. If this external language has been shaped by linguistic selection, then natural selection should, in turn, favor those individuals who are best at understanding that kind of language. Linguistic selection can be expected to weed out the less functional forms, so language learners can rely on the functionality of the language they have to deal with. This allows an expectation of functional forms to be built into listeners by natural selection. New forms that are first selected by linguistic selection can then be consolidated by natural selection. As with lactose intolerance, natural selection adapts the species to the behavior that is already in place.

The combination of natural and linguistic selection has the happy consequence that both those who favor innatist explanations and those who emphasize learning turn out to be at least half right. Learning is needed not only for the child who learns a language, but it was also crucial in guiding the development of increasingly functional language. As this happened, however, the language itself provided an environment in which those individuals who had a greater capacity to learn language (those, in other words, with a superior universal grammar) would have been better able than others to survive and reproduce. The extraordinary result is children who are able to invent a creole in a single generation, using no other evidence than the examples of a chaotic pidgin.

9

Step-by-step to grammar

In this chapter, I will draw on two quite different lines of evidence that have been used to make inferences about the stages by which syntax developed. On the one hand, I will ask which aspects of syntax would have been useful without other aspects, and in that way suggest what must have come first. On the other hand, I will consider a set of well-known historical processes that, I am sorry to say, are known by the cumbersome term "grammaticalization." By using these together it is possible to make some reasonable guesses about the stages of linguistic evolution.

Syntacticians have not often been tempted to ask what grammatical constructions would be useful by themselves and without the support of others. Some linguists have even found it hard to imagine a partial syntax, and that interferes with any urge to speculate about the steps by which syntax developed. If you either have it or you don't have it, there isn't much point in asking about steps along the way. Ray Jackendoff finally cut through this Gordian knot when he proposed several stages, each of which is characterized by more complex syntax than the earlier stages, but each of which would, nevertheless, be both possible and useful without the stages that follow. The stages are hypothetical, of course. In modern languages, everything always comes tangled up together, so we can never observe the stages in anything like their pure form. Nevertheless, Jackendoff offers a plausible sequence by which the syntax that we use today could have developed, step by step, from very simple beginnings. The earliest syntax could have developed at the same time as phonology was getting underway, but since syntax would have had no purpose without words, it could not possibly have begun until enough words were available to make syntax useful.

The second line of evidence, "grammaticalization," refers to the way that, over the course of centuries, the words and phrases of a language tend to be squeezed more and more tightly together. This is the long-term result of speakers' urge to say things fast. Changes take place as speakers and hearers interact in daily conversation. Speakers are always tempted to talk rapidly, and cut corners. They reduce the stress on words, abbreviate, and even omit the least important words and affixes. Listeners always have to scramble to keep up. Children, hearing or mishearing the rapid speech of adults, may model their own developing language on the abbreviated forms of their parents. With each succeeding generation, some constructions become just a bit more compact.

Examples can be found for every degree of contraction. For example, Americans find nothing wrong with sentences such as *I'll go pick up some Chinese food* where the two verbs, *go* and *pick up*, are so tightly bound to one another that *go* might even be regarded as an auxiliary verb. This construction must have grown out of a less compacted, *I'll go and pick up some Chinese food*, where the verbs are separated by *and*, and indeed, the British still prefer the longer form. The American sentence is just slightly more compacted than the British one, so it counts as a bit more grammaticalized. Spoken language often shows a somewhat more advanced stage of grammaticalization than writing. We accept *I'd've* in speech, in a sentence such as *I'd've gone if I hadn't been so tired*, but we have not yet started to write it. *I'd've* probably shows the direction in which the language is moving.

From one point of view, grammaticalization looks like a one-way process. Loose sequences of words are drawn into increasingly fixed and regular constructions. Some words are reduced in length and stress until they become glued to other words as prefixes or suffixes. Words and parts of words may then be ground away still further, until they finally disappear. We can observe all these processes of compaction and reduction in our own languages, but they become unambiguous only over the course of several centuries. Written records show how all the phases of grammaticalization contributed to the gradual transformation of old English to modern English, and of Latin to the modern Romance languages.

Languages, of course, cannot forever become more tightly compacted without becoming ambiguous. As soon as contraction and word loss threaten clarity, new ways have to be found to express the lost meanings. Often, this is accomplished by adding new words and forming new phrases. We may write *I have an idea*, but when we talk we are likely to contract this to *I've an idea*. If this seems too clipped to be fully clear and explicit, we can then reinforce it with *got* and say *I've got an idea*. Words are abbreviated and squeezed together, but then other words are added to strengthen the meaning.

It may be helpful to think of the grammaticalization cycle as just a bit like an assembly line or, better perhaps, a disassembly line. Look at the assembly line at one moment and it looks much as it does at any other moment, with bits showing every degree of assembly. Nevertheless, the individual bits are constantly changing as they move down the line. On an assembly line, the bits grow steadily more complex. In language, the bits are steadily ground away but as quickly as some bits disappear new ones enter the language.

Grammaticalization has probably been underway for a much longer time than our historical records can show, very likely since the time when language first began in the human species. Even at the earliest stages of language, we can imagine listeners struggling to keep up with careless or impatient speakers. Those who understood best would always have an advantage over their less proficient contemporaries, but each advance in the listeners' skill would leave speakers free to talk even more quickly, to abbreviate even further, to leave out more. Since it is in the listener's interest to have everything stated clearly and explicitly, while the speaker's interest is to finish as expeditiously as possible, listener and speaker are pushed into endless competition. We struggle with this competition every time we have to ask "what did you say?" or "hunh?"

Through hundreds of millennia and thousands of generations, natural selection surely favored listeners who were increasingly adroit at understanding ever more compacted speech, but this selection is invisible in the few thousand years for which we have written records. We can see the erosion of forms in contemporary languages but, in the short run, whenever these bring dangerous ambiguities listeners push speakers to slow down or to add extra words. Over the much longer timescale of biological selection, language itself became a part of the environment in which natural selection occurred, and as skill at comprehension rose, speakers were able to pack their words ever more tightly together. Many of the most complicated features of our own languages emerge when independent words are bound together, first into phrases and then into words, and when the pieces begin to be eroded away.

Several of Jackendoff's stages run parallel to the stages of the grammaticalization cycle. By considering both together, it is possible to triangulate on a sequence that could have led to the kind of complex syntax that we find in our own languages. In the rest of this chapter, I will follow Jackendoff and outline a series of stages, each building on what had gone before. Some such sequence must have led to modern syntax. Jackendoff did not speculate about the selective forces that might have fostered his various stages, but I will be less cautious. I will assume that, at every stage, comprehension had to precede production.

A summary is called for. I have suggested four different ways by which change can come to language. These take place on very different timescales, but since all four could have been underway simultaneously, they are easy to confuse.

First, even within the span of a single human life, every part of a language is subject to random changes. The parts of a language act a bit like the molecules of air: They jiggle around all the time. Unlike the movements of individual molecules, however, we can watch as the changes in a language gradually accumulate. New words come into fashion. Old words drop out. Pronunciation changes relentlessly, though slowly enough to be less obvious than the coming and going of words. Even syntactic constructions gain or lose popularity. The changes carry the language steadily away from its antecedents, and their very randomness helps dialects to diverge, but the changes do not alter the character of the language. Random changes make the language neither simpler nor more complex, neither more nor less functional. They have no bearing on the evolution of the capacity for language, but we need to be careful not to confuse the random changes with other types of changes that matter more for evolution.

Second are the changes that are part of the grammaticalization cycle. These are best seen in written records that span several centuries. No more than random changes do these result in languages of a new type, but they differ from random changes because the individual changes are unidirectional and progressive. Since there is a good deal of randomness in exactly which bits of language happen to be grammaticalized at which times, varying grammaticalization helps dialects to diverge, but so far as we can tell, the resulting languages do not differ in complexity, efficiency, or usefulness. The importance of grammaticalization for evolution is that it gives us hints about the ways in which complexities could have been introduced into language even during its early stages.

Third is linguistic selection, which was described in the previous chapter. This takes place when some forms of the external language are selected by children in preference to others as models for their own new internal language. Linguistic selection must be presumed to have taken place over an even longer timescale than grammaticalization, so it is not visible either in our own languages or in the historical records of earlier languages. Unlike either random change or grammaticalization, however, linguistic selection could have brought about a significantly new type of language. If children base their own new internal language on a biased sample of the external language, each generation will have a somewhat different internal language than their parents. Linguistic selection should lead to increasingly functional language. This alters the environment in which natural and sexual selection take place.

Fourth and last, are the changes brought about by natural and sexual selection. These required by far the longest timescale of any of the four kinds of change. Understanding how natural and sexual selection brought language into being is, of course, our ultimate goal, but both grammaticalization and linguistic selection probably played crucial parts in allowing natural and sexual selection to work.

Let's start by assuming that single words have come to be in wide use, but that each is used independently, never joined in any sort of construction with another word. Can we imagine a series of plausible steps that would lead toward the kind of language we know today? The first question to ask is: How did pairs of words start to be used together?

Strings of words. The grammaticalization cycle seen in modern languages begins when words or phrases follow each other with no explicit sign of their connection. If I call out *Bill!* and then *Come here!* the first word has a clear and meaningful relation to the meaning of the phrase that follows, but nothing about the form of the words makes that relationship explicit. Even the intonation of the two parts may indicate little about their relationship, though more unified intonation is also possible. A simple change to a unified intonation could be the first step toward grammaticalization.

The very first language users would have had nothing except single words, but as the numbers of words grew, and as speakers became increasingly skilled at using them, words would sooner or later begin to bump up against one another. At first, this must have happened without any communicative intent, but even a speaker who does not join words intentionally may still give a listener enough clues to let her draw her own conclusions. Something could be inferred simply by noticing that two words were used in close succession, and when they drew close enough, something similar to the first stages of grammaticalization must have taken place.

Signalers could hardly have resisted grouping their signs in a way that reflected their own thoughts and their own focus of attention. If only because a speaker's attention is more likely to stay fixed on something for a short period than for a longer one, two words used in quick sequence are more likely to refer to the same phenomenon than two words separated by a long gap. When used beside one another, a word meaning "rock" and a word meaning "hot" might be guessed to mean that "hot" has something to do with "rock." The name for a place and the name for a fruit might be understood as implying that the fruit will be found at that place. If people had personal names, a name might be used along with another word that described what the person named was busy with. *Apple John*, to be sure, could have many meanings: *John has an apple, John wants an apple, I have John's apple,* or any number of other things. In order to narrow the meaning, listeners would need to pay attention to the context in which they heard the words, but two words would give much better clues to a speaker's focus of attention than just one. Even at this very simple stage, we can see how linguistic selection could have prepared for natural selection. Young learners who are exposed to words would notice and imitate some sequences more easily than others. Pairs of words used in close succession would surely be noticed and imitated more easily than pairs of more distantly separated words. Gradually, linguistic selection would consolidate the use of word sequences, and then natural selection could go to work and favor individuals with a superior endowment for recognizing the sequences.

From the start, prosody would have provided one important indication of how words were grouped. The iconicity of intonation—stress indicating the important points, pitch moving up when more is to follow but falling at the conclusion—might have been understood by listeners whether or not the speakers even realized that they were varying their pitch or volume. Even today, the information carried by prosody passes largely unplanned by the speaker, and receives only minimal conscious attention from the hearer. We have a strong sense that we plan our words and sentences, but we are only rarely aware of planning our prosody. It would surely be advantageous for learners to be able to perceive and draw conclusions from the way words are grouped, and there must have been steady selective pressure favoring those who were skillful at it. Once hearers were able to make inferences about the relations between adjacent words and about their meanings, speakers would have had an incentive to put words beside each other deliberatively, and to make the grouping explicit by a unified intonation. When two-word clusters were well established, the step to three- and four-word clusters would certainly have come more easily. Even without consistent word order, groups of three or more words would convey increasingly serious messages.

Meaningful word order. Before listeners can make inferences based on word order, speakers need to arrange their words in ways that reflect meaning; but speakers have good reasons for arranging their words, quite apart from helping their listeners. The earliest consistencies in word order were probably nothing more than iconic reflections of the way speakers ordered their ideas. Modern word order has been rigidified by habit and by consistent syntax, but the pressures of iconicity would have been felt as soon as words began to be bunched together. Today, people who try to communicate in a language they barely know easily resort to strict temporal order as a way to make themselves clear. *Come, shh, look, kangaroo* is hardly an elegant way to talk, but it suggests the order in which events might happen. Even at the start, temporal sequence may have been the most natural way to order words.

Other regularities of word order are more subtle. In modern languages, "agents" tend to come before "goals." The agent is the one who causes or initiates some action, and the goal is whatever is affected by the action. Chronology is not unambiguous here, but by first naming the one who acts, and by naming the one who is affected later, we talk as if the cause comes first and the result follows. We interpret *Bill shoved Tom* to mean that *Bill* did the shoving and that *Tom* was affected by it. Of course, the rules of English require us to order our words in this way, but the linguistic rule is, itself, an iconic reflection of our understanding of how the world works.

Still another tendency in many, perhaps all, languages is to put the new information last. If we say *The travel agent is on the third floor*, the chances are good that we were already talking about the travel agent and are now describing its location. If we have been talking about the third floor, and want to tell someone what is found there, we are more likely to say "The third floor has a travel agent." When we give the new information last we start by supplying some familiar context, and in that way set the stage. Only then, do we offer our new information. This is a way of supplying context and working up to the main point. It reflects the speaker's way of thinking, but it also helps the hearer to focus on the most significant part of the utterance. Stress is another way in which English speakers mark new information, so word order alone is not always a reliable guide, but in the absence of stress new information is most likely to come last.

Once the practice of using conventional word order was established in a few iconically clear ways, it would have been easier to devise useful but more arbitrary conventions, even where iconicity was unclear. Even if *black book* and *book black* do the job equally well, some consistent ordering convention can be helpful. Skill at sticking to chronology, and practice with ordering the agent and the new information would have opened the way for more arbitrary conventions. Here is a place where initial iconicity could have led to later conventionality, and where increasingly firm conventions could finally undermine iconicity. Here, too, is a place where skill at pattern recognition might be rewarded. Individuals with a superior ability to recognize patterns in the groups of words they hear should have had a considerable advantage over their duller contemporaries.

Phrase structure. Modern languages order their words in more intricate ways than anything describable as agent or as new or old information. In particular, our languages allow an entire phrase to be used in place of a single word. For example, *little black dog* can fit into the same spot in a sentence where the single word *dog* might stand alone. So, for that matter, can *shaggy little black and white dog that we found in the alley this morning*, or any number of even more complex phrases of arbitrary length and complexity. It is this ability to replace a single word with a multi-word phrase that allows languages to be recursive, since once a word has been expanded into a phrase, the individual words within the phrase can be expanded again. Some scholars have focused on recursion as the decisive step in the evolution of human language. This strikes me as an unnecessary fixation on a single event, a Rubicon that must be crossed in order to reach true language, but recursion is certainly important, and it gives language a hierarchical phrase structure—words within phrases, within larger phrases, and so on.

The first step was for listeners to recognize groups of words that belong together, and to locate some centrally important word within the group. Speakers might group words with related meanings into bunches, and mark the bunches by uniting them under a unified intonational contour, simply because that reflected their own conception of what they were trying to say. The iconicity of rising and falling pitches would have led speakers to raise their pitch when another group of words was about to follow, but to drop their pitch as they finished speaking. If, for example, a group of related words that formed something like a proto-noun phrase ended with a rising intonation, the listener would have a hint about where one group of related words ended and another began. Speakers might also have given extra stress to the most important word of a group, much as modern English tends to stress the most significant word of a phrase. This is an iconic reflection of the speaker's judgement of importance, but if listeners can pick up the stress difference, they will probably also locate the conceptual center of the phrase. That ought to help them untangle the relations among the words.

In modern languages, the order of words within phrases expresses the kind of iconicity I described in Chapter 5. The modifiers that stand closest to the noun are also those that are most specifically related to its meaning, as in *the old red iron steam engine*. The iconicity of both intonation and word order, then, could have led early speakers to organize their words, with no conscious intent at all, in ways that would help the listener to understand.

Language learners would also contribute to increasingly consistent word order. Children would most easily understand the sequences where intonation most clearly reflected groups of related words and where word order was most clearly iconic. If children patterned their own internal language on the examples from the external language that they understood most easily, they would nudge the language toward more consistent use of the most easily understood patterns. Then, as the external language gained regularity, natural selection would favor those who were best able to conform to regular word order. A start would be made at building in an expectation for consistent ordering.

Finally, the iconicity with which the process began could yield, in part, to arbitrary conventions. As it became easier to group words into bunches, and then to order the bunches with respect to one another, it would become possible to override iconicity and to converge on fully arbitrary ordering conventions. The result is the tightly controlled word order of modern languages, but the iconicity that we still find in both intonation and word order reflects the importance that iconicity must have had in getting the process started. Once it became easy to add words to a phrase, and once phrases could be used within larger phrases, the seeds of recursion had been sown.

Having gained the ability to learn large numbers of words and to order them consistently in ways that convey meaning, our ancestors became capable of a rudimentary sort of language. Perhaps this early language was not too different from the pidgin languages that, even today, are used among people who share no common native language. With plenty of words and some fairly consistent word order people could engage in serious communication on all sorts of topics. They would be able to organize themselves into communities of a kind that no other animal species had ever achieved. The phonology, words, and word order of such an early language would need to be learned, so different communities would settle on different conventions. Distinct languages would have come into existence

What such languages would have lacked were the morphological and syntactic complexities that increase the speed, efficiency, and clarity by which the words of modern languages can be joined. Just as important, perhaps, they may have been less effective than later languages as tools for impressing one's companions, striving for leadership, or advertising oneself as a desirable mate.

For many linguists it is the complexities of morphology and syntax that have seemed to be the most diagnostic features of language. These are the features whose origins in both phylogeny and ontogeny have seemed most difficult to explain. Once we admit that some aspects of syntax can be useful even in the absence of others, however, the problem can be broken down into less daunting steps. We need no longer look in awe at the complexity of syntax or resort to a miraculous mutation to explain it. Jackendoff offers several steps by which increasingly complex syntax could have gradually emerged. I will offer a few guesses about how selection, whether linguistic, natural, or sexual, might have fostered these steps. Focusing on the listeners helps to make sense of what happened.

Function words. Most of the words of a language refer to concepts for objects, ideas, actions, states, or qualities. These words call attention to things and events, both those in the world and those in our imaginations. These are the "content words," usually nouns, verbs, or adjectives that give us the means to talk about whatever interests us. In addition to these content words, all modern languages also have "function" words whose job is to relate the content words to each other. We have words that show how the parts of the discourse are related (*and, but, moreover*), others that show relationships of space and time (*next to, above, before, after, then*), quantity (*some, more, always*), and causation (*therefore, because*). Still other words show negation and turn statements into questions. Function words are useless at the one-word stage. Lonely single words have no other words to relate to, so they have no need for words that relate. As words cluster into ever larger bunches, ways to organize them are urgently needed.

Many of the function words whose history we know developed from content words. We can see how function words are created when words for concrete concepts accumulate abstract meanings. *Back*, a concrete word for a very concrete part of the body, begins to be grammaticalized in the British English *at the back of*, and it is more thoroughly grammaticalized in the American *in back of*. The Chinese word *gĕi* originally meant "give" and it can still have that meaning, but *gĕi* can now also be used as a preposition meaning "to." The literal, word-for-word meaning of *Wŏ jiĕ gĕi tā sān* is "I lend *give* him [an] umbrella" but the sentence is now more naturally translated as "I lend *to* him [an] umbrella." *Gĕi* has developed from a verb meaning "give" to a preposition that labels a recipient, just as *to* labels a recipient in English.

Words that are already abstract can become even more abstract. Spatial terms sometimes acquire a temporal meaning, as when *going to* adds a future meaning to its original directional sense. Temporal terms, in turn, may take on causative meanings. *Since* was originally a temporal term, but in *Since you won't, I will* it picks up a causative meaning. English *have* can still refer to possession and *be* can still mean existence, but both have become so deeply involved in the tense system that they can lose their older meanings. *Where have they gone?* and *What can he be doing?* have nothing to do with possession or existence. Definite articles such as *the* are most often derived from demonstrative adjectives such as *this* or *that*. Indefinite articles usually develop from a word for the number *one* as is shown clearly by French *un* or German *ein* and more obscurely by English *an*, all of which are derived from words that originally meant "one." The older meaning of *will* is still found in *willpower* and *against his will*, but the word is now more often used for the future tense. In modern languages we can see a slow but long-term drift for words with relatively concrete meanings to collect increasingly abstract and relational meanings. These are the kinds of shifts that could have stretched the meanings of words in very early languages.

The first function words of the earliest languages would have had to develop from words with more concrete meaning. There is really no other place for them to come from. The stretching of meaning required to change a concrete word into a function word recalls the even earlier stage of language when single words were stretched to be used in an increasingly wide range of situations. Listeners must have played a large part in both kinds of stretching. Listeners need to find as much meaning as possible in what they hear, and it is when a listener perceives a relational sense in a word like English *back* or Chinese *gěi* "give" that it becomes a function word.

Grammatical classes. The distinction between function words and content words may have been the first step toward the division of words into grammatical classes—parts of speech—but the division might have come, instead, with something more like our own nouns, verbs, and adjectives. From the time when words first began to be used together, people must have had a need to talk about the objects of their world, and also to describe their characteristics and their actions. The objects are the relatively enduring phenomena: *man, woman, lion, sun, club, tree.* Their actions are more transient: *walk, fall, die, break.* Their qualities fall somewhere between: *hot, dark, sweet.* Words that convey these concepts anticipate our nouns, verbs, and adjectives, but they could become differentiated into parts of speech only as they were used in varying combinations with other words.

Many of the earliest word combinations could have linked a word for an object with a word for a quality or action: *fruit sweet; close lion; woman fall; cry child.* At first, the words might have been uttered in either order, but consistent word order would have made comprehension easier. Linguistic selection should have encouraged regularity and pushed a community toward a consistent pattern. If the word that named the object was regularly placed first while words for qualities or actions came second, we would have a basis for recognizing at least two parts of speech, those that came first and those that came second. Once word order was reasonably fixed, the language would have incipient nouns, verbs, and adjectives.

Semantic roles and grammatical functions. When trying to understand how the clauses and sentences of modern languages are organized, we need to distinguish what are sometimes called "semantic
roles" from "grammatical functions." The semantic roles express the
meanings that connect the various parts of the sentence. In *Mary
smashed the glass with the hammer, Mary* is the agent who does the
job, *glass* is the goal that suffers its effect, and *hammer* is the instrument
by which the task is accomplished. Often, as in this example, the
semantic roles correspond neatly to grammatical functions. Here,
the semantic role of agent is expressed by the grammatical function
of subject, the goal by the object, and the instrument by a prepositional
phrase. If that were all that there was to it, we might not need to
distinguish semantic roles from grammatical functions, but language is
not so simple. In *The hammer smashed the glass, hammer* still has the
semantic role of instrument, but now, instead of being expressed by a
prepositional phrase, it has become the subject of the sentence. In *The
glass smashed,* it is *glass* that has become the subject, but it is still the
thing acted on so it is still the goal. In other words, while the prototypical subject may be the agent, it is also possible for either the goal or
the instrument (or words with a number of other semantic roles) to act
as a subject. This variation in the assignment of semantic roles to
grammatical functions is what forces us to distinguish the roles from
the functions. From either point of view, however, we have one or
more names for things (*Mary, glass, hammer*) held together by a word
for an action (*smashed*). Before there was syntax, there could only have
been semantic roles, so we are faced with a question: How did grammatical functions become separated from semantic roles?

Anyone who is inclined toward linguistic determinism must be
tempted to notice a sentence pattern that is found in all languages
and that allows several noun phrases to be used as satellites of a verb.
Could this universal sentence pattern influence the way we see the
world? We seem to understand the world around us as a collection of
objects that act on each other in all sorts of ways, and it is not
impossible that our understanding is influenced by our language.
I am more tempted by a different view. Perhaps our minds were
designed by natural selection to see the world in this way long before
we had any language. Perhaps other mammals organize their worlds

much as we do, full of objects that act on one another. When language came along, it could have simply reflected the pre-existing design of our minds. We do not need to worry about whether the world is *really* constructed of objects that act on one another. If our minds were constructed so as to let us interpret the world in this way, that would be quite enough to account for the structure of our sentences.

The first verbal expression of this view of the world would certainly have used expressions that were closer to the semantic roles of agent, goal, and instrument, than to the grammatical functions of subject, object, and prepositional phrase. The listener's first job was to figure out who or what did it, what it was done to, and what was used to do it. Often this could easily be inferred from the meaning of the words. *Glass, hammer, Mary, smashed* is not likely to mean anything except *Mary smashed the glass with the hammer.* Other examples would be more ambiguous, though it might help to guess that an early word represents the agent while a later one gives new information.

In some cases, however, word order is not enough to avoid ambiguity, and one solution is to use relational words to show the role of each word: *Using hammer acting Mary against glass smashed.* From the vantage point of modern languages these look a bit like prepositions, or even case markers, but at first, they would express the semantic relations among the words rather than their grammatical functions. Certainly the listener would be helped by being able to rely on either consistent word order or relational words that clarify the function of each content word. Then, as fluency increased we could expect conventionalization and grammaticalization to make word order more rigid, and relational markers more obligatory. Having become fixed and obligatory, words and word order would become emancipated from the meanings with which they started. A word or affix that once meant "this is the agent" might be used with a word meaning the instrument or even one meaning the goal, if one of those was the most salient noun. Instead of indicating a particular semantic role, the marker would then indicate the most salient argument of the verb. In that way it would become a marker of the subject, rather than of the agent, and grammatical functions would be separated from semantic roles.

Affixes and compounds. Complex words come in two forms. Compounds are built from two independent words. Inflected words have a dominant central part with one or more prefixes or suffixes hanging on as satellites. In most compounds, such as *footstep* or *blackboard*, the individual parts are easily identified, but with the passage of time the parts sometimes fuse and become obscured. *Breakfast* is derived from words that once suggested "breaking a fast," but the reduced pronunciation of the compound has obscured its origins. Where we know the history of prefixes and suffixes, we often find that they have also developed from independent words but they may show extensive phonological reduction. Frequently used words can be gradually worn down in size and reduced in stress until they lose their independence by being glued to another word. Perhaps we can see an early stage of affixation when we glue *-like* to the ends of words, as in *whale-like* or *adjective-like*. Although *like* can be added quite freely to another word, it retains the pronunciation and meaning of the independent word. A later stage of affixation is seen when *not, had, am,* and *are* are contracted and attached to another word: *can't, you'd, I'm, you're.* These contracted forms are transparently related to the full forms, but other affixes, such as plural *-s* and past tense *-ed*, no longer have any relationship to any independent word.

Contraction, affixation, erosion, and reinforcement must have begun as soon as two words were used together. As some bits were ground away, others remained, and all sorts of fiddly irregularities began to find their way into languages. The competing needs of the speaker for speed and of the hearer for clarity introduce some of the worst complications and irregularities of language, and they keep language from ever quite stabilizing. The contraction of words and their conversion into affixes would have begun as soon as hearers became proficient enough to extract meaning from reduced forms and when speakers began to exploit their hearers' skills.

Reduction and loss of affixes. The final stage of the grammaticalization cycle is the loss of some bits from the language. Affixes are particularly subject to loss. They are usually short and weakly stressed, and even though glued onto other words, they continue to be eroded away. Old English had much more elaborate noun and verb inflections than modern English. Nouns had case suffixes and verbs had markers for person and number, but in the course of several centuries most of these suffixes have now disappeared. The third person singular *-s* of verbs, and the plural -*s* and possessive -'*s* of nouns are now all that remain of person and case markers, while -*ed*, -*en*, and -*ing* remain to show tense. Other suffixes that once helped a listener to understand have disappeared.

When inflections go, ambiguities arise, and since speakers always abbreviate, listeners are continually challenged by language that teeters on the brink of unintelligibility. Those who were good at understanding must always have had an advantage in survival, but better comprehension simply allowed speakers to abbreviate even further. Over the long time span of human evolution, the tendency to compress and abbreviate must have pressed relentlessly in the direction of highly compacted languages. Fluent understanding allowed fluent speaking to follow.

The stages of language evolution that I have proposed in this chapter are, admittedly, speculative. We cannot know the precise sequence by which grammar developed, but we can find entirely plausible processes that would drive the changes. These would have allowed a sequence of small steps to carry a very simple language to the kind of complex language that we use today. A loosely gathered group of words could, by infinitesimal steps and through thousands of generations, have gained more structure until our modern kind of grammar became possible. We do not have to appeal to some magical mutation that blessed us with language. We do not have to look for an abrupt step where it all started or another abrupt step where the pieces all came together. Some aspects of syntax would have been useful without others. Learners could have selected increasingly functional languages. As listeners became more skillful, they liberated speakers to use ever more complex and compacted forms, and speakers would always keep up the pressure by speeding up their speech until it challenged the listener. All these forces working together resulted in human beings who are capable of the kind of intricacies that we find in the languages that we use today.

10

Power, gossip, and seduction

There was a time, not so many decades ago, when anyone who thought at all about the evolution of language took the reasons for its selection to be more or less self-evident. We use language today for every sort of practical purpose, to exchange information, to coordinate our daily lives, and to instruct the young, so it seemed only reasonable to suppose that, from its earliest days, hunters and gatherers used language for the much same purposes. Our ancestors needed to cooperate and to pass on their technology to the next generation just as we do, and language should have been useful in planning and coordinating the food quest, in reaching agreement on where to meet and where to camp, or in explaining to a young person how to build a shelter. Language is an eminently practical tool.

Practical purposes like these offer us plausible explanations for why the earliest stages of language would have been advantageous, but they don't help us much in explaining the peculiarly complex type of languages that all of us now use. In the kinds of societies in which language evolved, subsistence needs ought to have been fully satisfied with a much simpler language than we use, perhaps no more than a rudimentary pidgin. What selective advantages would be offered by the baroque syntax or the enormous vocabulary of near synonyms that characterize all human languages today? To a highly verbal linguist or primatologist who puzzles over the evolution of language, the advantages of being able to talk in a complex and nuanced way may seem so obvious as to hardly require discussion. Nevertheless, the selective pressures that would have fostered the development and perpetuation of verbal complexity should not be taken for granted. In this chapter, I will suggest several purposes, other than subsistence, for which language could have been used. Even now, some of our most treasured uses of language have little to do with practical subsistence, and once language got started, these nonsubsistence uses could have driven language to ever increasing complexity.

The human bones that remain from the European Upper Paleolithic, beginning about 35,000 years ago, are distinguished from modern bones only by a certain robustness. People with bones like these look modern enough to have been able to handle a language of the same type and the same degree of complexity as the languages we use today. If Japanese or English had been available to them, the children of the upper Paleolithic could have learned these languages with no more difficulty than children who are born today. At a minimum, then, the full capacity for language was in place 35,000 years ago, more than 20,000 years before the beginning of agriculture or urban life. Our language capacities were perfected in small and technologically simple societies, where subsistence was based on gathering edible wild plants and hunting wild animals. When we ask what reproductive advantage men and women gained by using language that was lexically, phono-logically, and syntactically more complex than their neighbors, we need to consider the conditions of life in preurban and preagricultural communities. It was in such communities that language began, and it was in such communities that it reached its modern degree of com-plexity.

We can agree that a modest amount of language ability would have been useful for cooperating in hunting and gathering, but it is not at all clear that this technology would be helped by the kind of complex language that all modern human beings use. Excellent coordination in hunting would have been possible with a far less intricate language than ours. Lions manage splendidly effective cooperative hunting with no language at all. In the direct and personal kinds of attack and defense that faced our evolving ancestors, the noise of talking must often have been more dangerous than total silence, and an intricate language would have been useless. A single word or a single cry would have been a more helpful way to warn a fellow australopithecine of an attacking lion than a paragraph of polished prose. Even today, when precise coordination under tense conditions is required, we usually strip our language down to unambiguous essentials. *Duck!* is a far more effective warning than *Please lower you head in order to move it out of the way of that flying rock.*

Language would have been more useful for the initial planning of foraging and hunting than for actually conducting these activities, but a few thousand words, along with a bit of loose syntax and the kind of iconic and indexical gesturing that we still use with spoken language, should have been quite enough to tell others about the location and condition of berries and roots or the likely movements of animals. A complexly nuanced language with tens of thousands of subtle near synonyms does not seem to offer any special advantage for the subsistence activities of these people, so we are left with a puzzle: Why do we have such elaborate languages if, in the kinds of societies in which language evolved, simple languages would have served as well?

Would the education of the young in subsistence techniques profit from more subtle linguistic skills than the practice of subsistence among mature adults? Words might have helped with the demonstration and teaching of technological skills, even if they were not needed for the actual use of these skills. The pedagogical use for language, like its use in subsistence, has an initial plausibility, and it is true that in our own society we make extensive use of language in technical education. In hunting bands and village communities, however, education for subsistence, like the practice of subsistence, could certainly have been accomplished with a far less complex or subtle language than the people who live in these communities actually use.

My own observations of language use in a nonwestern society could, I believe, be duplicated by the observations of many ethnographers who have lived among hunters and gatherers or among people with a simple agricultural technology. The Garos, slash-and-burn farmers of northeastern India among whom I once lived, performed their technical tasks with a minimum of verbal coordination. People knew what needed to be done, knew how to do it, and knew when to do it. Whatever coordination was required by the technology could easily have been achieved with a pidgin-like language of restricted vocabulary and simple sentence structure. Even the technical education of young people required only a modest use of language.

I wanted to learn the technical skills of my hosts and, in my western way, I would occasionally ask someone to explain how to tie a knot or how to hold a knife when cutting bamboo. The only technical instruction I could ever elicit would come when a man would reach for my tool and materials, demonstrate the manner in which the job should be done, and then hand them back along with the injunction: "Do it like that." Nor did children receive much more in the way of technical education than I did. Of course, children learned all sorts of other things with the help of language—what would happen if they were impolite to their mother's brother, how to placate the spirits, which cousins are improper marriage partners, and much more—but subsistence and technical activities required little language either in use or in teaching the next generation. Even deaf mutes learned the technology well enough to do their share of the family work.

In band and village communities, which were the only places where anyone lived until the first cities were built a mere five or six thousand years ago, technology could be easily observed and easily understood. The people of such communities could practice their technology and pass it on to their children without complex language. Humans imitate so easily that basic technical skills can be learned simply by watching and copying. Something about hunting and gathering communities endowed us with more language than those societies needed for practical subsistence. What, then, was the driving force behind the development of complex language? We need to look at the social uses of language.

I share a growing consensus that our intelligence evolved primarily as a means for dealing with other individuals. Ours is primarily a social intelligence, and language is one product, and one part, of that intelligence. In preurban societies, and even in our own, language in its most delicately nuanced form is used, not so much for basic subsistence tasks, as for establishing, maintaining, and refining social relationships. It is when dealing with people, not material objects, that we call on our richest linguistic resources.

It is in defining ourselves in relation to others, in conducting interpersonal negotiations, in competing, in manipulating, in scheming to get our own way, that the most subtle aspects of language become important. We need language for arguing our case, for claiming our rights, for leaving just the right degree of ambiguity, for talking our way out of tight spots, for outdoing our rivals in our many intricate forms of verbal competition. When disputes grow dangerous, we need language as an alternative to violence. We need our very best language for winning a lover.

When we look beyond subsistence activities, and recognize interpersonal relationships as the primary arena for complex and modulated language, new and different selective pressures are seen to be plausible. Before describing these, however, I need to take a detour and consider the nature of linguistic and individual variability.

Selection can take place only when the trait under selection is heritable, that is when it is variable and when at least some of its variation is due to to genetic variability. This has to mean that, during the period when the ability to use increasingly complex language was evolving, individuals must have varied from one another in their inherited capacity for language. To attribute individual differences in language ability to genetic differences badly violates the egalitarian assumptions that linguists usually hold about language, but the capacity for language surely did evolve, and it could not have done so without a variable genetic base upon which selection could work. Heritable differences in linguistic ability must have contributed to varied reproductive success.

The bias against searching for genetically based differences in linguistic skills is so strong that linguists are reluctant to give any attention at all to individual differences in language use or ability. The study of aphasia and other speech abnormalities forces the investigator to consider idiosyncratic linguistic traits, but most linguists deal with the language of what we are pleased to call "normal" people, and we have hung back from searching for individual differences among them. The orthodox linguistic attitude toward variability is expressed by Chomsky's explicit injunction that "Linguistic theory is concerned primarily with an ideal speaker-listener, in a completely homogeneous speech community..." Linguists have seen language as a shared system, and it has been the shared aspects of language that have interested them.

The sociolinguists have shown us how important some sorts of linguistic variation are. They have pointed to the ways in which ethnic groups, social classes, men and women, young and old, and every other social category one might think of, differ in the way they speak, but even the sociolinguists have stopped short of looking for individual differences that might be attributed to inherited capacity. For the most part, linguists have systematically, even deliberately, ignored the possibility that individuals might differ in their linguistic ability, and even the most fine-grained sociolinguistic studies have stopped short of attributing linguistic differences to individual differences. We have repeatedly asserted that all normal human beings learn to speak the language of their community but we have rarely stopped to ask whether all these normal people speak in exactly the same way. We have examined the commonalities of speakers, not their individual differences.

There are good reasons for the skittishness about individual differences. The measurement of linguistic skills is a big business in the United States. Advancement in both education and employment often rests on the results of tests that are intended to measure verbal aptitude. Linguists have found much to criticize in these tests, for they reduce what must be a multitude of separate skills to simplistic global measures, and they ignore the reality of dialect variation. They are surely biased in favor of the fortunate children who speak the dialect of the middle and upper class. The serious difficulties posed by any attempt to sort out truly individual differences from differences that reflect class, ethnic membership, bilingual background, age, sex, or an apparently limitless range of other sociological variables have made many linguists skeptical of the whole enterprise. The manifestly dangerous biases of many verbal aptitude tests have even encouraged some of us to throw our hands up in horror at the very suggestion that aptitude differences can be measured or that they even exist. Even if they do exist and even if they can be measured, it may seem prejudicial to mention them.

The refusal to acknowledge individual variability, however, bumps up against some other stubborn intuitions and observations. Everyone who is not a linguist seems to have utter confidence that people differ substantially in their linguistic skills. When not wearing their professional hats, even linguists recognize some of their acquaintances as "articulate," "fluent," "taciturn," "glib," "slow-spoken," or "polished speakers." Some people use more elaborate vocabulary than others. Some people talk a lot but never say much of anything. People in every society seem to recognize some among their fellows as having outstanding linguistic skills—as arguers, orators, raconteurs, bards, punsters, rhyme makers, or, in literate societies, as writers. We admire high linguistic skill. The simplification implicit in verbal aptitude tests that reduce all variability to a single scale seems unwarranted, but to conclude that there are no individual differences at all would be just as wrong.

We need to recognize two kinds of individual differences. On the one hand, inconsequential variability in pronunciation or even voice quality, special development of some areas of vocabulary, or idiosyncratic differences in syntactic detail tell us nothing about linguistic aptitude. On the other hand, some differences can be ranked along a scale, as demonstrating greater or lesser linguistic ability, as allowing more or less complexity, as better or worse for some purpose. Of the two, linguists have been much more willing to investigate nonranked differences. We may be able to agree that people exhibit all sorts of idiosyncrasies in their speech while denying that these reflect any underlying difference in ability or contribute in any way to differential success at any activity.

If, however, we suppose our own language to be in any way "better," "more developed," "more complex," or "capable of more subtlety" than the language of our ancestors of, let's say, a million years ago, we have to be concerned with rankable differences. Language could not have evolved unless individuals differed in their rankable abilities and unless selection favored those with better language. Surely there was an evolutionary trend through time in such matters as the size of vocabulary that individuals could control, the complexity of grammatical detail with which they could cope, and the skill with which they could offer or follow a logical argument. This evolution must have been built on differences that existed within once-living populations. In the rest of this chapter, therefore, I will not be concerned with nonrankable idiosyncratic differences but will, of necessity, focus on the more sensitive issue of rankable differences. I must, in particular, consider those aspects of rankable linguistic abilities that reflect, at least in part, genetic variability. I do not see how we can talk about the evolution of language unless we are willing to admit that individuals have differed in their inherited linguistic abilities. Rankable differences in linguistic skill must have been around for a long time. Even primatologists who have worked with chimpanzees have noted clear individual differences in their ability to acquire signs.

What remains is to ask why the most capable Paleolithic men and women, those who could handle more complex language than most of their contemporaries, managed to raise more than the average number of children. Among the possibilities that have been proposed are that high language ability would have allowed more useful gossip, more relevant conversation, more skillful courtship, and a more effective pursuit of leadership. All of these could have worked together to give a reproductive advantage to those who could understand and speak with skill. Since I have something of a vested interest in language and leadership, I will start with an argument that I first made in the 1980s. The rest of the chapter will then describe other social advantages of complex language that make the argument considerably more persuasive than it was when I first offered it.

Two relationships that are characteristic of most preurban societies would, when taken together, give a clear selective advantage to high language ability. First, leaders are often acknowledged, within their community, to possess special and admirable linguistic skills. Second, leaders manage, with considerable regularity, to father more than the average number of children and to raise a larger proportion of their children to maturity. If better speakers become leaders and if leaders raise more children, we have a mechanism that would drive the selection for better linguistic skills. Can we take these relationships seriously? It is somewhat easier to justify the second relationship, so I turn to that one first.

The relationship between rank and the number of children is supported by demographic studies in widely varying populations, and it can even be seen as the human expression of the much more widespread tendency for the dominant males of many species to produce more than their share of offspring. Men are capable, biologically, of siring a very large number of children, but they are usually limited by their restricted access to women. Men who can command the reproductive powers of more than a single woman can easily produce extra children. The best-studied human example may still be that of the Yanomamo Indians of Venezuela and Brazil. Napoleon Chagnon and his colleagues give careful figures to show that Yanomamo headmen, because of both polygyny and quicker remarriage after the loss of an earlier wife, have more wives than the average male. In a number of respects, including language, headmen are described as more capable than the average male, and they father approximately twice as many children as other men.

The tendency for wealthy and high-ranking men to father more than the average number of children has been demonstrated repeatedly. As just one example, among the mid-nineteenth-century Mormons of Utah, men with high church rank had markedly more children than average, almost entirely because they had more wives. Compensating for the men who father many children are others who have none at all, and in human populations, as indeed in populations of other animals, males vary considerably more than females in the number of their offspring.

In addition to having more wives, chiefs and other men of high status often control more human and material resources than others, and they are often able to use these resources to benefit their own children. In this way, they may be better able to keep their children alive long enough to produce grandchildren. Martin Daly and Margo Wilson describe an area in central India where "the fertility of (monogamous) couples showed no relationship to the husband's income, but the number of *surviving* children increased with increasing affluence." Thus even in the absence of polygyny, we can expect that high status will be reflected in a larger number of surviving children than the average, at least when resources are scarce, as they must often have been in prehistoric times.

Since women face a strict biological ceiling on how many children they can bear, their reproductive success is considerably less variable than that of men, at least in the first generation. This means that discussions of reproductive potential can sound sexually biased to those sensitive to hints of male–female differences. In spite of the smaller variation in the numbers of children born to women, however, women with superior social skills should be able to attract more successful fathers for their children, and women certainly contribute to the acquisition of resources. In these ways, a woman's social skills should join with those of her mate to affect the number of children who survive. In addition, through their genetic contribution to their sons, women also contribute to the variable reproductive success of the next generation. The variable genetic contribution of women may become unambiguous only with the generation of their grandchildren, but it is no less important for that. The reproductive variability of men becomes apparent more quickly, so it is easier to measure, and since men have monopolized most formal positions of leadership, it is also with men that we can more easily test the possibility that language, leadership, and reproduction are all related.

The relation between language ability and leadership is not as easy to quantify as is the relation between status and numbers of offspring, but the impressions of a good many ethnographers make it seem plausible. Striking evidence for the high language skills of leaders was gathered in a book edited by Maurice Bloch called *Political Language and Oratory in Traditional Society*. The case studies in this collection suggested that, in a remarkably wide range of societies, leaders are good talkers.

In describing the people of Mount Hagen in the Western Highlands of Papua New Guinea, for example, Andrew Strathern says:

A man can...retain prominence...for long periods of time well into his old age and one of the resources he has at hand for doing so is his ability to speak.
Prominent men are speech-makers. A man can raise numerous pigs and give many away in *moka*, [ceremonial exchange] but he cannot effectively influence his fellow-men unless he can use speech persuasively...most big-men are in fact good speakers, although some are much more persuasive and fluent than others.

David Turton describes the very different society of the Mursi of pastoral East Africa, but his conclusions are similar,

One does not have to attend many meetings in a particular locality before coming to recognize the more influential men of the area. They are the speakers who are listened to without interruption and whose speeches tend to come toward the end of a debate, not because there is any set order of speakers, but because the very nature of their contributions reduces the need for further discussion.

Since it is thus through consensus alone that public meetings reach agreement, it is not surprising that the most frequently mentioned attribute of an influential man is his ability to speak well in public.

It is not only the tone of a speech, but also the skill with which it is constructed that seems to impress an audience. Mursi public speeches tend to be very allusive ... but some men appear to excel in the subtlety with which they employ allusions and images in their speeches, thereby achieving a terseness of style which is much appreciated by the audience.

In his study of early classical Greece, E. A. Havelock describes the relation of language and leadership in this way:

... within limits, the community's leadership lay with those who had a superior ear and rhythmic aptitude, which would be demonstrable in epic hexameter. It would also however show itself in the ability to compose *rhemata*—effective sayings which used other devices besides the metrical, such as assonance and parallelism. Again, the good performer at a banquet would be estimated not exclusively as an entertainer but as a natural leader of man ... the effective judge or even general tended to be the man with the superior oral memory ... The general effect was to put a great premium on the intelligence in Greek social transactions and to identify intelligence with power. By intelligence we specially mean a superior memory and a superior sense of verbal rhythm.

Even in our own society, of course, those who reach influential positions, not only in government but in spheres such as business or education, tend to be recognized as highly verbal individuals. The type of language that Americans have deemed to be suitable for political activities has varied from the florid to the terse, but in every era, some styles are admired and judged to be more effective and persuasive than others. A technically skilled horticulturist, machinist, jeweler, sculptor, or dentist can practice his trade without being good with words. If he aspires to leadership, he needs good language.

These examples all come from societies that are technologically more developed than those in which language first developed, but the relationship was probably just as important much earlier. Although the resources of hunting and gathering communities did not ordinarily allow the kind of institutionalized chiefdoms found in more settled societies, men must still have varied in their degree of influence, and men must always have needed skillful language to gain recognition as leaders.

As a social activity, of course, it is not enough for language to be spoken. Language also needs to be understood, or at least appreciated, but even an average speaker can recognize outstanding language in others. Since we can always understand a wider range and variety of speech than we can use, we can appreciate and be persuaded by those who speak more skillfully than we do ourselves. Nonpoets can be moved by poets.

Could it be that the demonstration of high linguistic ability is not so much a prerequisite for leadership as its consequence? Once he is in charge, a man may have new opportunities, both to acquire new linguistic skills and to exhibit linguistic talent that had previously lain dormant. Perhaps those who rise to leadership have more chance to talk on occasions that make them appear to have special skills. The apparent talent of leaders would then be an illusion. Fully to sort out what is cause and what is effect in the relation of leadership and language requires more careful ethnographic studies than have yet been done, but in the meantime, the examples we have strongly suggest that it helps to have linguistic talent to start with. Observers who have addressed the question write as if leaders bring their skills to office with them.

We have evidence, then, both for the usefulness of good language as a means for acquiring leadership and for the ability of leaders to raise more children than other men. Ten thousand generations of biased birth rates would have done wonders for language.

Ever since information theory was developed in the 1940s, engineers have been devising better ways to squeeze information through electric and electronic circuits, and the view that language is designed to exchange information has come to seem so obvious that it needs no discussion. We take it for granted that we talk, write, and send email in order to communicate information, and of course there is a truth to this view. We pass all sorts of information back and forth. Nevertheless, it is not at all obvious that it was the need for information that propelled the evolution of language. From an evolutionary point of view, in fact, it is very odd that we should be so eager to give away information. Information is valuable. Listeners should want to get all the information they can, but once they have it, they should keep it to themselves so that they can use it for their own advantage. Instead of saving it for guarded use at strategic moments, however, everyone seems eager to broadcast everything they know to the world. What do speakers gain by disgorging information so freely?

We use language in all sorts of situations and for all sorts of purposes, but its prototypical use is still ordinary conversation, chit-chat, shooting the breeze, schmoozing. Formal speeches, rituals, making plans, writing a novel, constructing a logical argument, and instructing the young are all hugely important to us, but no use of language beats conversation in the sheer amount of time that it occupies in our lives. Conversation is enjoyed among all people, everywhere, and it must have ancient evolutionary roots.

The rules of conversation are strict, though we may be only half-aware of them. A conversation requires at least two people and as many as four can be easily accommodated, but even a group of five begins to be big enough to encourage a split into two smaller ones. Only one person is allowed to speak at a time and we have subtle rules for taking turns. We know where we can break in and we know how to yield the floor to others.

Robin Dunbar has listened to what speakers in England talk about in their ordinary conversations, and their topics are unlikely to be much different from those enjoyed elsewhere. Dunbar found that people used as much as two-thirds of their conversational time talking about social matters: personal relationships, the people they like or dislike, their own personal experiences, and the behavior of others. No other topic came close. Politics, religion, work, sports and leisure, and everything else were all squeezed into just one-third of their talking time. Negative gossip and criticism of other people were not as important as we sometimes suppose them to be, for they occupied no more than 5 per cent of the time devoted to social relationships. Men and women did not differ in the total time they spent talking about social relationships, but they did differ in whom they talked about. Men talked more about themselves and women talked more about others. Dunbar interprets this as indicating that women engage in networking while men are more likely to indulge in advertising.

So what really interests people is people, both other people and themselves. Why are we so endlessly fascinated with the actions, intrigues, motivations, successes, and failures of everyone we know and even of those we don't know? Perhaps by learning how others have managed, we learn to manage ourselves. We may also glean valuable information about our friends and neighbors that helps us to deal with them more successfully later. Reports that someone has acted badly warn us against trusting him. Reports of honorable behavior may encourage future cooperation. We learn a great deal from ordinary conversation. Far from simply being idle chatter, conversation can be highly educational. The advantages to the listener are clear. Just why everyone is so eager to share what they already know is less obvious.

Perhaps we trade our own information in return for information received. This would be an example of so-called "reciprocal altruism" which is supposed to be one of the cornerstones of human and animal cooperation. You scratch my back; I'll scratch yours. We pass on information too eagerly for reciprocal altruism to be a convincing explanation, however. Since we can speak with several listeners at the same time, fascinating bits of information can spread quickly and widely, and it is unlikely that we can ever get paid back from everyone who profits from our information. If collecting valuable information is what conversation is all about, moreover, it should be easy to cheat. All a cheater would need to do would be to keep quiet, or if a return was demanded, to give back false information. Each of us is too eager to talk for us to suppose that the listener profits from a conversation more than the speaker. We compete with one another for the privilege of speaking, not for the privilege of listening. We can understand the eagerness that listeners have for information about the behavior of others, and we might have expected an evolutionary arms race, with ever more refined skills at collecting information competing with ever better skills for concealing it. Why are speakers so eager to cooperate?

A promising answer to this question is that we gain status by displaying our ability to provide interesting information at the right moment. Engaging in a conversation requires a high degree of skill. Never mind all the phonological and syntactic skills that are needed. Except for socially stigmatized forms, such as English double negatives, we tolerate a good many syntactic stumbles from our companions. We forget a foreign accent if the speaker talks about interesting things. What participants in a conversation really need to worry about is figuring out what they can say that will be appropriate. They are required to match their topics to what has been said before. Next time you are having a friendly conversation about the relative virtues of PCs and Macs, try out the perfectly accurate statement "New Jersey is across the Hudson from New York" and see how it helps you. Speakers must not repeat platitudes, but say things that others find new and interesting. Jean-Louis Dessalles summarizes all this by saying that speakers need to be "relevant" and he suggests that the most relevant comments offer information that is either surprising, pleasant, or unpleasant.

Participants in a conversation know that they will be judged by what they say. The speaker who is interesting to listen to, who develops ideas clearly and logically, and who can say them in clever ways is admired, but there are as many ways to lose in conversational competition as to win. Speak too much and others will resent having their own turn cut short. Speak too little and you will be judged as dull. Talk on the wrong topic and you will irritate. Speak without sense and you will not be invited back next time. Among our favorite topics of conversation are reports of our own activities, past and present. We constantly tell others what we have done, sometimes what we did this morning and sometimes, if we are old enough, what we did fifty years ago. If we can make our reports interesting, people will come back for more. If our stories are dull we are more likely to be avoided. Skill at conversation matters. We gain friends by speaking well; we lose them by speaking badly. Here, at a microcosmic level of human interaction, we compete for status.

Because we gain admirers by the quality of our conversation we may be tempted to embroider the truth, to make our stories a bit more exciting than the events they purport to describe. Listeners know this and they tolerate a bit of conversational license. We can enjoy a good story even if we don't fully believe every word. When we are tempted to go beyond artful exaggeration and to lie, we must be careful. An astute college dean once said to me, not entirely as a joke, "You have to be honest in this job. It's not a matter of principle, but if you start to lie, you can't remember what you have said to whom, and pretty soon you're in terrible trouble." I did not ask if he spoke from experience.

Perhaps it is the danger of such tangles that has given us an emotional warning whenever we are tempted to lie. Our own nervousness cautions us to be careful, and the nervousness may be visible enough to make others suspicious. We are not as good at lying as evolutionary theory and sheer self-interest might lead us to expect, but since lying can be risky, caution may be beneficial. Once people catch you in serious contradictions, and once they start to share this interesting and relevant information with their friends, you will lose badly in the competition for prestige. You would have fared even worse in a society of a few hundred people where everyone knew and depended on everyone else. Most of us simply don't have the skill to stray very far from the truth without getting caught. We can avoid danger by sticking reasonably close to reality.

Thanks to the eagerness of people to display their knowledge, we are able to learn important things from conversation and it is people that we learn most about. Since it is maneuvering through the social system that gives us the most difficult challenges of our lives, the information we gain by learning how others have behaved is extremely valuable. It is fortunate for the learner, then, that we are at least as eager to pass information on as to receive it.

The related idea that communication is manipulative comes from John R. Krebs and Richard Dawkins. Most of their examples are taken from studies of animal communication, but the principles apply equally well to human language. Their point is that anything you say can be interpreted as an attempt, in one way or another, to get someone to do something on your behalf. Ask the man sitting beside you to pass the salt, and you are hoping to use his muscles to achieve your own ends. Tell a good story and you will manipulate people's minds into admiring you. Instruct your child well, and you will teach him behavior that will help him to survive and to pass on your own genes. Reveal precious secrets by yielding to torture and you are desperately hoping to manipulate your torturer into easing up.

By using the word "manipulation" Krebs and Dawkins are deliberately provoking us, indeed manipulating us, into seeing familiar behavior from a fresh perspective. They are showing us that we can look upon speaking as selfish. Some uses of language give us immediate benefits, such as the salt that someone passes. More often, the rewards are much less direct, but by using language skillfully we do raise our status, not much on any one occasion perhaps, but we can hope, bit by bit, to make our reputation grow. Whether we see language as being used to boost our own reputation or as a way of manipulating others to our own benefit, therefore, comes down to the same thing. Little is so important to us as our standing among our fellows. If language can be used to manipulate others into granting high status, the speaker will have gained a priceless benefit.

Charles Darwin has been remembered primarily for his theory of natural selection. With this, Darwin offered us a thoroughly plausible mechanism by which nature's wonderful array of plants and animals could have evolved. Darwin is not quite so famous for a second theory, that of sexual selection. Natural selection is driven by pressure from the natural environment and especially by the pressure of other species; sexual selection is driven by the need to attract a mate. Natural selection adapts individuals to their environment; sexual selection adapts males and females to each other. Natural selection produces efficient survival machines; sexual selection leads to some of the most flamboyant products of evolution, and it probably played a major role in the evolution of language. Since sexual selection is not so widely understood as natural selection, I need to take a brief detour to describe how it works.

In any species whose members are divided into males and females, individuals need to overcome two challenges if they are to pass their genes on to the next generation. First, they must survive, of course, and if female mammals and birds are to keep their genes in the gene pool, they need to survive long enough not only to reproduce, but to provide maternal care. In addition to simple survival no member of a sexual species can pass on its genes without the assistance of a member of the opposite sex.

The challenge of finding a sexual partner is much more focused and intense than the long-term challenge of surviving. For the members of most species, the search for a partner remains latent, not only during immaturity but also during the seasons when breeding does not occur. It becomes an urgent matter when the season arrives. The challenge of finding a sexual partner is very different for males than for females. Females contribute much more to each of their offspring than do males. This, in fact, is the definition of what is it to be female, for the female egg is many times larger than the male sperm. All by itself, the mammalian egg contains enough material to get the embryo well started. Except for a single minute sperm, a hen gives her egg everything that is needed to create a whole chick. Having already invested so much, she must then protect her investment by taking on the job of brooding her eggs until they hatch, and then herding her chicks until they can manage on their own. Compared with the huge numbers of sperm that every male manufactures, a female produces only a tiny number of eggs. The male can afford to squander his sperm since, if another prospect comes along, he will always have more. A female must be careful not to waste her eggs. This means that the female needs to be choosy about her mates, for she will leave more successful progeny if she can find a male who provides her children with good genes.

In a species where the young remain dependent after birth, responsibility for their care is often exclusively the female's, and this added responsibility should make her even more cautious about selecting the right father. If she makes a mistake she will have only a few chances to do better. She will have only a limited number of opportunities to breed in her lifetime, and she needs to do her best each time. If males participate in childcare, as human fathers and many bird fathers are supposed to, the female ought to be careful to mate only with a male who will stick around long enough to do his job. So females need to compete for the best males. Males compete, instead, for the most females, but in the face of cautious females the male has a serious problem: How can he persuade as many of these choosy females as possible to mate with him instead of with a rival? Males use many tactics to compete. Some fight, some demonstrate their devotion by persistent courting, some birds display fancy feathers. Some are more successful than others.

One part of this argument seems so obvious to biologists that they can forget to make it clear to others, but anyone who finds this unfamiliar territory needs to understand that none of this "choosing" and "competing" needs to be done self-consciously. The mechanisms of selection, both natural and sexual, apply to apes and birds, as much as to human beings. They even apply to frogs and snails. Even if none of the participants in the game has any awareness about what they are doing, it is those particular females that make good choices and those particular males that are persuasive that leave the most genes for later generations. This means that the genes that lead to wise choices and successful persuasion will spread through the population. If a frog can make good choices without understanding heredity then so can a human being. A female of a species where males help to raise the young should choose a reliable male. She does not need to search deliberately for reliability, but she may still be attracted to qualities in her suitors that imply the genes that produce supportive behavior. It is easiest to write about these mechanisms by using words like "choose" and "compete," but these must not be interpreted as imply-ing deliberate choice or conscious competition.

No female, however choosy she may be, can directly judge the genes of her prospective mates, but she can judge the phenotypic traits of the male's body and behavior that are likely to reflect good genes. First, she can judge his state of health. If he is strong, vigorous, and resistant to disease, he has a good chance of fathering children who will also be strong, vigorous, and resistant to disease. Such a male will be a better prospect than a sickly weakling. This makes it advantageous for a male to display features that advertise his health, and a feature that burdens him with a handicap may be especially convincing. A brightly colored male bird may be in more danger from predators than one with dull plumage, but simply being able to thrive in spite of his bright colors is a sign of extra strength and vigor. Females that choose brightly colored mates have a good chance of choosing strong and healthy fathers for their children. If enough generations of females choose the most brightly colored mates, they will select for ever more gaudy plumage. Even though bright colors may attract predators, a male has no way to pass on his genes unless he attracts a female, so some reds and yellows may be well worth the risk. The whole point of the plumage is the risk.

Brightly colored males who escape predation are the best of all prospects. To make the right choices, females need to be attracted to bright plumage but they do not need to have bright plumage themselves, so they can afford to cling to dull but safer colors. It is the choices of repeated generations of females that have given such beautiful colors to so many birds, and that have given the gaudiest colors to males. Even dull-colored females can admire the bright colors of males. This is sexual selection.

The classic example of sexual selection is the tail of the peacock. A peacock's tail is not merely gaudy but terribly encumbering. It must be hard to fly if you have to carry around so much tail. Only the strongest and healthiest males can survive with the best tails, but it is these tails that peahens consistently choose. Female choice is so decisive that males gather in a single place where they compete to strut their stuff. Females inspect them, and then make their choice, and the males with the best tails consistently win the competition. If you are a peacock, you need to gamble. If you play it safe and grow a modest tail you may have a long life, but your genes will die with you. If your genes encourage you to gamble you may die young, but at least you will stand a chance of leaving some genes behind for the next generation. Under this kind of insistent selective pressure, changes can take place that, by the standards of natural selection, are both very rapid and very risky.

Sexual selection cannot work unless some males are more successful than others. Gaudy tails would not develop unless they made a difference in reproduction, and the greater the variation in male success, the more rapid the selection will be. Among peacocks almost all the young are fathered by a small fraction of the males, so evolution can proceed with great speed. It is female choice that sets the direction of evolution, and if females will mate only with males that have risked their lives, the willingness to take risks will rapidly spread through the male half of the population.

Once started, sexual selection can have a momentum of its own. To pass on their genes most successfully, females must produce sons who can attract females. If most females want males with flamboyant tails, it is best to mate with a large-tailed bird even if you don't happen to be so taken by them yourself. Only if you go along with the majority will you produce sons with the kind of tails that will maximize the number of your grandchildren. You will be left out if you don't jump on the bandwagon. Selective breeding means that genes for males with big tails and genes for females with a preference for big tails become united in the same animals. Together, they lead to ever bigger tails.

Sexual selection has a random quality that natural selection lacks. Nature is relatively stable. It exerts long-term pressures that that can pull plants and animals relentlessly, but unspectacularly, in a consistent direction. Of course, the environment can change and then the direction of selection will change as well, but most environmental changes are relatively slow, and sudden changes are infrequent. By comparison, sexual choice can be quixotic. Females can fixate on almost anything and start to choose males for that trait, pushing the trait to spread and to become more elaborate. Even a peacock's tail must have a limit, however. The very best tail is the one that females prefer over all others but that still allows its owner to survive. Since traits that are fostered by sexual selection may interfere with survival they can be unstable, and female preferences may change. Sexual selection may push now in one direction and now in another. It is unlikely to have as much long-term consistency as natural selection, but it promotes some of the most spectacular characteristics of living beings.

Most descriptions of sexual selection focus on female choice because it is usually more important than male choice. Males in most mammalian species simply don't need to be very choosy. Their problem, instead, is outdoing other males. When there is long-term bonding between sexual partners, however, the choice of a partner becomes almost as important for the male as for the female. A man can afford a short-term fling, but if he is to spend a lifetime with just one woman he needs to be careful to make the right choice. In a species where most females are already committed to someone else it may be a better strategy to invest great effort in courting a single desirable female, even if it means promising eternal faithfulness, than to hope to attract several. All human societies have some degree of polygyny. Sometimes it is socially recognized and accepted, sometimes it is strongly condemned, but it is never completely absent. Some men, everywhere, stray and cheat, but of course they cannot do so without some cooperation from women. Men stray so as to get more partners.

Women stray so as to get better partners. Evolution is not always politically correct.

Has sexual selection had a part in molding human nature? The evolutionary psychologist Geoffrey Miller believes that it has, and he even argues that we have a whole suite of traits that are difficult to explain in any other way. These include traits that we feel to be our among our most precious: music, art, religion, our creative intelligence, our ethical ideals, our sense of humor, and, not least, our language. These are ornamental and highly valued. They contribute little to the serious business of survival, but they are wonderfully helpful in attracting a mate. Miller attributes these to sexual selection, and in this section, I crib shamelessly from his engrossing book *The Mating Mind*.

Creative intelligence and language have more plausible survival value than music, art, or a sense of humor, but as I have already argued, the technology used in societies where language evolved did not need the ornate and intricate kind of language that we use today and so greatly admire. How would the ability to tell a lively story or sing a lovely song have contributed to anyone's survival? How, for that matter, would imaginative fictional worlds, or imaginary numbers, or speculations about what might be found on the other side of the moon contribute to subsistence? Spending the night singing or telling stories is more likely to interfere with tomorrow's hunt than to help. A hardworking, reliable, but unimaginative man, one who is never distracted by frivolities like song and dance or the urge to create a magnificent carving, ought to be a woman's best choice to supply the genes to mix with her own, and then to help her to support their children. Except that human women are no more attracted to such a dull but hardworking man than a peahen is attracted to a male with an efficient but scruffy tail.

In a species where a male's contribution to reproduction ends as soon as he has donated his genes, a female's choice is much more important than the male's. He needs to be more pleasing than all the other males. All she needs to be attractive is the ability to produce his children. In a species where males and females form long-term partnerships, however, male choice matters. If a man is going to be restricted to a single woman for much of his life, he needs to be as careful as she is before committing himself. A man can take the risk of being undiscriminating in a short-term affair. For a long-term partnership, his choice is as important as hers. This is why human beings spend so much time in courtship. We need the time to assess the quality of the candidates. We still make mistakes, but we do better than we would in a random shuffle.

Music, art, humor, and elaborate language are all prominent among human displays. They are our peacock's tail, ornaments that are wonderfully useful as displays even if they interfere with the more mundane matter of making a living. Women are attracted to men who are musical, artistic, funny, imaginative, and interesting conversationalists. Men, it turns out, are attracted to women who are musical, artistic, funny, imaginative, and interesting conversationalists. Women also like men, and men like women, who are kind, thoughtful, and helpful, and these qualities, too, could have been promoted by sexual selection. A good memory, the ability to plan ahead, a logical mind, and a taste for novelty would come as a bonus. Miller calls all these traits an "entertainment system" which potential mates find irresistible. We show off these traits even more often than peacocks show off their tails. We display our skills prominently during courtship, but we display them to impress one another on many other occasions as well.

Humans, we presume, began their separate evolutionary path as a species with no more pair-bonding or male assistance with child-rearing than is found among modern chimpanzees—essentially none. If pair-bonding developed gradually there must have been a time when males hung around and helped for a while, but when they were even more inclined than men are today to abandon the mothers and their children. Deserted mothers would be on the lookout for another helpful male to whom they could offer sex and from whom they could get some practical assistance. A prospective partner's best indication of fatherly devotion would be how kind and helpful he was to the children she already had and if, for a few thousand generations, females selected fathers who were kind to children, males would certainly evolve to new heights of paternal responsibility.

If sexual selection is so efficient, why are we not, by now, all thoughtful paragons of intellectual brilliance? One answer is that a suitor must not only persuade a potential mate but simultaneously defeat the competition. For this, a certain ruthlessness may be needed. Too much kindness and generosity might reduce the competitive edge. You might also do better to have some traits that set you apart and make you even more interesting than the others. There should be a selective advantage for the individual who is just a bit different. The balance between all the required skills is enormously complex and if the brain and mind don't get it all exactly right, reproduction will suffer. The brain, unfortunately, is subject to a constant rain of deleterious mutations. So many genes contribute to its development that damaging mutations are a constant problem. Selection gradually cleans up the defects, but it never quite catches up with new mutations.

Do skills such as language, sense of humor, art, and imagination give any indication of the underlying genetic quality of the individuals who have them? They surely do, for the very complexity of the human brain that makes all this attractive behavior possible, also makes the behavior an excellent indicator of quality. An enormous number of genes contribute to building a brain. The brain cannot function properly, unless everything develops in exactly the right way. By selecting a man whose humor, imagination, language, and music give evidence of a superior brain, a woman has a good chance of choosing the best genes to help her own genes survive, not only in her own children but beyond them to later generations. By choosing men who are kind, thoughtful, and helpful, mate choice could even have softened the competitive edge that is needed for natural selection.

Sexual selection is an enticing explanation for behavior that is difficult to explain by natural selection. It helps us to understand traits that contribute little to survival. Nevertheless, the theory is not without problems, and two of these need to be addressed.

First, sexual selection works so quickly but so inconsistently that it is unlikely to lead a species in a single direction over an extended period. Sexual selection can push a species in one direction only to change and pull it off in another. Following the replacement of the Australopithecines by the genus Homo, the human brain expanded relentlessly for two million years. If the growth of the brain had anything at all to do with the growth of our more intellectual and imaginative talents, then these, too, must have been expanding for as long as the brain was growing. That is a longer continuous development than would be expected for sexual selection.

One explanation for such a long development could come from "the handicap principle" that states that a good indicator of quality is the ability to overcome handicaps. A peacock's tail is a terrible handicap, so the peacock that can overcome such a handicap must be a very superior bird, the very bird that a peahen would want as the father of her chicks. Traits that handicap the male are less subject to whimsical change than traits that are neutral. Females may, however, be attracted to traits that do not handicap the males, and these traits can also be promoted by female choice. Women lack beards just as peahens lack fancy tails, and since women get along just fine without beards, beards are clearly not needed for survival. The male beard, therefore, is an excellent candidate for having once been the target of sexual selection. There must have been a time when the girls went for the guys with the best beards. Unlike a peacock's tail, however, a beard is not much of a handicap, so it is not a useful indicator of the health and vigor of its owner. An otherwise poor specimen might grow a magnificent beard. At some point in the course of our evolution, beards seem to have lost a good deal of their allure. If female preference for beards was still strong, shaving would surely be less popular. Traits that give a serious handicap offer a more honest indication of quality than neutral traits like a beard. Instead of being led astray by a beard, females do better by looking for partners who are strong enough to survive in spite of their handicaps. Perhaps the eagerness to exhaust oneself by staying up all night making music, or missing a chance to hunt in order to chip away all day at a useless wooden statue are, like the peacock's tail, attractive handicaps.

The brain itself is a serious handicap. Our large brains make childbirth far more dangerous for both mother and child than it is among other animals. In addition, in the jargon of evolutionary biologists, the brain is an extremely "costly" organ. It gobbles up a fifth of the calories required to support the human body, so it takes a lot of hunting and gathering to support a brain. If women have been choosing abilities that require a massive brain, and thus indirectly choosing brains that make these abilities possible, they have been selecting a trait that is a considerable handicap. If the brain was used primarily for frivolities that contributed little to survival, then sexual selection is the most likely explanation.

A second challenge to the theory of sexual selection, one that is even more serious than its speed, is that women are so much like men in their intellectual, verbal, and artistic abilities. Among other animals, traits that are attributable to female choice are usually much better developed in males than in females. Peahens do not develop elaborate but burdensome tails. In species where males fight for the privilege of mating, and where females accept the winner, the biggest and strongest males regularly sire the next generation. Males, in such species, are very much larger than the females. If men and women differ in musical, artistic, or linguistic ability, however, the differences are difficult to detect. If these traits have been fostered by sexual selection, why are they so well developed in women? If a peahen can manage with a scruffy tail, why can't a woman manage with scruffy language?

One possible explanation is that, once upright posture was taken care of, the most dramatic changes that transformed humans were primarily intellectual. Perhaps it takes a good intellect to appreciate another's intellect. To recognize the comic ability of a potential partner, a woman must have a sense of humor herself. To appreciate a musician, a woman needs some musical ability. It takes one to know one. I do not find this argument persuasive. The premise of this book is that comprehension is always better than production. All of us can understand more than we can say. If language, and so many other distinctive human traits, developed as a result of female choice, why did women's ability keep up with that of men? If a peahen can appreciate a fine tail without having one herself, why should a woman need fancy language to appreciate the fancy language of a man?

A more persuasive explanation, I believe, is that women are not the only ones to choose. Human males also have to find a long-term mate so they need to be almost as choosy as females. It is not only women who look for a sense of humor, an imaginative mind, and artistic ability when they contemplate a lifetime with a single partner. When choice is mutual, both sexes must do their best to satisfy the tastes of potential partners. Judging these traits is a difficult and complex task, but that is why we have courtship. It gives us time to judge.

Language is just one of the many mental capacities that, Miller believes, have been fostered by sexual selection, but it is a central capacity and at least as important as any of the others. Both men and woman have probably spent many hundreds of thousands of years choosing partners who were good at talking. The best advice to young people, for as long as language has made our ancestors human, would be: "Look for a spouse who is a joy to talk to, good at reporting the facts, but also good at telling stories, good at telling jokes, good at making the appropriate remarks at the appropriate moment." Young people should also search for a partner who is imaginative enough to experiment, for one of the traits that seems to have been bred into humans is a desire for novelty. We find it good to follow custom but we also find it good to try something new, to be just a little different. Language has to follow conventions, but unless it deviates just a bit from convention it grows dull. So: "Find a spouse who is imaginative enough to keep you interested. Look for the best entertainment machine and you will find a good parent for your children."

Sexual selection for intellectual abilities offers a possible explanation for an otherwise odd disparity between the expansion of the human brain and the paucity of archeological evidence for what this growing brain might have been used for. Fossil skulls show us that the human brain more than doubled in size in the last two million years, from less than 600 cc to more than 1200 cc today, and yet technology, to the extent that it can be judged from stone tools, advanced hardly at all until the last tenth of that time. The brain had expanded nearly to its modern size before technology shows much sign of change. If we can see nothing to show for it in the archeology, what in the world was all that brain expansion good for? One answer is that the brain was not being selected for technology at all, but for better music, language, and humor, and for the kind of imagination that could invent religion and tell stories. In this case, new behavior could have flowered with little noticeable impact on the surviving archeological record. The stagnant stone tools do not have to mean that either the mind, or the behavior and culture that the mind made possible, were stagnant. It means only that for most of the last two million years other things were more important to our ancestors than chipped flint.

Thanks to Geoffrey Miller, mate selection has become a serious candidate for an evolutionary explanation of the most dazzling of human talents. The ideas are sufficiently new and sufficiently complex that it would be astonishing if they did not need some rethinking and refinement before all the problems are resolved. Not everyone is convinced. Still, I expect that we will hear much more about sexual selection in the years to come.

I believe that it was selection for social skills more than for technical skills, that drove the evolution of complex language. The very earliest language may well have developed in response to subsistence needs, but it would have taken very little language to agree on where to meet, to tell others where to find ripe fruit, or to cooperate in hunting. The capacities that we have inherited from our late Paleolithic ancestors allow a far more complex language than was needed for subsistence. It must have been the social side of life that benefited most from language. It was dealing with people, not material objects, where complex language was needed. To be sure, complex language did preadapt us for all sorts of activities that are important to us today, including higher mathematics, double-entry bookkeeping, crossword puzzles, and the Internet, but language could not have evolved for such purposes because none of them existed during the Paleolithic era when language evolved. Between the earliest use of rudimentary language and the invention of writing, the pressures of both natural and sexual selection gave the most benefits to the individuals with the best social skills.

Leadership, skill at conversation, and the need to find a mate have all been offered in this chapter as calling for skill at language. Far from being alternatives, these are really all part of the same package. From slightly different perspectives they all describe ways in which language is used for social purposes, to gain an edge, to accomplish one's goals. The better our language, the better our chances in life and, most importantly, the better our chances for passing our genes on to later generations.

The evolutionary mechanisms proposed here suggest an engine that, once started, could have driven the evolution of the capacity for language over a very long period of time, quite plausibly for several million years. During this period, language could have improved more in response to social needs than to subsistence needs, but in the end, an increasingly complex language must have brought with it an increasing power of conceptualization. With that, our ancestors became preadapted for a radically new kind of civilization. Agriculture was followed by urban life, by writing, and by the ever-expanding accumulation of knowledge that made writing possible. None of this could have happened without language or without the kind of mind that made language possible.

11

What has language done to us?

Through most of this book I have offered some facts, some arguments, and a good deal of speculation about the path by which language might have emerged in the human species. Now, at the end, I want to raise a somewhat different question: What has language done to us? How has it changed our lives? For, whatever the selective pressures were that encouraged the emergence of language, and whatever the stages through which evolving language passed, we can have no doubt at all that language must be given a good deal of the credit (or is it blame?) for turning us into a most peculiar animal. Nothing is more important than language in the behavioral revolution that has made us so different from even our closest anthropoid kin. Above the level of basic physiology, we do precious little that is not, in some way, affected by language. What, then, has language done to us?

To ask how language has changed us is not quite such a speculative undertaking as to ask about the stages through which language passed. We can compare ourselves to other animals, inspect the ways they differ from us, and notice how language has contributed to whatever differences we find. Guesswork and inference do not loom quite so large as when we search for the lost forms of earlier language. Language changed the way we use our minds and it prepared us for the literate, urban, and technological society that our ancestors began to build about six thousand years ago.

I have argued that the most important advantages given to our Paleolithic forebears by intricate forms of language were more social than technical, and language still shapes every moment and every detail of all our social relationships. Even our vocabulary shows the importance of language in our social life. Think how many words we need to describe the precise purposes to which we put language. With the help of language we *accuse, advise, answer, challenge, claim, demand, deny, discuss, describe, encourage, explain, flirt, insult, invite, joke, learn, lie, negotiate, object, promise, pretend, question, reject, request, refuse, teach, threaten, warn,* and *woo.* Of course, this is only the beginning. We would have no trouble doubling and then redoubling the length of this list.

I constructed this sample of English words just after I had put together a similar list in a language that is spoken in the far northeast corner of India and that is known as "Garo." To produce the English list, I simply translated the words on the Garo list. The Garos are slash-and-burn hill farmers, to whom literacy has come only recently, but when I was living among these people and learning their language I was repeatedly surprised by the delicate distinctions they could make with their words, including the distinctions of their personal relationships. My surprise, of course, was misplaced, for even if their technology is, by our standards, simple, their social life and language are not. They need words to describe their use of language as badly as we do, and I have no doubt that the list of their words could be doubled and redoubled as easily as ours. It is not the specific richness and versatility of English that yields such a long list, but the richness and versatility of the minds that allow everyone to have languages of such complexity.

With language, we map the social divisions of our society. Men do not speak in the same way as women. Nor do children, adolescents, the middle aged, or the elderly, or the members of different social classes or occupations. Indeed, linguists have never examined a social distinction without finding it marked by linguistic differences. All of us also vary our language in ways that help to define our relationships to others. We speak in one way to important strangers and in a different way to close friends. We speak in one way to contemporaries and in another way to children, in one way to men and in another way to women. We also vary our speech to fit the occasion, making it more or less technical, legal, ceremonial, secular, formal, or informal. Individual personality is expressed more clearly by the way we talk than by anything else that we do. We cannot separate people's skill in handling their social relationships from their skill in handling the language of these relationships.

Language helps us to bring order to our social relationships, and in that way to build more complex societies than are possible for any other animal. In the small-scale societies in which all of our ancestors once lived and that can still be found on the margins of centralized nations, it has been the language of kinship that expressed the social organization most clearly. Kinship must have provided the earliest framework by which evolving humans organized their communities, just as it still provides the social framework for preliterate societies everywhere. We are not the only animal to recognize kin, of course. Closely related animals of many other species assist one another, and mammals generally recognize close kin well enough to avoid mating. Males and females of a few mammalian species, and of many more species of birds, form long-term mating bonds. Infant birds, like infant mammals, could not survive without parental care. Because humans are not the only mammals to have parents, children, mates, and siblings, something like kinship and something like families are recognizable among many animals, but we are the only species with a vocabulary that lets us follow kinship ties out to third cousins and beyond. Only humans can speculate about their great-great-grandparents or their great-great-grandchildren. As language grew more complex, it could be used to keep track of increasingly distant kinsmen, and with the help of our kinship terms, we can form far more extensive alliances than are possible for any other species. Later, an endlessly cross-cutting variety of other social categories—age, birth order, gender, residence, marital status, beliefs, skin color, language, ethnicity, nationality, education, occupation—whose recognition and definition were made possible by language, were used to organize the kinds of societies that we live in today.

If linguists think about the question at all, it is the cooperative potential of language, rather than its use in competition, that they like to emphasize. Human beings are not the only animals that can cooperate. Lions hunt in packs, and in his book, *Chimpanzee Politics,* Franz de Waal shows us how male chimpanzees can cooperate to assert leadership, and how females can cooperate with one another to find security in a social order where males dominate. Human beings, however, can use language, including the language of kinship, to cooperate in far more intricate ways than lions, or even chimpanzees. Early language has often been thought of as a tool that could help men to hunt more cooperatively, or give women a way to tell each other where the best roots and berries could be found. By emphasizing the role played by language in our social relations I should not leave the impression that it had no role to play in early subsistence. Language certainly gives us a way to convey information, and share wisdom. With language we can plan exactly how we will cooperate, what your role will be and what will be mine.

We use language to encourage loyalty not only to the immediate family, but also to the clan, the tribe, or even to something as abstract and remote as the modern nation. We find it less appealing to suggest that language may be even more important for competition than for cooperation, but the cooperation that language makes possible is often used as a way of forging alliances against others. When a man and woman agree to cooperate in building a family, they have simultaneously defeated their rivals. We build loyalties within a clan, tribe, or nation, in order to strengthen it in relation to other clans, tribes, or nations. We cooperate in order to compete, and language helps us to do both with more subtlety and skill than any other animal can muster.

Whether we like it or not, all animals, including human beings, compete, and language brings endless refinements to the means by which we do so. We constantly use language to persuade or to manipulate others into helping us. We use language to try to gain an edge over others, just as they use language to try to gain an edge over us. We constantly seek to persuade, to convince, to cajole, to seduce. Skill with language brings tangible rewards. We remember our successes and our failures, in considerable part, by how well we managed to present ourselves with words. We all remember, with sorrow or shame, those awful moments when we were unable to think quickly enough to give the most strategic response. We relish the memory of our verbal triumphs.

We use language to avoid violence, and we recommend talk as an alternative to violence. Whenever war threatens, we urge the belligerents to talk. No one should ever imagine that language has made us less violent than other animals, but it has surely changed the way in which we handle violence. Chimpanzees often live in peace with their fellows. Males can cooperate and even form close alliances with one another, but males also compete, and sometimes they fight over access to physical resources or over females. We now know that chimpanzees are capable of grisly violence. Two or more males sometimes gang up on another, and allied males may cooperate to kill an outnumbered enemy. We find it difficult not to see this in human terms and call it "murder."

We find this behavior disturbing because it reminds us so insistently of ourselves. We know all too well about male violence in our own species, but we do have one means that apes do not for extricating ourselves from trouble. An outnumbered man whose enemies threaten him with death is no more capable of physical self-defense than is an outnumbered chimpanzee, but a man may be able to remind his attackers that, even if he is killed, he has brothers back home who will avenge his death. We can talk through the consequences of our actions. We can calculate possible outcomes, and sometimes, if we are clever enough or lucky enough, we can successfully substitute talk for violence. The possibility of talking our way out of violence may not lower the overall level of human violence, but it does, sometimes, postpone it. We put off violence until the pressure builds and finally explodes in the particularly destructive episodes that we call "war," for if language allows us to avoid some kinds of relatively small-scale violence, it also gives us the means to organize our societies for our own unique forms of mass slaughter. Humans have no monopoly over violence, but language lets us organize our violence on a vastly greater scale than any other species can achieve.

Language must have been selected, first of all, as a way to communicate, but that does not imply that it evolved from an earlier system of primate calls. I have felt that our own primate calls and gestures have been too little altered by language to suppose that they could have been its source. The primate gestures and vocalizations by which we still communicate have not been radically changed by language, but our minds have. The changes that have come to our minds do not obscure the shared origins of human and other primate minds, but where our minds differ from those of chimpanzees, the differences are due, in large part, to language. The entanglement of the mind with language is exactly what we should expect if language emerged as a central component of a radically evolving mind.

Language gives us names for things. These are the spoken or gestured words by which we can call another person's attention to something that we have already been thinking about. This gives us the sense that we can almost peer into another mind. We can read someone else's mind in a way that is possible for no other animal. Once we have names, they also seem to float in our heads, so that even when we keep silent, we often feel that we think in language. Show people a number of abstract shapes and later ask them to identify the shapes that they have seen before. If you do nothing more than suggest "give them whatever names you like," you boost the accuracy of their memory. Simply by assigning a name to something we remember it better. You cannot tell an ape to give something a name, but human beings want names for everything. We find it perfectly reasonable to say "I know I've seen that kind of bird before, but I don't know what it is" as if knowing an arbitrary name that someone has bestowed on it, adds to our knowledge of the bird itself. Perhaps that is why a name like "Language Acquisition Device" or "Universal Grammar," persuades us that there must be some object in the world, maybe even a chunk of the brain, that corresponds to the name. Because it has a name, we feel it must be real.

By changing the way we think, language gives us new ways of working through puzzles. Viki, the chimpanzee who grew up in the Hayes household and who failed so badly to articulate words, was subjected to all sorts of tests that explored her ability to solve problems. For many kinds of simple problems, she performed very much as human children do, but she fell badly behind in tests for which children find language helpful. Viki could learn to differentiate two spots from three spots easily enough, but because she could not count, she was much worse than human children at distinguishing six spots from seven. In problems where a sequence of actions had to be performed in a fixed order, human children rehearsed the order verbally. Viki could not do this and she was much less successful than the children.

All mammals learn by experience, but we can sometimes avoid nasty experiments by imagining the outcome of various alternatives. We can play with possibilities in our minds, think about the likely outcomes of our choices. Considering alternatives does not always need words, of course. Animals need to weigh alternatives before making their own strategic decisions. Questions like "Should I fight or flee?" or "Where do I go in order to look for food?" had to be asked long before they were put into words, but as our choices become more complex, we find words increasingly helpful. With words we can define and distinguish the available alternatives. When decisions are difficult we find it helpful to talk over the alternatives with a friend. Literate people may even make written lists of the pros and cons of various choices. If we can think about the alternatives clearly enough, we may never need to experiment.

Language even lets us profit from the experiences of other people. With enough skill and luck, we can avoid repeating their unsuccessful experiments. If we can listen to their reports, we may not even need to watch their failures. I have expressed my skepticism about the need for elaborate language, either for practicing or for teaching the technology of preurban communities, but language is essential for teaching children the community's culturally acceptable social practices. Only with language can children learn about the social categories of their society, about the rules by which their people cooperate, or about the supernatural world that they do not directly experience. Rules, to be sure, sometimes become authoritarian and dogmatic, too sacred to be safely questioned, but at other times we do question our rules and even deliberately change them. Our rules do not prevent us from being the most adaptable of species.

For me, the deepest of the world's mysteries is that of human consciousness. Science has given us satisfying, if still incomplete, answers to many of the mysteries over which human beings have puzzled—the nature of the stars and planets, the origins of mountains and oceans, the relationship among species, biological reproduction—but science has hardly touched consciousness. As every tree and blade of grass should remind us, life does not require consciousness. Whether you believe that animals need to have consciousness depends, in part, on your attitudes toward mosquitoes and clams, but most of us would probably admit that some kinds of animals manage just fine with no more consciousness than a daffodil. For you and for me, however, nothing can be more real than our own consciousness, even if nothing is more difficult to explain. In spite of much recent discussion of the problem, I have not yet found a satisfying explanation for how an organic brain can yield the consciousness of our daily experience.

Do primates share our consciousness? What about other mammals? Any number of dog owners look into the eyes of their pets and are certain that they see consciousness, and yet the biologist Donald Griffin was treated as a radical because he very cautiously suggested that some animals might share our "awareness." The psychologist Julian Jaynes argued, apparently seriously, that consciousness did not come, even to human beings, until shortly before the age of Classical Greece. Every child must have faced the strange thought that we cannot even be quite certain of the consciousness of our own friends. Maybe, like the people I meet in my dreams, everyone else is just a figment of my own mind. If we cannot be certain about our friends, I see no way that we can ever be certain about which animals have consciousness and which do not.

The ability to talk may be the best indication we have of another's consciousness, and it has sometimes been taken for granted that it was language that brought us consciousness. The fact that people report themselves to be conscious may seem convincing, but even if animals do have consciousness, they cannot tell us about it. Deaf people who learn to sign only as adults, but who have clear memories of events that took place long before they had language, show us that consciousness can come before speech. It might be argued that deaf mutes have the kind of brain that could learn to speak if only their ears worked properly. Perhaps that kind of brain is all that is needed for consciousness. We are left in doubt about animals. I find it likely that some other mammals share our consciousness, but I can marshal no good arguments that would persuade a skeptic.

My own favorite theory of consciousness is still that of Nicholas Humphrey, who proposed that our consciousness is useful to us because it gives us a privileged insight into our own motivations, emotions, and behavior. Humphrey suggested that the self-insight that consciousness gives us helps us to interpret the behavior of others. By being able to understand ourselves, we become superb natural psychologists. Humphrey is himself a professional psychologist, but he suggests that all of us are better than any academic psychologist at understanding and interpreting one another's motives and behavior. We interpret the acts of others by relating them to our own feelings and motivations, and we can know these only because of our own consciousness. Humphrey avoids taking a stand on animal consciousness, but I would suppose that animals would profit, just as we do, by being able to use self-understanding as a means for interpreting the behavior of other members of their species. This might require them to have a theory of mind, however, something that has been difficult to demonstrate, and about which opinions remain divided. We know neither whether animals have consciousness nor whether the capacity for language is a prerequisite for consciousness.

Even if language does not actually create consciousness, of course, it may help consciousness along. Perhaps we can understand one another's behavior even better with language than without. Even such a simple matter as giving names to our emotions—anger, joy, amusement, envy, love, and pride—must help us come to terms with these emotions, just as names help us to deal with plants, animals, and physical objects. Verbal labels for our own emotions may help us to understand the emotions of others more easily. Talking about our inner lives and hearing the reports of the inner lives of our friends, must make those lives more real.

It has sometimes been argued that language evolved first as an internal system, a "language of thought" or "mentalese", and that it only later emerged into view as a form of communication. The difficulty with this view is that so much of spoken language appears to be specifically designed to pass from one person to another.

To be sure, language could not exist without a preexisting conceptual system. We might even give a name like "mentalese" or "language of thought" to that conceptual system, but giving it this name does not make it resemble the languages that we call English, Hungarian, or American Sign Language. Much of the apparatus of our languages is of no use whatever for thought, but essential for expressing meanings in a way that can be shared with someone else. Phonology, morphology, and syntax are needed only to allow meanings to be conveyed from one mind to another. Phonology is not needed for keeping concepts distinct, but it is essential for keeping the thousands of words of a language distinct. A language of thought would have no need of morphological distinctions such as verb agreement or case marking. Distinctions such as that between *him* and *himself* are essential for making our meaning clear to another person, but the ideas are perfectly clear in our minds before we ever put them into words. The syntax of deaf signing differs in so many ways from the syntax of spoken languages that we have to conclude that much of syntax is adapted not merely to communication but to the particular medium that is used. Signing takes place in three-dimensional space as well as in one-dimensional time, and it exploits the spatial dimensions in ways that are impossible for spoken language. Much of the syntax of spoken language is needed in order to squeeze multidimensional thought into the single dimension of time.

Once born as a means of communication, however, it could be that language reacts back on our minds and allows us to think in different ways. Our skills at classifying and categorizing, while foreshadowed in apes, are much more refined than theirs, and the refinements could have come when they were needed for more skillful word learning. Learning vocabulary sharpens our perceptions. We learn to discriminate among wines more easily if we assign names to various tastes. We can distinguish fifteen items from sixteen items only because we can give names to numbers and use the names for counting. Could we think about the difference between a misdemeanor and a crime, or between and angel and an elf without words that make them concrete? It is hard to imagine how any but the tiniest fraction of mathematics could exist without language.

We are tempted to see language doing much more. It has been claimed that the particular language that we speak influences the way we view the world, or even determines the way we think. The idea is an old one, and it crops up in many connections and in many forms. It is now often associated with the linguist Benjamin Lee Whorf who believed that varied languages guide their speakers to varying perceptions, and even to different ways of thinking. It was Whorf who described the world before it is organized by language as "presented as a kaleidoscopic flux of impressions." Taken at face value, this is sheer nonsense. No snail could scratch its way along the beach if its world were a kaleidoscopic flux of impressions. If the world contains things that are hoping to eat you, as well as other things that you are hoping to eat, you had better not be so confused by a kaleidoscopic flux that you cannot tell which is which. Nor is the world a kaleidoscopic flux to a prelinguistic child. Children could not even begin to learn a language if they did not have concepts for at least some of the distinguishable actions and objects that await names.

There are less implausible versions of the idea that language guides our perceptions. The most plausible but least exciting comes from the observation that the words of different languages divide the world of experience in different ways. As a result, it has been claimed, speakers are led to recognize differing segments of the world as belonging together. People who call their mother's brothers by one term but their father's brothers by another may distinguish these kinsmen more easily than do people who use a term like "uncle" for both. Different names may make it more natural to expect different behavior. On the other hand, the names may simply reflect the differences that are already there in the culture. In a society where men are expected to act one way toward their sister's children and another way toward their brother's children, their differing names may do no more than reflect the different behavioral expectations. Which comes first, the behavior or the names?

The most interesting claims now being made for the power of language to affect the way we think concern the way we talk about and think about space. Some people find it natural to describe locations with compass directions: "Use the cup that is on the northeastern corner of the table." In other places, people need to use "left" or "right." Perhaps people learn to think with compass directions when they hear others using the compass terms. On the other hand, all languages provide terms both for the compass directions and for "left" and "right," and we find great individual differences, even within our own culture. Some Americans find themselves baffled at a friend's suggestion that they meet on the northeast corner of 5th Avenue and 34th Street. The idea that spatial conceptions are molded by one's language remains controversial.

Certainly vocabulary tells us something about the society in which it is used. As technology changes so does the vocabulary. Everyone who has lived through the computer revolution knows how much new vocabulary we needed in order to play with the new gadgets. Do we need a new vocabulary in order to view the world in a new way? Even if we do, this may not matter much, because we learn new words so easily. We are never held back for long by the lack of a word. As soon as we need a new one, we invent one. As soon as we need to distinguish our mothers' brothers from our fathers' brothers, we find a way to do so, as I have just done in this very sentence.

Whorf was more interested in the way words are constructed and combined than in the words themselves, and he believed that different grammatical patterns encourage different ways of viewing the world. This is far more controversial than any claim about lexical differences reflecting cultural differences, and it is much more difficult to justify. I have been skeptical about the impact of grammar on thought ever since I began to learn the Garo language several decades ago. Its grammar was unfamiliar at first, but I did not feel that it required me to think in unfamiliar ways. Perhaps this does no more than reveal my own lack of imagination, but the decades since Whorf wrote have not been kind to his hypothesis, and I do not think we have yet uncovered any convincing evidence that differing linguistic structures affect world-view in any very interesting way. At the same time, it has to be acknowledged that Chomsky so radically altered the kinds of questions that linguists ask, that the era has hardly been favorable to Whorf's ideas. For many linguists, the universals of language have seemed more interesting than their differences. Anthropologists, always ready to revel in cultural differences, have taken Whorf considerably more seriously than linguists.

Instead of asking whether different languages encourage differing views of the world, we might ask, instead, whether the *universal* features of language affect the way that *all* of us think. Nearly all languages, for example, distinguish nouns from verbs. Linguists assign words to various parts of speech by their syntactic or morphological characteristics, not by their meanings. If an English word is used with articles and plurals we recognize it to be a "noun." If it is used with suffixes like *-ing* and third-person singular *-s* we call it a "verb." Thus *toy* is a noun in *The toys are broken* but a verb in *He's toying with quitting his job*. Nevertheless, "things" (whatever that means, and that is part of the problem) are most often named by nouns, while "actions" are more often named by verbs. Are things and actions, then, created only by our language? Or is it more likely that the division between nouns and verbs builds on and reflects the way in which human beings already viewed the world before they had language? Perhaps language confirms, rather than creates, a view of the world.

The subjects of our sentences are often agents that perform the action named by the verb. We say *Mary tickled Bill, Florence broke the window,* and *He's swimming. Mary, Florence,* and *He* are the agents who take initiative, who do the *tickling, swimming,* or *breaking.* Do sentences like these encourage us to imagine that other subjects are also active agents? Does this idea leak over into the way we interpret sentences such as *Fred wants a pickle, The lightning struck the radio tower,* or *John can see her?* Fred takes no action at all and lightning surely lacks the initiative we expect of an agent. When John sees her, light-waves impinge on John's retina, so, if anything, he is the recipient of the action rather than its agent. Perhaps our language encourages us to imagine John to be an agent, even when he is doing nothing except reacting to light-waves.

Causality is a notoriously difficult concept but it is a concept that is built into English, as it is probably built into every language. The difference between a verb used intransitively and transitively is usually a matter of causality. We can say *the paper tears,* but we can also say *I tear the paper,* which can be paraphrased as *I cause the paper to tear.* Many languages have causative markers that turn a word with an intransitive meaning such as "see" into a word with a transitive meaning such as "show." Does our notion of causality come from our language? Or did we have a concept of causality long before we had language, and simply incorporate the idea into our language?

We cannot do without words, but words can lead us badly astray. If we need to talk about something for which we have no precise word, we find another word that seems reasonably close to the meaning we want, and we thereby stretch the word's earlier meaning. As soon as we use the same word for a variety of things, however, we can be misled into supposing that all those things are the same. By using the word "gesture" both for the visible movements of our hands and for the largely invisible movements of our vocal organs, we may fool ourselves into believing that there would have been no problem, in the course of human evolution, in shifting from an earlier language of manual gestures to a later language of vocal gestures. We cannot have a separate word for every single one of our thoughts and concepts, but it is easy to forget the differences that we hide behind a common name.

We give names to imaginary conceptions as easily as to those that stand for objects and actions that we take to be real, but once we have given a name to some idea, we may come to believe in the reality of the idea even if it exists only in our imagination. Most of us are confident that Santa Claus is not real, but human beings have believed in a great variety of elves, ghosts, gods, and spirits for whom the empirical evidence is no better than it is for Santa Claus. People kill each other to defend or advance their competing beliefs about totally unverifiable beings. Is it language that makes such acts possible?

Once, many years ago, I lived for six weeks in a poor agricultural village near the city of Varanasi in northern India. A young woman who must have been about eighteen years old and who appeared to be totally deaf lived in the house next door. Like everyone else in the village, her parents were farmers of modest means, and I do not believe that she had ever had a single day of schooling. She had no regular contact with other deaf mutes, so she had never had any opportunity to learn an established sign language. Of course she used gestures to communicate with the other members of her family, but everyone else in her household was able to hear and to speak, while their communication with the young deaf woman was limited to gestures. In spite of her deafness and her resulting isolation, I was continually astonished, as I watched her and the other members of her family, by her apparent normality. She dressed as other young women of her age dressed. She worked in the kitchen and around the house doing a young woman's work. She went to the fields and shared in the labor of agriculture. She squatted as other women squatted, and she used the appropriately self-effacing postures of a young village woman of her age. As far as I was able to judge, she pulled her full weight in the economic activities of her household. Watching her was one of the experiences that has made me skeptical of the importance of language for preindustrial technology. Here was a person who had no language at all, but who appeared to participate fully in the technical tasks of her family and community. She had learned everything by watching and by imitating, and she had needed no language to do so.

I did ask myself what she missed, and of course, she missed a great deal. Her understanding of kinship, for example, must have been rudimentary. She could see how the people of her large extended family behaved toward one another and she must have felt particularly close ties with some of them. Perhaps she observed the pregnancies of her sisters-in-law and grasped the fact that pregnancies ended with the arrival of new babies. She could watch mothers nursing their babies so she must have understood something about the special bonds that unite women with their own children. She could watch herself and the other children in her family and neighborhood grow and gradually become more independent, even while maintaining the special tie to the women who had once nursed them. Even in a society where husbands and wives never display the slightest hint of affection in public, she must have noticed that some men and women had special bonds. She must have developed theories of some sort to explain the relationships among the people among whom she lived, but beyond the limits of her observations there must also have been unfathomable mysteries. Could she have isolated the relationships that we name with words like *aunt, uncle,* and *grandfather,* to say nothing of *second* or *third cousin*?

She must have learned to expect the passage of the sun, the moon, and the seasons, but her understanding of the way people divide time into weeks or hours must have been very limited. She could see the altars in her home, and the statues of Hindu deities, but she could not have known that the statues represented gods. Indeed, she could have known nothing at all of the gods, spirits, ghosts, and demons that were familiar to everyone else. She could watch worshipers and learn to mimic their behavior, but she could hardly have understood the meaning that her own movements held for others. She had no way of knowing about the Hindu doctrine of rebirth. She could hardly have had a full understanding of concepts like truth or falsity, justice or cheating, honesty or deceit. She knew no stories. She knew nothing about the world beyond the narrow confines of her home and her village. She had heard no tales of earlier times and she had few ways to anticipate the future. She could not plan because she did not know the plans of others.

On the other hand, the world of my young deaf neighbor was nothing remotely like the "kaleidoscopic flux of impressions" that Whorf imagined to be the condition of a prelinguistic child. She could distinguish different kinds of objects from one another and she knew how each object was used. She did not need the conventional words of her community to react conventionally to the physical objects around her. Beyond the concrete world of physical objects, however, were more abstract realms that were closed to her. Kinship systems, village boundaries, principles of justice, stories of what follows death, all these are creations of language. Only language lets us know realms that reach far beyond our own neighborhoods. With words we create heavens and hells, and with words we invent big bangs and theories of evolution. Without words there would be no mythological realms, neither the Olympian realm of the Greek gods, nor the realm of the Flintstones of television. We give names to the concrete objects and actions of the world around us, but by the very act of naming we also bring other more abstract concepts into existence. A child can learn preindustrial technology by watching and copying. We cannot teach our children about kinship, heaven, honor, or truth except through the medium of language, and yet these become as real and important to us as the tangible objects that we can see and touch.

Language is far too complex and far too well designed to have developed in any way except by a long period of selection. There is simply no other explanation for the kind of adaptive complexity we find in language. Language cannot be just a lucky byproduct of something else. We cannot doubt, however, that language was an essential pre-adaptation for the kind of civilization that started with the growth of cities five or six thousand years ago. The ability to learn and use language evolved among stone-tool-manufacturing hunters and gatherers of the lower Paleolithic, but without language, we could not have invented the very different kind of life we lead today.

Consider literacy. We ought to be astonished that human beings are able to read and write. We can attribute understanding and speaking to a long period of natural selection and to a gradual growth of the capacity for language learning, but humans have written their languages for little more than five thousand years, not nearly enough time for the capacity for writing to have been built into our minds as a specialized skill. There can have been no selection for literacy during the old stone age because there was no writing for which humans might have been selected. Even today, a few people who appear to have entirely normal ability with oral language find it difficult or impossible to learn to read. In a society without writing, dyslexics would never be recognized as different from anyone else. The ability to become literate is not, therefore, an automatic consequence of the ability to understand and to speak. From an evolutionary perspective, all populations, even today, are new to writing, so why are we not all dyslexic? Far from being dyslexic, most people, once they have the chance, are able to learn to read and write very successfully. Where spelling is less chaotic than in English, they are even able to learn quite quickly. In some mysterious way, spoken language has preadapted most of us, although not quite all of us, for written language. Having given us the ability to count, language also preadapted us, or some of us, for mathematics and for the kind of science that is expressed in mathematical formulas.

The cognitive abilities entailed by an improving language helped to create a species that was capable of producing the refined art and tool assemblages that we find in the upper Paleolithic, and capable, later, of inventing the revolutionary civilization that began with agriculture and then developed into urban life. Spoken language was all that was needed in small bands or villages where everyone was intimately acquainted, but cities, and then the ever larger nations and empires that followed, could not have developed without writing. Urban civilization brought, for the first time, record keeping, codified legal systems, bureaucracy, the accumulation of recorded knowledge, science, expanding technology, and formal education. Social stratification became sharper and a division of labor brought kings and bureaucrats, traders and priests. None of the social and technical inventions that have come with increasing speed ever since cities were first built would have been possible without the language that had evolved in an earlier and different era. Complex language evolved as a delicate instrument for engaging in ever more intricate social relationships, and language continues to serve that purpose. Now, it also permits the vastly more complex organization of modern society, a use for which it was never designed.

Languages have to be learned, but they must also be shared. A language would do us no good if it did not match the language of the other members of our community, but we cannot speak a language without learning it. This seems obvious, for it says no more than that our languages are a part of our culture, passed down from one generation to the generation that follows. Nevertheless, behavior that is both shared and learned is unusual in the animal world. Shared behavior is widespread, and so is learned behavior, but behavior that is both shared and learned is not.

All dogs bark, so barking is shared behavior but it is so narrowly determined by the animal's inheritance that learning plays hardly any part in its development. Raise a puppy in complete isolation from other dogs, and it will soon bark as enthusiastically as all the rest. Most forms of animal communication are like barking. They are inherited as part of the genetic endowment of each individual and they need little contribution from learning.

At the same time, mammals, if not insects or clams, have plenty to learn, but most of what they learn is not widely shared with others. In many species, for example, each animal needs to learn its territorial boundaries. It learns to find its way around within the boundaries, and learns where the resources are to be found. Since the members of a species have different territories, however, each animal has to acquire its own unique territorial knowledge and it does not need to share that knowledge with others. Barking is shared but not learned. Territorial boundaries are learned but not shared.

Languages, however, are both shared and learned. Like any communication system, of course, a language would help no one if it were not shared. Most animal communication requires little learning, so why does language need so much? The answer that I gave in Chapter 7 was that the few million years in which the ability to use language evolved were simply not long enough to build everything into our genes. Indeed, all the vast complexities of a language could not possibly be squeezed into the available DNA. The only way we could acquire such a complex skill as language was to build in a lot of empty storage capacity and then rely on learning to fill it up. The brain evolved in a way that permitted language, but the details need to be filled in by experience. Because we must talk with each other, we need a language that resembles the language of our kinsmen and neighbors. Because language must be learned, people who have no need to communicate can learn very different languages.

The least unambiguous examples of nonhuman animal behavior that is both shared and learned, which is to say behavior that is cultural, are bird songs and the communication of some cetaceans such as dolphins and humpback whales. Because they are, in part, learned from neighbors, the bird songs of some species and the songs of some whales can, like languages, be fairly called "traditional." Language, bird songs, and the songs of humpbacks vary from one group to another, and they all change gradually through time. It may seem surprising that the best examples of animal culture, as well as the single most distinctive example of human culture, are all systems of communication, but this is not simply coincidence. Because they are used for communication, bird songs, whale songs, and language all have to be shared, while most learned behavior does not. It is the dual quality of being both learned and shared that makes bird songs and whale songs, along with language, traditional forms of behavior that are subject to cultural variation.

Languages are much more complex than the songs of either whales or birds, so they need a correspondingly long period of learning. By evolving into the kind of animal that could learn so much language and sustain such differing linguistic traditions, we may also have become the kind of animal that can also sustain other kinds of traditions. We can pass traditions of every sort from one generation to the next, so it is not only our language that is culturally variable but also our kinship practices, our religion, our ideas about government, our art, and our technology—just about everything that matters to us. It is tempting for a linguist to wonder if it was the need to learn the cultural tradition of a language that has given us, as a byproduct, the ability to learn and to share so much else. Language may have preadapted us for the ability to learn, and then pass on to the next generation, the many varying cultural traditions that characterize humankind.

Human beings cannot stop themselves from searching for explanations or from constructing theories, and any but the simplest theory requires language. When we hear the word "theory" we think first of science, where a systematic effort is made to construct theories that will explain the phenomena of the world around us, and where a deliberate effort is also made to find data that tests whether a theory can account for the observations. The deliberate construction and testing of theories is a relatively recent, and still rather unusual, intellectual enterprise, but even people who are innocent of modern science have always had theories. We now assign some of our less deliberately constructed theories to the category that we call "religion." "Doctrine" is a more familiar word than "theory" for religious teachings, but religious doctrines, no less than scientific theories, offer explanations for the nature of the world in which we live and for our place within this world. Religious doctrines, like scientific theories, help people to make sense of the vagaries of nature and of humankind. They bring a kind of coherence to the world that lies around and within us, and that is not always as orderly or predictable as we would like it to be.

Only one real difference distinguishes a scientific theory from a religious doctrine, but it is an important one. In science, we are supposed to search deliberately for data that undermines our theories. In this way we test our theories and eliminate those that do not fit the facts. In religion, we attempt, almost as deliberately, to ignore or reject any data that contradicts the doctrine. Doubt about a religious doctrine can be met by encouragement to deepen one's faith, rather than by a search for data that will subject the theory to empirical test. Even the difference between skeptical testing and comfortable faith can be exaggerated, however. Scientists can become so committed to their favorite theories that they refuse to acknowledge embarrassing data, while even long-cherished religious doctrines can be forced to yield when sufficient contradictory evidence accumulates. People who have attributed disease to malevolent spirits, and who have sacrificed animals as the best means to appease those spirits, can have their faith seriously undermined when they see how effectively penicillin does the job. Hardly anyone any longer takes seriously the possibility of a geocentric universe, although it was once a firm article of religious faith. The heliocentric theory explains the positions and apparent motion of the wandering planets so much more successfully than the older geocentric theory did, that the geocentric theory finally had to yield.

Believers in both religious and scientific theories, then, can resist empirical disproof, but both must finally succumb. Still, the difference between religious and scientific theories is important. When scientific theories do not accord with the facts, they are abandoned considerably more easily than religious doctrines. Newton's laws, once as empirically successful as any scientific theory ever proposed, yielded with hardly a whimper when Einstein's relativity came along and accounted for some extra observations. Creationists have fought for a century and a half against the theory of natural selection, but in the end, their battle is unlikely to be any more successful than was the resistance of the Catholic Church to the heliocentric solar system.

Human beings constantly construct less exalted theories than the grand doctrines of science and religion. Modest theories, that no one would dignify as either science or religion, help us to interpret and understand what happens around us. A mechanic tries out alternative explanations in order to understand why a car will not start. Computer programers search for a reason why their programs do not perform as they should. Like a mechanic or a scientist, the programer tries to narrow the range of explanations by experimenting with alternative procedures.

Even for more trifling matters than a failing car or computer, we search for explanations: "Where is that book that I remember leaving on the table this morning?" "Could John have gotten it into his head to clean up?" "Did I take it to the office with me?" "Have I, after all, forgotten where I left it?" Or, "Why did Mary seem so withdrawn?" "Was she feeling sick?" "Is she worried about her mother?" "Could it be because she saw me talking to Suzy?" We constantly make such modest guesses and construct such modest theories to explain the most mundane details of our daily life. I doubt if other animals form even the simplest theory, and they are certainly free of the more elaborate theories that we would recognize as either scientific or religious. Human beings cannot stop themselves from theorizing. Would we have theories if we had no language?

Linguists sometimes suggest that we need to construct a theory in order to learn a language. Although we may start with universal grammar, we go on to construct a theory of one particular language, and as I suggested in Chapter 4, the ability to find patterns is a prerequisite for language. Like little linguists, children start by collecting data. The talk that swirls around them bathes them in data, and on the basis of these data, children must construct their own internal grammars. Since nobody tells children how the language works, they need to figure it out for themselves. Whatever the complexity of the universal grammar that has been built into their heads by natural selection, plenty remains to be learned, not just words and pronunciations, but the idiosyncratic grammatical patterns of their community's language. One way of describing what children do, (which is to say, one theory by which we can try to understand what they do) is to say that children make guesses (hypotheses) about what they hear, and then use these guesses as a theory that guides them as they construct their own new sentences. At first, their incomplete theory can produce no more than crude baby talk, but as they hear more of the language they refine their hypotheses, and test them by forming new sentences. Gradually, they build up a theory of grammar that is close enough to the theory already held by older people to let them join their elders in talk.

Of course, children do not construct their theories self-consciously, but there is a sense in which children can be said to need a theory. They need to form generalizations about the language before they can produce new utterances of their own, and their generalizations are complex enough that it is reasonable to think of them as constituting a sort of theory, even if it is unconscious. If this is a plausible way to think of the manner in which we all learned our first language, it suggests that everyone is born with the ability to devise theories that account for at least some of the data in their environment. A linguist must be tempted by the idea that the kind of expertise needed to develop a linguistic theory may equip us to build other kinds of theories as well. Could the skillful eagerness with which human beings construct theories of all sorts be a byproduct of the need to construct a theory of a language?

This may be claiming too much for language. Admittedly it expresses a language-centered view of humanity, a view that may be especially appealing to linguists. It is not too much, however, to recognize the importance of language in all theory building, both religious and scientific, and to point out that we have to use language whenever we describe or teach our theories. Simple technology can be conveyed by demonstration and imitation, but the theories that describe optics, radioactive decay, DNA, natural selection, reincarnation, or life after death can only be explained, or learned, with the help of language. The most elegant theories of modern science are now stated in mathematical form, but even mathematics amounts to a kind of language. Only a talking animal could have invented such a refined variety of language as mathematics.

I will end this book on a very personal note. I have spent almost four years of my life living among the people known to the world as "Garos." Two of these years were in the 1950s, a half century ago, when I lived in a village in the hills of northeastern India. The rest of the time was passed in other small Garo villages that lie across the border in Bangladesh. Many Garos are now wet rice farmers, but those I lived among during the fifties supported themselves by slash-and-burn farming. The membership of Garo villages was, and is, very stable. Many young men change villages when they marry, but most women, and a good many men as well, remain in their natal villages for their entire lives. A mobile westerner finds it hard to grasp just how well people get to know each other after living for fifty years in a single village of a few hundred people. They cooperate and they quarrel. They marry and, occasionally, they cheat on their spouses. They trade labor and they assemble for rituals. They know who is lazy and who is hard working, who drinks too much, who is clever, and who is foolish. Over the years, they watch some families accumulate wealth and watch others, through bad luck or bad management, grow poor. People die but others are born. But whatever happens, however much they like each other or hate each other, they go on living in neighboring houses. I have often asked myself, as I sat with Garo friends: "What, after all these years, can they still have to talk about?" But of course they keep talking. Like everyone else, they fill their days with chatter. Serious or frivolous, wise or foolish, always there is talk.

They feel talk to be essential. One of the things that I find most difficult about living among Garos is how hard it is to get away from people. Their insistent curiosity is exhausting. I look forward to retreating into my room, to closing the door, to being alone. Garos don't understand this, for they don't like to be alone. In particular, Garos do not like to sleep in a room alone. Babies share their parents' bed. Young people want room-mates. Old widows take a grandchild into their room as a companion. When I first went to live in the village of Gaira in Bangladesh, people asked me if I wouldn't be afraid to be alone, or if not afraid, wouldn't I be lonely? Wouldn't it be good to have someone else sharing my room so I would have someone to talk to? They are tolerant of my eccentricities and they permit me to have my private room, but people still ask from time to time if I am not lonely, all by myself, without anyone to talk to.

Talk is important to the Garos as it is to all of us. We never run out of things to say. We are a strange species, and, as much as anything else, it is language that has made us strange. We will never know all the details of how language got started or of how it developed in the human species, but the better we can guess, the better will be our understanding of the talking ape.

Notes

Chapter One

3. Phylogeny of the apes: Begun (1999).

6. Comprehension, and production in children: Frasier, Bellugi, and Brown (1963).

7. Recognizing the mother's language: Mehler et al. (1988); Moon, Cooper, and Fifer (1993); DeCasper and Spence (1986).

7. Name recognition by infants: Mandel, Jusczyk, and Pisoni (1995).

7. Comprehension in home-reared chimpanzees: Kellogg and Kellogg (1933); Hayes and Nissen (1971).

9. Comprehension of English by Kanzi, the bonobo: Savage-Rumbaugh et al. (1993).

14. Origin of animal signals: Tinbergen (1952).

17. Social need for language: Humphrey (1976); Dunbar (1996); Miller (2000a).

18. Crucial mutation for language: Bickerton (1990). However, see Calvin and Bickerton (2000); Bickerton (2003) for a revised opinion.

Chapter Two

24. Universals of facial expressions: Ekman (1972).

25. The manner in which I describe human communication here owes much to Charles Hockett's classic use of "design features" to compare human and animal communication: Hockett (1959, 1960).

28. Expression of emotion and intention: Darwin (1998 [1872]); Ekman and Friesen (1969).

32. Gordon Hewes collected accounts of the experience of the first European explorers to encounter people in the Caribbean and Pacific islands. These travelers described how they were able to communicate well enough to get food and directions from the local people even when they shared no common language whatever: Hewes (1974a).

32. Universality of facial expressions: Ekman (1972); Ekman and Friesen (1969, 1971); Izard (1971, 1980); strong skepticism expressed about uni-

versals: Russell (1994, 1995); Fridlund (1994); replies to attacks by Russell and Fridlund, convincing in this author's opinion: Ekman (1994); Izard (1994).

32. The high tide of the behaviorist understanding of language: Skinner (1957). The beginning of the end of this view of language: Chomsky's review of Skinner's book, Chomsky (1959).

33. Learning and heredity: For a clear and accessible account of Chomsky's view of learning, see Neil Smith (1999), especially pp. 26–7, 117–19, 169, 178. Smith also gives a good introduction to many other aspects of Chomsky's thinking.

34. Double articulation: Martinet (1949); duality of patterning: Hockett (1959).

36. Voluntary control of facial muscles: We can control our facial muscles voluntarily, but when we do so, we do not use the same neurological mechanisms that we use under the pressure of emotion. Spontaneous facial expressions of emotion are controlled by the limbic system, while more voluntary movements of the face are cortically controlled. For most of us, these two pathways converge so intimately that we never need to be aware that different processes are involved, but pathological conditions reveal the difference. People with brain lesions in the cortical motor strip can suffer a severe paralysis on one side of their face that leaves them with no voluntary control over the muscles. The same muscles, however, react normally to emotion. Someone whose voluntary "smile" is badly one-sided can react to a joke with a fine bilateral smile. Other kinds of lesions, especially those in the basal ganglia, leave the voluntary control of the facial muscles unimpaired. In this case, however, the victim's face remains deadpan, whatever his emotions. Such people do not smile in response to a joke or to greetings from a friend; Rinn (1984).

38. The classic and still excellent account of the nature of sign language is Klima and Bellugi (1979); Wilbur (1987) is also a good survey.

38. Deaf signing as equivalent to spoken language: Stokoe (1960).

40. Speed of speaking and signing: Bellugi and Fischer (1972).

41. Emblems: Ekman and Friesen (1969); quotable gestures: Kendon (1992).

44. Gesticulation: McNeill (1992).

44. Intonation: Bolinger (1986).

Chapter Three

48. Hominin: The human line, including both Australopithecus and Homo, has been traditionally designated as "hominid". Now that chimpanzees and bonobos are recognized as being so closely related to humans, they are increasingly recognized as hominids as well. The smaller group still needs its own term, and it is now increasingly designated as "hominin".

48. Language evolution seen from the primate perspective: Miles (1983: 33–44); Cheney and Seyfarth (1990).

48. Impoverished primate calls: Bickerton (1981: 220).

50. Vervet alarm calls: Struhsaker (1967); Seyfarth, Cheney, and Marler (1980a, 1980b); and especially Cheney and Seyfarth (1990).

50. Vervet grunts: Cheney and Seyfarth (1990: 114–20).

53. Graded and discrete animals calls: Marler (1976, 1982); Marler and Mitani (1988).

54. Graded calls of chimpanzees: Marler (1976).

55. Learning of bird songs: Marler (1970); Catchpole and Slater (1995).

55. Whale songs: Tyack and Sayigh (1997); Payne (2000).

55. Hints of learned communicative behavior among primates: Marler and Mitani (1988); Mitani et al. (1992); Hauser (1992); Mitani and Brandt (1994); Mitani et al. (1999).

55. Learned traditions among primates: Whiten et al. (1999).

56. Songs of humpback whales: Payne (2000); Tyack and Sayigh (1997).

57. Gibbon songs: Geissmann (2000); Gelada baboon songs: Richman (1987).

57. Voluntary character of vervet alarm calls: Cheney and Seyfarth (1990: 144–9).

59. Young chimp leading others away from food: Goodall (1986).

59. Paul's screaming tactic: Byrne and Whiten (1988).

59. Skepticism about deception by apes: Tomasello and Call (1997: 233–42).

60. Homology of human and ape gesture-calls: van Hooff (1972, 1976). See also ample later confirmation of van Hooff's observations: Chevalier-Skolnikoff (1973); Preuschoft (1992); Preuschoft and van Hooff (1995, 1997).

61. Human laughter: Provine (2000).

61. Play face: Schmidt and Cohn (2001).

61. "Throughout this time...": Savage-Rumbaugh and Lewin (1994: 106–7).

Chapter Four

70. Viki: Hayes and Nissen (1971).

70. "Toward the end . . .": Hayes and Nissen (1971: 88).

71. Kaleidoscopic flux: Whorf (1956).

72. Recognition of individuals: Boesch and Boesch-Achermann (2000: 234).

72. Personal relationships among chimpanzees: de Waal (1982).

73. Quine's problem: Quine (1960).

73. Capacities needed for word learning: Bloom and Markson (1998).

73. Shared attention by small children: D. Baldwin (1991).

73. Recognizing a *blurg*: Bloom (1997).

73. Failure of chimps to understand pointing: Tomasello and Camaioni (1997).

74. Blocked view understood by chimpanzees: Hare et al. (2000).

75. Imitation by infants: Meltzoff and Moore (1977).

75. Imitation and mirror neurons: Considerable interest has been directed toward so-called "mirror neurons" that react both when an individual performs an action such as grasping and when he observes a similar action being performed by someone else. Some such identification of one's own behavior with the behavior of others would seem to be necessary for imitation: Rizzolatti and Arbib (1998); Arbib (forthcoming).

75. Birds imitating their neighbors: Marler (1970); Catchpole and Slater (1995).

75. Imitation by whales and dolphins: Tyack and Sayigh (1997); Payne (2000).

76. Skepticism about imitation: Tomasello (1996); Tomasello and Call (1997: 308–10).

77. Imitation by orangutans: Russon and Galdikas (1993, 1995).

77. Chimpanzee teaching: Boesch and Boesch-Achermann (2000: 245).

77. General review of imitation in apes: Byrne and Russon (1998).

78. Cultural variation in apes: Whiten et al. (1999).

78. Converging pant-hoots: Marshall et al. (1999).

78. One chimp assumes another's pant-hoot: Boesch and Boesch-Achermann (2000: 235).

78. Variable vocalization among rhesus monkeys: Hauser (1992).

78. Icons, indices, and symbols: Peirce (1940).

79. Viki's iconic gestures: Hayes and Nissen (1971: 107).

79. Kubie: Tanner and Byrne (1996).

80. Booee's understanding of iconic gestures: Savage-Rumbaugh and Lewin (1994: 36).

80. Kanzi's iconic gestures: Savage-Rumbaugh and Lewin (1994: 134).

80. Positions for copulation: Savage-Rumbaugh and Lewin (1994: 112).

82. Word learning: Markman (1989); Bloom (2000).

82. Learning grammatical patterns in childhood: Tomasello (2003).

83. Recognizing "words" such as *tibudo*: Saffran, Aslin, and Newport (1996).

83. Distinguishing ABB from AAB sequences: Marcus et al. (1999).

83. Tamarins recognizing ABB and AAB sequences: Hauser et al. (2002).

87. Adaptation to a changing environment: Boyd and Richerson (1985).

88. Starting points for language: Bloom (1998).

89. Deaf children creating a new sign language: Kegl and McWhorter (1997); Kegl, Senghas, and Coppola (1999).

89. Language as byproduct: Chomsky (1991: 50).

90. Single mutation: Bickerton (1990).

90. William Paley and the eye: Paley (1802 [1951]).

90. Mutations and hurricanes: Pinker (1994: 361).

90. Deaf mutes remembering: S. Schaller (1991).

91. Features of language needed for communication: Bloom (1998: 213); Hurford (2002).

91. Language first used for thought: Burling (1993: 37).

Chapter Five

92. Saussure on arbitrariness: Saussure (1959: 69).

94. Peirce's typology of signs: Peirce (1940).

94. Hand gestures: McNeill (1992, 2000).

94. Gesticulation: Kendon (1993, 1997).

97. Syntactic iconicity: Haiman (1985); Givón (1989); Matthews (1991: 12).

98. Iconicity shown by word order: Bybee (1985) gives a more extensive example of the iconicity of the order of items, but her examples concern the order of verbal affixes rather than of separate words.

98. Motivated language in children: Slobin (1985).

99. High and low pitch: These relate to the pervasive metaphor in English, and probably of many other languages, of "up and down". "Up" is associated with vigor, activity, health; down with the opposite: G. Lakoff and Johnson (1980).

99. "In the course of an action...": Bolinger (1985: 99).

100. Humming intonation: Bolinger (1986: 211).

100. Variation in stress: Bolinger (1978: 474).

101. Meanings of pitch: Ohala (1994).

101. Polite speech: Brown and Levinson (1987: 267–8).

101. Deferential speech of women: R. Lakoff (1975: 17).

Chapter Six

105. Young chimpanzee communication: Tomasello et al. (1985, 1989, 1994, 1997).

107. Ontogenetic ritualization: Tomasello and Call (1997: 299–302).

112. Sumerian writing: Kramer (1963).

112. Iconic signs: Frishberg (1975); Klima and Bellugi (1979).

113. Cinnamon roll and videotape recorder: Klima and Bellugi (1979: 11).

116. Conventionalization of gestures by deaf children: Goldin-Meadow (1993).

116. Deaf children's stories: Goldin-Meadow (1993: 65–6).

117. Two users needed for arbitrariness: Goldin-Meadow (1993: 78).

117. Nicaraguan sign language: Kegl and McWhorter (1997); Kegl, Senghas, and Coppola (1999); Senghas and Coppola (2001).

118. Creoles: Bickerton (1981); Sankoff (1980).

118. Motivated but incorrect word order: Slobin (1985).

118. Children's negations: Klima and Bellugi (1966).

Chapter Seven

122. Human vocal tract: Lieberman (1968, 1984); Lieberman and Crelin (1971); but see also the cautionary argument of Fitch (2002).

123. Visual language before audible: Hewes (1973); Armstrong, Stokoe, and Wilcox (1994, 1995); Corballis (2002); Arbib (forthcoming).

123. Ape signing: Gardner and Gardner (1969).

124. Articulatory "gestures": Armstrong, Stokoe, and Wilcox (1994: 57–8).

124. Darwin on music: Darwin (1930 [1871]: 585).

125. Jesperson on song: Jesperson (1922: 434).

125. Evolution of music: Wallin, Merker, and Brown (2000).

125. Parallels between music and language: Livingstone (1973); Lerdahl and Jackendoff (1983).

125. Whale songs: Payne (2000); Tyack and Sayigh (1997).

125. Gibbon duetting: Geissmann (2000: 107); see also Richman (1987, 2000) on gelada baboons.

126. Imitation among whales: Tyack and Sayigh (1997); Payne (2000); among birds: Catchpole and Slater (1995).

126. Synchrony in frogs and fireflies: Merker (2000).

126. Regular beats of language: Pike (1945); Couper-Kuhlin (1993).

127. Common ancestry of music and language: Brown (2000).

127. Motherese: Falk (forthcoming).

128. Split between music and language: Brown (2000).

128. Parallels between music and language: Lerdahl and Jackendoff (1983).

130. Meaning of the first words: Wray (2002).

134. Brain size, intelligence, and verbal ability: Wickett et al. (2000).

135. Animal discrimination of formants: Fitch (2002); Sommers et al. (1992).

135. Animal discrimination of speech sounds: Kuhl and Miller (1975).

136. Vocal tract changes: Lieberman (1968, 1984); Lieberman and Crelin (1971).

136. Low larynx in some mammals: Fitch (2002).

137. Syllables: McNeilage (1998); McNeilage and Davis (2000).

138. Infinite use of finite means: Humbolt (1972 [1836]).

138. Proteins, chemical compounds, and words: Abler (1989); Studdert-Kennedy (1998, 2000).

139. Duality of patterning: Hockett (1960); Martinet (1949).

139. Comparative difficulty of speech sounds: Lindblom and Maddieson (1988).

141. The brain: Deacon (1997); Marcus (2004).

142. Complexities of lexical meaning: Jackendoff (2002).

143. Language instinct: Pinker (1994).

143. The number of genes in the human genome was once estimated to be 100,000 or more. 30,000 is now regarded as more likely: Marcus (2004).

Chapter Eight

145. Late and sudden language: Bickerton (1990); Berwick (1998).

145. Gradual syntactic development: Tomasello (2003); Burling (2002).

145. Bickerton backs away from the single mutation: Calvin and Bickerton (2000); Bickerton (2003).

146. Chomsky on evolution: Onomothy (1975: 59, 1991: 50).

146. Language evolving by selection: Pinker and Bloom (1990).

146. Punctuated equilibrium: Eldredge and Gould (1972).

146. Single mutation: Crow (2002).

147. 100,000 year punctuations: Gould (1982).

148. Mitochondrial "Eve": Templeton (1993); Stoneking (1994); Ayala (1995).

149. FOXP2: Lai et al. (2001); Enard et al. (2002); Marcus and Fisher (2003); Fisher (forthcoming); Simon Fisher, personal communication.

149. Colonization of Australia: O'Connell and Allen (2004).

150. Upper Paleolithic: Whallon (1989); Mellars and Stringer (1989).

150. Brain expansion: De Miguel and Henneberg (2001); Lee and Wolpoff (2003); Aiello (1996).

152. Rubicon: Bickerton (2003).

153. Poverty of stimulus: Pinker (1994); Anderson and Lightfoot (2002).

153. End of behavioral psychology: Chomsky (1959).

153. Unimportance of what comes from the outside: So far as I am aware, Chomsky has never said, in so many words, that what comes from the outside is relatively unimportant, but the thrust of his writing seems to push in that direction: his consistent focus on universal grammar; the suggestion that "learning" is a pretheoretical concept; the comparison of language acquisition to puberty—it just grows; the suggestion that we should be more concerned with I-language, than with E-language. Even

the doctrine of parameters seems to be a metaphor that is intended to play down the need for learning. Parameters do not need to be "learned" at all, but only "set." Indeed, they are set by mere "triggering." For an accessible account of Chomsky's ideas, see Smith (1999).

154. Language organ: Anderson and Lightfoot (2002).

155. Noninnatist views: Tomasello (2003); Sampson (1997).

156. Naga pidgin: Sreedhar (1974).

158. Selection for good language genes: Pinker and Bloom (1990); Newmeyer (1991).

159. Arena of use: Kirby and Hurford (1997); Kirby (1999).

159. External language and DNA: It is interesting to note a parallel. Both DNA and external language have two functions. DNA defines the proteins that build and maintain an organism. In addition, it serves as a template for replicating itself so that a new individual can come into existence. External language is the stuff of conversation among mature speakers. It gives us a way to exchange information, manipulate others, and display our talents. In addition, external language serves as a template that immature speakers can use to construct their own new internal language, a language that will come close to replicating the internal language of the previous generation. Both DNA and external language are replicators, and both use the organism to produce copies of themselves.

160. Selection of easy-to-parse examples: Kirby (1999); Kirby and Hurford (1997).

161. Creoles: Rickford (1987); Sankoff (1980); Bickerton (1981).

161. Nicaraguan sign language: Kegl and McWhorter (1997); Kegl, Senghas, and Coppola (1999).

162. Baldwin effect: Baldwin (1896); Hinton and Nolan (1987). For a negative evaluation of the Baldwin effect, see Yamauchi (2001).

Chapter Nine

164. Grammaticalization: Lehmann (1982); Heine, Claudi, and Hünnemeyer (1991); Bybee, Perkins, and Pagliuca (1994); Hopper and Traugott (1993).

164. Sequence of syntactic features: Jackendoff (2002).

164. Sequence of stages: Jackendoff (2002: ch. 8).

171. Agents and Goals (Patients): Comrie (1981); Jackendoff (2002: 247–51).

173. Recursion as critical: Hauser, Chomsky, and Fitch (2002).

174. Complex syntax: Jackendoff (2002: 253–64).

175. Relational (functional) words: Jackendoff (2002: 253–4).

175. Chinese *gěi* "give": Lehmann (1982).

Chapter Ten

181. Language as a practical tool: Lancaster (1968: 454); Hewes (1974b: 15); Peters (1974: 89).

182. Lion hunting: G. Schaller (1972).

183. Language in pedagogy: Hewes (1974b: 18); Bruner (1972: 701).

183. Garo pedagogy and technology: Burling (1963).

184. Social uses of language: Humphrey (1976); Jolly (1966); Dunbar (1996); Dessalles (1998); Locke (1998); Miller (2000a).

185. The ideal speaker-listener: Chomsky (1965: 3).

186. Measurement of linguistic aptitude: Wolfram (1976).

186. Class differences in language: Much work has gone into demonstrating the linguistic equivalence of the language of different social groups. The disabilities faced by speakers of nonstandard dialects are the result of social prejudices, not of their own linguistic failure. See Labov (1972).

188. Individual differences among chimpanzees: Fouts and Couch (1976); Premak (1983); Savage-Rumbaugh and Lewin (1994: 60–1).

188. Language and leadership: Burling (1986).

188. Yanomamo headmen: Chagnon, Flinn, and Melancon (1979: 317–19).

189. Headmen's wives: Chagnon and Irons (1979: 384).

189. The ability of headmen: Neel (1980: 283).

189. Wealth, rank, and number of children: the Turkmen of Iran: Irons (1979); the Kipsigis in Kenya: Borgerhoff-Mulder (1987); the Mukogodo, also of Kenya: Cronk (1991); north India: Casimir and Rao (1995); the Gabra of Kenya: Mace (1996).

189. Mormon polygyny: Mealey (1985).

189. Male–female variability in reproduction among animals: Clutton-Brock, Guiness, and Albon (1982).

189. Central India: Daly and Wilson (1983: 333), citing Driver (1963).

190. Reproductive success of women: Hrdy and Williams (1983).

190. Political oratory: Bloch (1975).

190. Mt. Hagen: Strathern (1975: 186, 187).

191. The Mursi: Turton (1975: 173, 176, 177).

191. Classical Greece: Havelock (1963: 126).

191. Oratory in the US: Cmiel (1990).

192. Information theory: Shannon and Weaver (1949).

193. Topics of conversation: Dunbar (1996: 123).

194. Gender differences: Dunbar (1996: 176).

194. Status gained by providing relevant information: Dessalles (1998, 2000).

196. Conversation as manipulation: Krebs and Dawkins (1984).

197. Sexual selection: Darwin (1930 [1871]); Cronin (1991); Miller (2000a, 2000b).

199. Handicaps as evidence of health: Zahavi and Zahavi (1997).

202. Sexual selection and the mating mind: Miller (2000a); on music (2000b).

205. Overcoming handicaps: Zahavi and Zahavi (1997).

207. Expansion of the brain: De Miguel and Henneberg (2001).

208. Language for early subsistence: Bickerton (2002).

Chapter Eleven

213. Chimpanzee cooperation: de Waal (1982).

214. Chimpanzee violence: Wrangham and Peterson (1996); de Waal (1982).

216. Viki's counting: Hayes and Nissen (1971).

217. On consciousness: Humphrey (1984); Jackendoff (1987); Edelman (1989); Dennet (1991, 1995); Crick (1994).

217. Animal awareness: Griffin (1976).

217. Greek consciousness: Jaynes (1977).

217. Deaf-mute consciousness: S. Schaller (1991).

218. Nicholas Humphrey on consciousness: Humphrey (1976).

218. Language emerging from thought: Bickerton (1995).

218. Language designed specifically for communication: Bloom (1998); Hurford (2002).

219. Language of thought: Fodor (1975).

219. One-dimensional speech: Hurford (2002).

219. Interrelation of language and thought: Carruthers and Boucher (1998); Jackendoff (1996); Bloom (1998).

219. Skill at categorization: Markman (1989).

219. Words and wine discrimination: Bedford (1993).

219. Language needed for computation: Clark (1998).

220. "Kaleidoscopic flux": Whorf (1956).

221. Words and concepts for space: Pederson et al. (1998); Li and Gleitman (2002); Levinson et al. (2002).

223. Misleading words: Jackendoff (1996: 28).

223. Vocalizations as gestures: Armstrong, Stokoe, and Wilcox (1995: 57–8).

226. No explanation for language design except selection: Pinker and Bloom (1990).

228. Bird songs as cultural: Marler (1970); Catchpole and Slater (1995).

228. Whale songs: Tyack and Sayigh (1997); Payne (2000).

230. Resistance to heliocentrism: Sobel (1999).

231. Language learning as theory construction: Chomsky (1959: 57).

Glossary

Agent. The actor who initiates the action described by a sentence. *John* is the agent in *John built a house.*

Analog. A method of processing or presenting information that is continuously variable, as by an analog computer, or a speedometer needle. Contrasts with "digital."

Analogous. Having the same function but different evolutionary origins, as the wings of insects and the wings of birds. Contrasts with "homologous."

Arbitrary. A relationship that is purely conventional. Specifically, a conventional relation between the form of a word (its pronunciation or shape) and its meaning.

Brachiation. Swinging by the arms as a means of locomotion, ordinarily from tree branches.

Calls. Usually used for animal vocalizations, but used in this book also for the analogous (and sometimes homologous) nonverbal vocalizations of human beings.

Compounds. Words constructed from two other words: *homemade, mousetrap, handbag,* etc.

Consonant. A speech sound with a restricted or obstructed flow of air through the vocal tract, such as the sounds represented by *p, b, m, ch, s.* Contrasts with "vowel."

Conspecific. A member of the same species.

Content words. Words that refer to things and that are used primarily to convey meaning. Most nouns, verbs, and adjectives, such as *girl, jump, careful,* are content words. Contrasts with "function words."

Contrast. A characteristic of the sound system of languages, in which two sounds do not grade into one another. In English, and in most languages, *p* is in contrast with *b* so that there can be no compromise or halfway point between these speech sounds. Intermediate sounds do exist, but English speakers interpret these intermediate sounds as if they are either one thing or the other, not something in-between.

Digital. A method of processing or presenting information that is broken into discrete units, as in a digital computer, an abacus, or a digital watch. Contrasts with "analog."

246

Displacement. A characteristic of communication systems that can be used to refer to things and events that are distant in time or space. Displacement is more characteristic of human language than of human or animal gesture-calls. Bee dancing, however, is a striking example of displaced communication.

Dislexia. A condition in which a person with otherwise normal intelligence and verbal ability finds it very difficult or impossible to learn to read and write.

Duality of Patterning. A characteristic of human language, in which one set of patterns is used to organize distinctive but meaningless speech sounds, but a different set of patterns organizes the meaningful words and phrases.

Form. The physical sound or shape of a bit of language, as the pronunciation of a spoken word or the hand shape used for a deaf sign. Contrasts with "meaning." The form of "dog" is a sequence of three speech sounds. The meaning of "dog" is "domestic canine."

Formants. Frequency bands that are found in resonant speech sounds, primarily in vowels. Each vowel is characterized by a particular pattern of formants.

Function words. Words that are used primarily to show how other words are related to one another. Most articles, conjunctions, and prepositions are function words: *the, and, of.* Contrasts with "content words."

Gesticulation. The waving of the hands and associated movements of the head and body that accompany, and work closely with, spoken language.

Gesture-calls. Used in this book to refer to the audible and visible communicative signals of animals, and to the analogous, and sometimes homologous, nonverbal signals of human beings, such as our cries, laughs, smiles, and frowns.

Goal. The entity that is affected by or undergoes the action initiated by an agent. *House* is the goal in *John built a house.* Sometimes called "patient" or "recipient."

Grading. A characteristic of some forms of human and animal communication, in which the signs are variable and lack sharp boundaries betweem them. Human giggles grade into laughs, and laughs grade into guffaws. Characteristic of analog signals.

Grammatical functions. See "semantic roles."

Grammaticalization. The process by which, over time, linguistic constructions become squeezed more tightly together: loose constructions are gradually stabilized; function words are formed, often from content words; words become affixes; words or affixes are deleted.

Heritable. The part of a trait's variability that is attributable to genetic inheritance. Eye color is highly heritable since it depends largely on inheritance. Hair style has low heritability since it depends upon the fashion of the moment.

Hominin. Used increasingly today for the branch of primates that split from the Chimpanzees and Bonobos and led to modern humans. The hominins include Australopithecus, Homo erectus, and Homo sapiens. This group was once known as "Hominids" but with the recognition of the close relationship of humans to chimps and bonobos, these apes are increasingly included within the hominids, thus requiring a new word for the smaller human group.

Homologous. Having the same evolutionary origins, but not necessarily the same function. The wings of birds are homologous with the forelimbs of reptiles and with human arms, but their functions are different.

Icon, iconicity. A sign that resembles the thing it stands for, as a picture, an onomatopoetic word, or a hand gesture that outlines the shape of an object.

Imitation. Often used as a synonym of "mimicry" but sometimes restricted to the use of mimicry to achieve a particular goal. In this sense, a parrot mimics, but does not imitate. A child who watches you use scissors and then copies your movements in order to cut is imitating.

Index, indexicality. A sign that points to, or has some logical relationship with, the object for which it stands. Smoke in an index of fire. An arrow can be an index of the thing it points to.

Inflection. The process by which words undergo changes to show tense, case, number, gender, etc., often by means of prefixes or suffixes.

Instrumental behavior. Behavior such as moving about, eating, watching, scratching, yawning, that is not intended to communicate, but from which observers may nevertheless learn something.

Intonation. The patterns of pitch, rhythm, and volume that are characteristic of language.

Language. Used in this book in the narrow sense, for those systems of human communication to which we give such names as Italian, Korean, or Navaho. Communicative forms such as so-called "body language" are excluded from this narrow definition of "language."

Morphology. The formation of words from smaller parts, from prefixes, suffixes, and word roots. "Morphology" is often used in contrast with "syntax," which refers to the way phrases and sentences are formed from words, but "syntax" is sometimes used more generally to include morphology as well.

Motivated. A communicative sign that is not arbitrary. Motivated signs include icons that resemble the object they refer to, and indices that point to the object or have some logical association with it.

Ontogeny. The path of growth and maturation in the individual. Contrasts with "phylogeny," which is the path of change in an evolving species or set of species.

Paralanguage. Signals that are used in close association with language but that are not usually considered to be a part of language itself. Paralanguage includes gesticulation and tone of voice.

Phenotype. The observable characteristics of an organism that result from the interaction of the genotype (the genetic inheritance) with environmental influences.

Phoneme. A contrastive unit of the sound system of language. The unit of sound that would be represented by a single letter in an ideal spelling system. The sounds generally represented in English by *p, t, g, s, z* are phonemes. Both vowels and consonants are phonemes.

Phonetics. The study of the sounds of speech, their production, and acoustics.

Phonology. The study and analysis of the organization of speech sounds. "Phonetics" refers to the physical nature of sounds. "Phonology" refers to the way they are organized within languages.

Phylogeny, phylogenetic. The way that species are related through evolutionary history. Chimpanzees are phylogenetically closer to us than dogs are.

Productive. Capable of being constructed by a general rule. The regular plural, for example, is productive in English because speakers are able, easily, to construct the plural of a previously unknown word: the plural of *blurg* is certainly *blurgs*.

Proposition. The meaning of a sentence, especially a meaning that can be judged as true or false. A statement. Propositional meaning, as opposed to emotional or intentional meanings.

Prosody. The features of pitch, loudness, tempo, and rhythm of spoken language, which help to show how the words relate to one another and which typically convey more about the speaker's emotions and intentions than about propositional meanings.

Quotable gestures. Conventional gestures such as thumbs up, a head shake, or an okay circle that have such well-defined forms and meanings that it is possible to quote them. Also known as "emblems."

Glossary

Quotable vocalizations. Used in this book, by analogy with "quotable gestures," to refer to meaningful and conventional vocalizations that do not conform to the usual phonological patterns of the speaker's language: *tsk-tsk, oh-oh, uh-uh, shhh*, the Bronx cheer, etc.

Recursive rule. A grammatical rule that can be repeated. A very simple recursive rule allows us to speculate about our *great-great-great-grandchildren*. A slightly more complex recursive rule allows us to tell the story of "This is the house that Jack built."

Reference, referent. Reference describes the manner in which a sign refers to something. The **referent** is the an object, process, action, or quality to which a sign refers. The furry four-legged animal is the referent of the word *dog*.

Ritualization. The process by which animal signals, such as a dog's snarl, are built into the inherited nature of the members of a species.

Semantic roles. The participants named in a sentence, such as the agent who performs the action, the goal who is affected by it, the instrument that is used, and so on. These are assigned to various **grammatical functions** such as subject, object, indirect object, or prepositional phrase.

Sign. 1. Anything that means or refers to something else: a word, a nod, scream, dark sky. Peirce distinguished three types of signs: icons, indices, and symbols. 2. Specifically, a gesture used in the sign language of the deaf that has a conventional form (shape) and a meaning. A sign, in this sense, has the same role in deaf signing that a word has in spoken language.

Symbol. An arbitrary sign. A sign whose form (shape, pronunciation) has no physical or logical relation to its meaning. Contrasts with "motivated signs," which include both icons and indices.

Syntax. The patterns by which words are organized into phrases and sentences. "Grammar" is often used as a synonym for "syntax" but "grammar" is sometimes used to include morphology and, less often, even phonology as well as syntax.

Theory of Mind. The recognition that other individuals have minds comparable to one's own. Normal human beings take for granted that other people can see, hear, think, wonder, plan, and conspire. We operate with the theory that others have minds much like our own—a "theory of mind." There has been much debate about whether, or the extent to which, chimpanzees or other animals have a theory of mind.

Vowel. A speech sound with a relatively open vocal tract that allows the air to escape freely. Contrasts with "consonant."

Bibliography

Abler, William (1989), "On the particulate principle of self-diversifying systems," *Journal of Social and Biological Structures* 12: 1–13.

Aiello, Leslie C. (1996), "Hominine preadaptations for language and cognition," in Paul Mellars and Kathleen R. Gibson (eds.), *Modelling the Early Human Mind*. Cambridge: McDonald Institute Monograph Series, 89–99.

Anderson, Stephen R. and Lightfoot, David W. (2002), *The Language Organ: Linguistics as Cognitive Physiology*. Cambridge: Cambridge University Press.

Arbib, Michael A. (forthcoming), "From monkey-like action recognition to human language: an evolutionary framework," *Behavioral and Brain Sciences*.

Armstrong, David F., Stokoe, William C., and Wilcox, Sherman E. (1994), "Signs of the origin of syntax," *Current Anthropology* 35: 349–58.

—— —— —— (1995), *Gesture and the Nature of Language*. Cambridge: Cambridge University Press.

Ayala, Francisco J. (1995), "The myth of Eve: molecular biology and human origins," *Science* 270: 1930–6.

Baldwin, Dare A. (1991), "Infants' contribution to the achievement of joint reference," *Child Development* 62: 875–90.

Baldwin, J. Mark (1896), "A new factor in evolution," *American Naturalist* 30: 441–51.

Bedford, F. (1993), "Perceptual learning," in Douglas L. Medin (ed.), *The Psychology of Learning and Motivation*. San Diego, CA: Academic Press, 1–60.

Begun, David R. (1999), "Hominid family values: morphological and molecular data on relations among the great apes and humans," in Sue Taylor Parker, Robert W. Mitchell, and H. Lyn Miles (eds.), *The Mentalities of Gorillas and Orangutans*. Cambridge: Cambridge University Press, 3–42.

Bellugi, Ursula and Fischer, Susan (1972), "A comparison of sign language and spoken languages," *Cognition* 1: 175–200.

Berwick, Robert C. (1998), "Language evolution and the minimalist program: The origins of syntax," in James R. Hurford, Michael Studdert-Kennedy, and Chris Knight (eds.), *Approaches to the Evolution of Language: Social and Cognitive Bases*. Cambridge: Cambridge University Press, 320–40.

Bickerton, Derek (1981), *Roots of Language*. Ann Arbor, MI: Karoma.

Bickerton, Derek (1990), *Language & Species*. Chicago: University of Chicago Press.

—— (1995), *Language and Human Behavior*. Seattle: University of Washington Press.

—— (2002), "Foraging versus social intelligence in the evolution of proto-language," in Alison Wray (ed.), *The Transition to Language*. Oxford: Oxford University Press, 207–25.

—— (2003), "Symbol and structure: a comprehensive framework for language evolution," in Morton H. Christiansen and Simon Kirby (eds.), *Language Evolution*. Oxford: Oxford University Press, 77–93.

Bloch, Maurice (ed.) (1975), *Political Language and Oratory in Traditional Society*. New York: Academic Press.

Bloom, Paul (1997), "Intentionality and word learning," *Trends in Cognitive Science* 1: 9–12.

—— (1998), "Some issues in the evolution of language and thought," in Denise Dellarosa Cummins and Colin Allen (eds.), *The Evolution of Mind*. New York: Oxford University Press.

—— (2000), *How Children Learn the Meanings of Words*. Cambridge, MA: MIT Press.

—— and Markson, Lori (1998). "Capacities underlying word learning," *Trends in Cognitive Science* 2: 67–73.

Boesch, Christophe and Boesch-Achermann, Hedwige (2000), *The Chimpanzees of the Taï Forest: Behavioral Ecology and Evolution*. Oxford: Oxford University Press.

Bolinger, Dwight (1978), "Intonation across languages," in Joseph H. Greenberg (ed.), *Universals of Human Language, II: Phonology*. Stanford: Stanford University Press, 471–524.

—— (1985), "The inherent iconism of intonation," in John Haiman (ed.), *Iconicity in Syntax: Proceedings of a Symposium on Iconicity in Syntax, Stanford, June 24–26, 1983*. Amsterdam: J. Benjamins, 97–108.

—— (1986), *Intonation and its Parts: Melody in Spoken English*. Stanford: Stanford University Press.

—— (1989), *Intonation and its Uses: Melody in Grammar and Discourse*. Stanford: Stanford University Press.

Borgerhoff-Mulder, Monique (1987), "On cultural and reproductive success: Kipsigis evidence," *American Anthropologist* 89: 617–34.

Boyd, Robert and Richerson, Peter J. (1985), *Culture and the Evolutionary Process*. Chicago: University of Chicago Press.

Brown, Penelope and Levinson, Stephen C. (1987), *Politeness: Some Universals in Language Usage*. Cambridge: Cambridge University Press.

Brown, Steven (2000). "The 'musilanguage' model of music evolution," in Nils L. Wallin, Björn Merker, and Steven Brown (eds.), *The Origins of Music.* Cambridge, MA: MIT Press, 271–300.

Bruner, Jerome S. (1972), "Nature and uses of immaturity," *American Psychologist* 27: 687–708.

Burling, Robbins (1963), *Rengsanggri: Family and Kinship in a Garo Village.* Philadelphia: University of Pennsylvania Press.

—— (1986), "The selective advantage of complex language," *Ethology and Sociobiology* 7: 1–16.

—— (1993), "Primate calls, human language and nonverbal communication," *Current Anthropology* 34: 25–37.

—— (1999), "Motivation, conventionalization, and arbitrariness in the origin of language," in Barbara J. King (ed.), *The Origins of Language: What Nonhuman Primates can Tell us.* Santa Fe, NM: School of American Research Press, 307–50.

—— (2002), "The slow growth of language in children," in Alison Wray (ed.), *The Transition to Language.* Oxford: Oxford University Press, 297–310.

Bybee, Joan L. (1985), "Diagrammatic iconicity in stem-inflection relations," in John Haiman (ed.), *Iconicity in Syntax: Proceedings of a Symposium on Iconicity in Syntax, Stanford, June 24–26, 1983.* Amsterdam: J. Benjamins, 11–47.

—— Perkins, Revere, and Pagliuca, William (1994), *The Evolution of Grammar: Tense, Aspect, and Modality in the Languages of the World.* Chicago: University of Chicago Press.

Byrne, Richard W. and Russon, Anne E. (1998), "Learning by imitation: a hierarchical approach," *Behavioral and Brain Sciences* 21: 667–721.

—— and Whiten, Andrew (eds.) (1988), *Machiavellian Intelligence: Social Expertise and the Evolution of Intellect in Monkeys and Apes.* Oxford: Clarendon Press.

Calvin, William H. and Bickerton, Derek (2000), *Lingua ex Machina: Reconciling Darwin and Chomsky with the Human Brain.* Cambridge, MA: MIT Press.

Carruthers, Peter and Boucher, Jill (eds.) (1998), *Language and Thought: Interdisciplinary Themes.* Cambridge: Cambridge University Press.

Casimir, Michael J. and Rao, Aparna (1995), "Prestige, possessions, and progeny: cultural goals and reproductive success among the Bakkarwal," *Human Nature* 6: 241–72.

Catchpole, Clive K. and Slater, P. J. B. (1995), *Bird Song: Biological Themes and Variations.* Cambridge: Cambridge University Press.

Chagnon, Napoleon A., Flinn, Mark V., and Melancon, Thomas F. (1979), "Sex ratio variation among the Yanomamo Indians," in Napoleon A. Chagnon and William Irons (eds.), *Evolutionary Biology and Human Social Behavior: An Anthropological Perspective.* North Scituate, MA: Duxbury Press.

Chagnon, Napoleon A., Flinn, Mark V., Melancon, Thomas F., and Irons, William (1979), *Evolutionary Biology and Human Social Behavior: An Anthropological Perspective.* North Scituate, MA: Duxbury Press.

Cheney, Dorothy L. and Seyfarth, Robert M. (1990), *How Monkeys See the World: Inside the Mind of Another Species.* Chicago: Chicago University Press.

Chevalier-Skolnikoff, Suzanne (1973), "Facial expression of emotion in nonhuman primates," in Paul Ekman (ed.), *Darwin and Facial Expression: A Century of Research in Review.* New York: Academic Press, 11–90.

Chomsky, Noam (1957), *Syntactic Structures.* The Hague: Mouton.

—— (1959), "Review of B. F. Skinner (1957), *Verbal Behavior,* New York: Appelton-Century-Crofts," *Language* 35: 26–58.

—— (1965), *Aspects of the Theory of Syntax.* Cambridge, MA: MIT Press.

—— (1975), *Reflections on Language.* New York: Pantheon.

—— (1991), "Linguistics and cognitive science: problems and mysteries," in Asa Kasher (ed.), *The Chomskyan Turn: Generative Linguistics, Philosophy, Mathematics and Psychology.* Oxford: Blackwell.

Clark, Andy (1998), "Magic words: how language augments human computation," in Peter Carruthers and Jill Boucher (eds.), *Language and Thought: Interdisciplinary Themes.* Cambridge: Cambridge University Press, 162–83.

Clutton-Brock, T. H., Guinness, F. E., and Albon, S. D. (1982), *Red Deer: Behavior and Ecology of Two Sexes.* Chicago: University of Chicago Press.

Cmiel, Kenneth (1990), *Democratic Eloquence: The Fight over Popular Speech in Nineteenth-Century America.* New York: W. Morrow.

Comrie, Bernard (1981), *Language Universals and Linguistic Typology.* Chicago: University of Chicago Press.

Corballis, Michael C. (2002), *From Hand to Mouth: The Origins of Language.* Princeton: Princeton University Press.

Couper-Kuhlin, Elizabeth (1993), *English Speech Rhythm: Form and Function in Everyday Verbal Interaction.* Amsterdam: J. Benjamins.

Crick, Francis (1994), *The Astonishing Hypothesis: The Scientific Search for the Soul.* New York: Scribner.

Cronin, Helena (1991), *The Ant and the Peacock: Altruism and Sexual Selection from Darwin to Today.* Cambridge: Cambridge University Press.

Cronk, Lee (1991), "Wealth, status, and reproductive success among the Mukogodo of Kenya," *American Anthropologist* 93: 345–60.

Crow, T. J. (2002), "ProtocadherinXY: a candidate gene for cerebral asymmetry and language," in Alison Wray (ed.), *The Transition to Language.* Oxford: Oxford University Press, 93–112.

Daly, Martin and Wilson, Margo (1983), *Sex, Evolution, and Behavior*. Boston: Willard Grant.

Darwin, Charles (1930 [1871]), *The Descent of Man and Selection in Relation to Sex*. New York: D. Appleton and Company.

—— (1998 [1872]), *The Expression of the Emotions in Man and Animals*, 3rd edn. ed. Paul Ekman. New York: Oxford University Press.

Dawkins, Richard (1986), *The Blind Watchmaker*. New York: W. W. Norton and Company.

De Miguel, C. and Henneberg, M. (2001), "Variation in hominid brain size: how much is due to method?" *Homo* 52/1: 3–58.

Deacon, Terrence W. (1997), *The Symbolic Species: The Co-evolution of Language and the Brain*. New York: W. W. Norton and Company.

DeCasper, Anthony J. and Spence, Melanie J. (1986), "Prenatal maternal speech influences newborns' perception of speech sounds," *Infant Behavior and Development* 9: 133–50.

Dennett, Daniel Clement (1991), *Consciousness Explained*. Boston: Little, Brown and Co.

—— (1995), *Darwin's Dangerous Idea: Evolution and the Meanings of Life*. New York: Simon and Schuster.

Dessalles, Jean-Louis (1998), "Altruism, status and the origin of relevance," in James R. Hurford, Michael Studdert-Kennedy, and Chris Knight (eds.), *Approaches to the Evolution of Language: Social and Cognitive Bases*. Cambridge: Cambridge University Press, 130–47.

—— (2000), "Language and hominid politics," in Chris Knight, Michael Studdert-Kennedy, and James R. Hurford (eds.), *The Evolutionary Emergence of Language*. Cambridge: Cambridge Univerisity Press, 62–80.

Driver, Edwin D. (1963), *Differential Fertility in Central India*. Princeton: Princeton University Press.

Dunbar, Robin I. M. (1996), *Grooming, Gossip, and the Evolution of Language*. Cambridge, MA: Harvard University Press.

Edelman, Gerald M. (1989), *The Remembered Present: A Biological Theory of Consciousness*. New York: Basic Books.

Ekman, Paul (ed.) (1972), *Emotion in the Human Face: Guide-Lines for Research and an Integration of Findings*. New York: Pergamon Press.

Ekman, Paul (1994), "Strong evidence for universals in facial expressions: a reply to Russell's mistaken critique," *Psychological Bulletin* 115: 286–7.

—— and Friesen, Wallace V. (1969), "The repertoire of non-verbal behavior: categories, origins, usage, and coding," *Semiotica* 1: 49–98.

—— —— (1971), "Constants across cultures in the face and emotion," *Journal of Personality and Social Psychology* 17: 124–9.

Bibliography

Eldredge, N. and Gould, Stephen J. (1972), "Punctuated equilibria: an alternative to phyletic gradualism," in Thomas J. M. Schopf (ed.), *Models in Paleobiology*. San Francisco: Freeman, Cooper, 82–115.

Enard, Wolfgang, Przeworski, Molly, Fisher, Simon E., Lai, Cecillia S. L., Wiebe, Victor, Kitano, Takashi, Monaco, Anthony P., and Pääbo Svante, (2002), "Molecular evolution of FOXP2, a gene involved in speech and language," *Nature* 418: 869–72.

Falk, Dean (forthcoming). "Prelinguistic evolution in early hominins: whence motherese?" *Behavioral and Brain Sciences*.

Fisher, Simon E. (forthcoming). "Dissection of molecular mechanisms underlying speech and language disorders," *Applied Psycholinguistics*.

Fitch, W. Techumseh (2002), "Comparative vocal production and the evolution of speech: reinterpreting the descent of the larynx," in Alison Wray (ed.), *The Transition to Language*. Oxford: Oxford University Press, 21–45.

Fodor, Jerry A. (1975), *The Language of Thought*. New York: Crowell.

Fouts, Roger S. and Couch, Joseph B. (1976), "Cultural evolution of learned language in chimpanzees," in Martin E. Hahn and Edward C. Simmel (eds.), *Communicative Behavior and Evolution*. New York: Academic Press, 141–61.

Fraser, Colin, Bellugi, Ursula, and Brown, Roger (1963), "Control of grammar in imitation, comprehension, and production," *Journal of Verbal Learning and Verbal Behavior* 2: 121–35.

Fridlund, Alan J. (1994), *Human Facial Expression: An Evolutionary View*. San Diego, CA: Academic Press.

Frishberg, Nancy (1975), "Arbitrariness and iconicity: historical change in American Sign Language," *Language* 51: 696–719.

Gardner, R. Allen and Gardner, Beatrice T. (1969), "Teaching sign-language to a chimpanzee," *Science* 165: 664–72.

Geissmann, Thomas (2000), "Gibbon songs and human music from an evolutionary perspective," in Nils L. Wallin, Björn Merker, and Steven Brown (eds.), *The Origins of Music*. Cambridge, MA: MIT Press, 103–23.

Givón, Talmy (1989), *Mind, Code, and Context: Essays in Pragmatics*. Hillsdale, NJ: Lawrence Erlbaum Associates.

Goldberg, Adele E. (1995), *Constructions: A Construction Grammar Approach to Argument Structure*. Chicago: University of Chicago Press.

Goldin-Meadow, Susan (1993), "When does gesture become language? A study of gesture used as a primary communication system by deaf children of hearing parents," in Kathleen R. Gibson and Tim Ingold (eds.), *Tools, Language and Cognition in Human Evolution*. Cambridge: Cambridge University Press, 63–85.

Goodall, Jane (1986), *The Chimpanzees of Gombe: Patterns of Behavior.* Cambridge: Harvard University Press.

Gould, Stephen J. (1982), "The meaning of punctuated equilibrium and its role in validating a hierarchical approach to macroevolution," in Roger Milkman (ed.), *Perspectives on Evolution.* Sunderland, MA: Sinauer, 83–104.

Griffin, Donald R. (1976), *The Question of Animal Awareness: Evolutionary Continuity of Mental Experience.* New York: Rockefeller University Press.

Haiman, John (ed.) (1985), *Iconicity in Syntax: Proceedings of a Symposium on Iconicity in Syntax, Stanford, June 24–26, 1983.* Amsterdam: J. Benjamins.

Hare, Brian, Brown, Michelle, Williamson, Christina, and Tomasello, Michael (2002), "The domestication of social cognition in dogs," *Science* 298: 1634–6.

—— Call, Josep, Agnetta, Bryan, and Tomasello, Michael (2000), "Chimpanzees know what conspecifics do and do not see," *Animal Behavior* 59: 771–85.

Hauser, Marc D. (1992), "Articulatory and social factors influence the acoustic structure of rhesus monkey vocalization: a learned mode of production?" *Journal of the Acoustical Society of America* 91: 2175–9.

—— Chomsky, Noam, and Fitch, W. Techumseh (2002), "The faculty of language: what is it, who has it, and how did it evolve?" *Science* 298: 1569–79.

—— Weiss, Daniel, and Marcus, Gary (2002), "Rule learning by cotton-top tamarins," *Cognition* 86: B15–B22.

Havelock, Eric Alfred (1963), *Preface to Plato.* Cambridge, MA: Harvard University Press.

Hayes, Keith J. and Nissen, Catherine H. (1971), "Higher mental functions of a home-raised chimpanzee," in Allan M. Schrier and Fred Stollnitz (eds.), *Behavior of Nonhuman Primates: Modern Research Trends.* New York: Academic Press, 59–115.

Heine, Bernd, Claudi, Ulrike, and Hünnemeyer, Friederike (1991), *Grammaticalization: A Conceptual Framework.* Chicago: University of Chicago Press.

Hewes, Gordon W. (1973), "Primate communication and the gestural origin of language," *Current Anthropology* 14: 5–12.

—— (1974a), "Gesture language in culture contact," *Sign Language Studies* 4: 1–34.

—— (1974b), "Language in early hominids," in Roger W. Wescott (ed.), *Language Origins.* Silver Springs, MD: Linstock Press, 1–33.

Hinton, G. and Nolan, S. (1987), "How learning can guide evolution," *Complex Systems* 1: 495–502.

Hockett, Charles F. (1959), "Animal 'languages' and human language," in James N. Spuhler (ed.), *The Evolution of Man's Capacity for Culture.* Detroit, MI: Wayne State University Press, 32–9.

Bibliography

Hockett, Charles F. (1960), "The Origin of Speech," *Scientific American*, October: 89–96.

Hooff, Jan A. R. A. M. van (1972), "A comparative approach to the phylogeny of laughter and smiling," in R. A. Hinde (ed.), *Non-Verbal Communication*. Cambridge: Cambridge University Press, 209–41.

—— (1976), "The comparison of facial expressions in man and higher primates," in M. von Cranach (ed.), *Methods of Inference from Animal to Human Behavior*. Chicago: Aldine, 165–96.

Hopper, Paul J. and Traugott, Elizabeth Closs (1993), *Grammaticalization*. Cambridge: Cambridge University Press.

Hrdy, Sarah Blaffer and Williams, George C. (1983), "Behavioral biology and the double standard," in Samuel K. Wasser (ed.), *Social Behavior in Female Vertebrates*. New York: Academic Press, 3–17.

Humbolt, Wilhelm von (1972 [1836]), *Linguistic Variability and Intellectual Development*, trans. G. C. Buck and F. A. Raven. Philadelphia: University of Pennsylvania Press.

Humphrey, Nicholas K. (1976), "The social function of the intellect," in P. P. G. Bateson and R. A. Hinde (eds.), *Growing Points in Ethology*. Cambridge: Cambridge University Press, 303–17.

—— (1984), *Consciousness Regained: Chapters in the Development of Mind*. Oxford: Oxford University Press.

Humphries, Tom, Padden, Carol, and O'Rourke, Terrence J. (1994), *A Basic Course in American Sign Language*. Silver Spring, MD: T. J. Publishers.

Hurford, James (2002), "The roles of expression and representation in language evolution," in Alison Wray (ed.), *The Transition to Language*. Oxford: Oxford University Press, 311–34.

Irons, William (1979), "Culture and biological success," in Napoleon A. Chagnon and William Irons (eds.), *Evolutionary Biology and Human Social Behavior: An Anthropological Perspective*. North Scituate, MA: Duxbury, 257–72.

Izard, Carroll E. (1971), *The Face of Emotion*. New York: Appleton-Century-Crofts.

—— (1980), "Cross-cultural perspectives on emotions and emotion communication," in Harry C. Triandis and W. Lonner (eds.), *Handbook of Cross-Cultural Psychology: Vol. 3 Basic Processes*. Boston: Allyn & Bacon, 185–222.

—— (1994), "Innate and universal facial expressions: evidence from developmental and cross-cultural research," *Psychological Bulletin* 115: 288–99.

Jackendoff, Ray (1987), *Consciousness and the Computational Mind*. Cambridge, MA: MIT Press.

—— (1996), "How language helps us think," *Pragmatics & Cognition* 4: 1–34.

—— (2002), *Foundations of Language: Brain, Meaning, Grammar, Evolution.* Oxford: Oxford University Press.

Jaynes, Julian (1977), *The Origin of Consciousness in the Breakdown of the Bicameral Mind.* Boston: Houghton Mifflin.

Jespersen, Otto (1922), *Language: Its Nature, Development and Origin.* London: G. Allen & Unwin.

Jolly, Alison (1966), "Lemur social behavior and primate intelligence," *Science* 153: 501–6.

Jusczyk, Peter W. (1997), *The Discovery of Spoken Language.* Cambridge, MA: MIT Press.

Kegl, Judy A. and McWhorter, John (1997), "Perspectives on an emerging language," in Eve V. Clark (ed.), *The Proceedings of the Twenty-eighth Annual Child Language Research Forum.* Stanford: CSLI, 15–38.

—— Senghas, Ann, and Coppola, Marie (1999), "Creation through contact: sign language emergence and sign language change in Nicaragua," in Michel DeGraff (ed.), *Language Creation and Language Change: Creolization, Diachrony, and Development.* Cambridge, MA: MIT Press, 179–237.

Kellogg, Winthrop N. and Kellogg, Luella A. (1933), *The Ape and the Child: A Study of Environmental Influence upon Early Behavior.* New York: McGraw-Hill.

Kendon, Adam (1992), "Some recent work from Italy on quotable gestures (emblems)," *Journal of Linguistic Anthropology* 2: 92–108.

—— (1993), "Human gesture," in Kathleen R. Gibson and Tim Ingold (eds.), *Tools, Language, Cognition in Human Evolution.* Cambridge: Cambridge University Press, 43–62.

—— (1997), "Gesture," *Annual Review of Anthropology* 26: 109–28.

Kirby, Simon (1999), *Function, Selection, and Innateness: The Emergence of Language Universals.* Oxford: Oxford University Press.

—— and James Hurford (1997), "Learning, culture and evolution in the origin of linguistic constraints," in Phil Husbands and Inman Harvey (eds.), *Fourth European Conference on Artificial Life.* Cambridge, MA: MIT Press, 493–502.

Klima, Edward S. and Bellugi, Ursula (1966), "Syntactic regulation in the speech of children," in John Lyons and R. J. Wales (eds.), *Psycholinguistics Papers: The Proceedings of the 1966 Edinburgh Conference.* Edinburgh: Edinburgh University Press, 183–203.

—— —— (1979), *The Signs of Language.* Cambridge, MA: Harvard University Press.

Kramer, Samuel Noah (1963), *The Sumerians: Their History, Culture and Character.* Chicago: University of Chicago Press.

Bibliography

Krebs, John R. and Dawkins, Richard (1984), "Animal signals: mind-reading and manipulation," in John R. Krebs and N. B. Davies (eds.), *Behavioural Ecology: An Evolutionary Approach*, 2nd edn. Oxford: Blackwell, 380–402.

Kuhl, Patricia K. and Miller, James D. (1975), "Speech perception by the chinchilla: voiced–voiceless distinction in alveolar plosive consonants," *Science* 190: 69–72.

Labov, William (1972), *Language in the Inner City: Studies in the Black English Vernacular*. Philadelphia: University of Pennsylvania Press.

Lai, Cecillia S. L., Fisher, Simon E., Hurst, Jane A., Vargha-Khadem, Faraneh, and Monaco, Anthony P. (2001), "A forkhead-domain gene is mutated in a severe speech and language disorder," *Nature* 413: 519–23.

Lakoff, George and Johnson, Mark (1980), *Metaphors We Live By*. Chicago: University of Chicago Press.

Lakoff, Robin Tolmach (1975), *Language and Woman's Place*. New York: Harper and Row:

Lancaster, Jane (1968), "Primate communication systems and the emergence of human language," in Phyllis C. Jay (ed.), *Primates: Studies in Adaptation and Variability*. New York: Holt, Rinehart, and Winston, 439–57.

Lee, Sang-Hee and Wolpoff, Milford H. (2003), "The pattern of evolution in Pleistocene human brain size," *Paleobiology* 29: 186–96.

Lehmann, Christian (1982), *Thoughts on Grammaticalization: A Programatic Sketch*. Köln: Arbeiten des Kölner Universalien-Projekts.

Lerdahl, Fred and Jackendoff, Ray (1983), *A Generative Theory of Tonal Music*. Cambridge, MA: Harvard University Press.

Levinson, Stephen C., Kita, Sotaro, Haun, Daniel B. M., and Rasch, Björn H. (2002), "Returning the tables: language affects spatial reasoning," *Cognition* 84: 155–88.

Li, Peggy and Gleitman, Lila (2002), "Turning the tables: language and spatial reasoning," *Cognition* 83: 265–94.

Lieberman, Philip. (1968), "Primate vocalization and human linguistic ability," *Journal of the Acoustical Society of America* 44: 1574–84.

—— (1984). *The Biology and Evolution of Language*. Cambridge, MA: Harvard University Press.

—— and Crelin, Edmund S. (1971), "On the speech of Neanderthal man," *Linguistic Inquiry* 2: 203–22.

Lindblom, Björn and Maddieson, Ian (1988), "Phonetic universals in consonant systems," in Larry M. Hyman and Charles N. Li (eds.), *Language, Speech, and Mind: Studies in Honour of Victoria A. Fromkin*. London: Routledge.

Livingstone, Frank B. (1973), "Did the australopithecines sing?" *Current Anthropology* 14: 25–9.

Locke, John L. (1998), *The De-Voicing of Society.* New York: Simon and Schuster.

Mace, Ruth (1996), "Biased parental investment and reproductive success among Gabbra pastoralists," *Behavioral Ecology and Sociobiology* 38: 75–81.

Mandel, Denise R., Jusczyk, Peter W., and Pisoni, D. B. (1995), "Infants' recognition of the sound patterns of their own names," *Psychological Science* 6: 314–17.

Marcus, Gary (2004), *The Birth of the Mind: How a Tiny Number of Genes Creates the Complexities of Human Thought.* New York: Basic Books.

—— and Fisher, Simon E. (2003), "FOXP2 in focus: what can genes tell us about speech and language?" *Trends in Cognitive Science* 7: 257–62.

—— Vijayan, S., Bandi Rao, S., and Vishton, P. M. (1999), "Rule learning by seven-month-old infants," *Science* 283: 77–80.

Markman, Ellen M. (1989), *Categorization and Naming in Children: Problems of Induction.* Cambridge, MA: MIT Press.

Marler, Peter (1970), "Birdsong and speech development: could there be parallels?" *American Scientist* 58: 669–73.

—— (1976), "Social organization, communication, and graded signals: the chimpanzee and the gorilla," in P. P. G. Bateson and R. A. Hinde (eds.), *Growing Points in Ethology.* Cambridge: Cambridge University Press, 239–80.

—— (1982). "Avian and primate communication: the problem of natural categories," *Neuroscience and Biobehavioral Reviews* 61: 87–94.

—— and John Mitani (1988), "Vocal communication in primates and birds: parallels and contrasts," in D. Todt, Goedeking, P., and Symmes, D. (eds.), *Primate Vocal Communication.* Berlin: Springer-Verlag, 3–14.

Marshall, Andrew J., Wrangham, Richard W., and Arcadi, Adam Clark (1999), "Does learning affect the structure of vocalizations in chimpanzees?" *Animal Behavior* 58: 825–30.

Martinet, André (1949), "La double articulation linguistique," *Travaux du Cercle Linguistique de Copenhague* 5: 30–8.

Matthews, Peter. H. (1991), *Morphology.* Cambridge: Cambridge University Press.

McNeilage, Peter F. (1998), "Evolution of the mechanism of language output: comparative neurobiology of vocal and manual communication," in James R. Hurford, Michael Studdert-Kennedy, and Chris Knight (eds.), *Approaches to the Evolution of Language: Social and Cognitive Bases.* Cambridge: Cambridge University Press, 222–41.

—— and Davis, Barbara L. (2000), "Evolution of speech: the relation between ontogeny and phylogeny," in Chris Knight, Michael Studdert-Kennedy, and

James R. Hurford (eds.), *The Evolutionary Emergence of Language: Social Function and the Origins of Linguistic Form*. Cambridge: Cambridge University Press, 146–60.

McNeill, David (1992), *Hand and Mind: What Gestures Reveal about Thought*. Chicago: University of Chicago Press.

McNeill, David (ed.) (2000), *Language and Gesture*. Cambridge: Cambridge University Press.

Mealey, Linda (1985), "The relationship between social status and biological success: a case study of the Mormon religious hierarchy," *Ethology and Sociobiology* 6: 249–57.

Mehler, Jacques, Jusczyk, Peter, Lambertz, Ghislaine, Halsted, Nilofar, Bertoncini, Josiane, and Amiel-Tison, Claudine (1988), "A precursor of language acquisition in young infants," *Cognition* 29: 143–78.

Mellars, Paul and Stringer, Chris (eds.) (1989), *The Human Revolution: Behavioural and Biological Perspectives on the Origins of Modern Humans*. Princeton: Princeton University Press.

Meltzoff, A. N. and Moore, M. K. (1977), "Imitation of facial and manual gestures by human neonate," *Science* 198: 75–8.

Merker, Björn (2000), "Synchronous chorusing and human origins," in Nils L. Wallin, Björn Merker, and Steven Brown (eds.), *The Origins of Music*. Cambridge, MA: MIT Press.

Miles, H. Lyn (1983), "Apes and language: the search for communicative competence," in Judith de Luce and Hugh T. Wilder (eds.), *Language in Primates: Perspectives and Implications*. New York: Springer-Verlag, 43–61.

Miller, Geoffrey F. (2000a), *The Mating Mind: How Sexual Choice Shaped the Evolution of Human Nature*. New York: Doubleday.

—— (2000b), "Evolution of human music through sexual selection," in Nils L. Wallin, Björn Merker, and Steven Brown (eds.), *The Origins of Music*. Cambridge, MA: MIT Press.

Mitani, John C. and Brandt, Karl L. (1994), "Social factors influence the acoustic variability in the long-distance calls of male chimpanzees," *Ethology* 96: 233–52.

—— Hasegawa, Toshikazu, Gros-Louis, Julie, Marler, Peter, and Byrne, Richard (1992), "Dialects in wild chimpanzees?" *American Journal of Primatology* 27: 233–43.

—— Hunley, K. L., and Murdoch, M. E. (1999), "Geographic variation in the calls of wild chimpanzees: a reassessment," *American Journal of Primatology* 47: 133–52.

Moon, Christine, Cooper, Robin Panneton, and Fifer, William P. (1993), "Two-day-olds prefer their native language," *Infant Behavior and Development* 16: 495–500.

Neel, James F. (1980), "On being headman," *Perspectives in Biology and Medicine* 23: 277–94.

Newmeyer, Frederick J. (1991), "Functional Explanations in Linguistics and the Origins of Language," *Language and Communication* 11: 3–28.

O'Connell, J. F. and Allen, J. (2004), "Dating the colonization of Sahul (Pleistocene Australia–New Guinea): a review of recent research," *Journal of Archaeological Science* 31: 835–53.

Ohala, John J. (1994), "The frequency code underlies the sound-symbolic use of voice pitch," in Leanne Hinton, Johanna Nichols, and John. J. Ohala (eds.), *Sound Symbolism*. Cambridge: Cambridge University Press, 325–47.

Paley, William (1802[1851]), *Natural Theology, or Evidence of the Existence and Attributes of the Deity, Collected from the Appearances of Nature*. Boston: Gould and Lincoln.

Payne, Katherine (2000), "The progressively changing songs of humpback whales: a window on the creative process in a wild animal," in Nils L. Wallin, Björn Merker, and Steven Brown (eds.), *The Origins of Music*. Cambridge, MA: MIT Press, 135–50.

Pederson, Eric, Danziger, Eve, Wilkins, David, Levinson, Stephen, Kita, Sotaro, and Senft, Gunter (1998), "Semantic typology and spatial conceptualization," *Language* 74: 557–89.

Peirce, Charles Sanders (1940), "Logic as semiotic: the theory of signs," in J. Buchler (ed.), *The Philosophical Writings of Peirce*. New York: Dover, 98–119.

Peters, Charles R. (1974), "On the possible contribution of ambiguity of expression to the development of proto-linguistic performance," in Roger W. Wescott (ed.), *Language Origins*. Silver Springs, MD: Linstok Press, 83–102.

Pike, Kenneth L. (1945), *The Intonation of American English*. Ann Arbor: University of Michigan Press.

Pinker, Steven (1994), *The Language Instinct*. New York: William Morrow.

—— and Paul Bloom (1990), "Natural language and natural selection," *Behavioral and Brain Sciences* 13: 707–84.

Premak, David (1983), "The codes of man and beast," *Behavioral and Brain Sciences* 6: 125–67.

Preuschoft, Signe (1992), "Laughter and smile in Barbary macaques (*Macaca sylvanus*)," *Ethology* 91: 220–36.

—— and Hooff, Jan A. R. A. M. van (1995), "Homologizing primate facial

Bibliography

displays: a critical review of methods," *Folia Primatologica (Basel)* 65: 121–37.

Preuschoft, Signe (1997), "The social function of 'smile' and 'laughter': variations across primate species and societies," in Ullica Segerstråle and Peter Molnár (eds.), *Nonverbal Communication: Where Nature Meets Culture.* Mahwah, NJ: L. Erlbaum, 171–89.

Provine, Robert R. (2000), *Laughter: A Scientific Investigation.* New York: Viking.

Quine, Willard V. O. (1960), *Word and Object.* Cambridge, MA: MIT Press.

Richman, Bruce (1987), "Rhythm and Melody in Gelada Vocal Exchanges," *Primates* 28: 199–223.

—— (2000), "How music fixed 'nonsense' into significant formulas: on rhythm, repetition, and meaning," in Nils L. Wallin, Björn Merker, and Steven Brown (eds.), *The Origins of Music.* Cambridge, MA: MIT Press, 301–14.

Rickford, John R. (1987), *Dimensions of a Creole Continuum.* Stanford: Stanford University Press.

Rinn, William E. (1984), "The neuropsychology of facial expression: a review of the neurological and psychological mechanisms for producing facial expressions," *Psychological Bulletin* 95: 52–77.

Rizzolatti, G. and Arbib, Michael A. (1998), "Language within our grasp," *Trends in Neurosciences* 21: 188–94.

Russell, James A. (1994), "Is there universal recognition of emotion from facial expression? A review of the cross-cultural studies," *Psychological Bulletin* 115: 102–41.

—— (1995), "Facial expressions of emotions: what lies beyond minimal universality?" *Psychological Bulletin* 118: 379–91.

Russon, Anne E. and Galdikas, Birute M. F. (1993), "Imitation in free-ranging rehabilitant orangutans (Pongo pygmaeus)," *Journal of Comparative Psychology* 107: 147–61.

—— —— (1995), "Constraints on great apes' imitation: model and action selectivity in rehabilitant orangutan (*Pongo pygmaeus*) imitation," *Journal of Comparative Psychology* 109: 5–17.

Saffran, Jenny R., Aslin, Richard N., and Newport, Elissa (1996), "Statistical learning by 8-month-old infants," *Science* 274: 1926–8.

Sampson, Geoffrey (1997), *Educating Eve: The Language Instinct Debate.* London: Cassell.

Sankoff, Gillian (1980), *The Social Life of Language.* Philadelphia: University of Pennsylvania Press.

Saussure, Ferdinand de (1959), *Course in General Linguistics.* New York: Philosophical Library.

Savage-Rumbaugh, E. Sue and Roger Lewin (1994), *Kanzi: The Ape at the Brink of the Human Mind*. New York: John Wiley and Sons.

—— Murphey, Jeannine, Sevcik, Rose A., Brakke, Karen E., Williams, Shelly L., and Rumbaugh, Duane M. (1993), *Language Comprehension in Ape and Child*. Monographs of the Society for Research in Child Development. Serial No. 233, 58, 3–4.

Schaller, George B. (1972), *The Serengeti Lion: A Study of Predator-Prey Relations*. Chicago: University of Chicago Press.

Schaller, Susan (1991), *A Man Without Words*. New York: Summit Books.

Schmidt, Karen L. and Cohn, Jeffrey F. (2001), "Human facial expressions as adaptations: evolutionary questions in facial expression research," *Yearbook of Physical Anthropology* 44: 3–24.

Senghas, Ann and Coppola, Matie (2001), "Children creating language: how Nicaraguan sign language acquired a spatial grammar," *Psychological Science* 12: 323–8.

Seyfarth, Robert M., Cheney, Dorothy L., and Marler, Peter (1980a), "Vervet monkey alarm calls: semantic communication in a free-ranging primate," *Animal Behavior* 28: 1070–94.

—— —— —— (1980b), "Monkey responses to three different alarm calls: evidence of predator classification and semantic communication," *Science* 210: 801–8.

Shannon, Claude E. and Weaver, Warren (1949), *The Mathematical Theory of Communication*. Urbana: University of Illinois Press.

Skinner, B. F. (1957), *Verbal Behavior*. New York: Appleton-Century-Crofts.

Slobin, Dan. I. (1985), "The child as a linguistic icon maker," in John Haiman (ed.), *Iconicity in Syntax: Proceedings of a Symposium on Iconicity in Syntax, Stanford, June 24–26, 1983*. Amsterdam: J. Benjamins, 221–48.

Smith, Neil (1999), *Chomsky: Ideas and Ideals*. Cambridge: Cambridge University Press.

Sobel, Dava (1999), *Galileo's Daugher: A Historical Memoir of Science, Faith, and Love*. New York: Walker & Co.

Sommers, M. S, Moody, D. B., Prosen, C. A., and Stebbins, W. C. (1992), "Formant frequency discrimination by Japanese macques (*Macaca fuscata*)," *Journal of the Accoustical Society of America* 91: 902–9.

Sreedhar, M. V. (1974), *Naga Pidgin: A Sociolinguistic Study of Inter-Lingual Communication Pattern in Nagaland*. Mysore: Central Institute of Indian Languages.

Stokoe, William C. (1960), *Sign Language Structure: An Outline of the Visual Communication Systems of the American Deaf*. Studies in Linguistics:

Occasional Papers 8. Buffalo, NY: Department of Anthropology and Linguistics, University of Buffalo.

Stoneking, Mark (1994), "In defense of 'Eve'—a response to Templeton's critique," *American Anthropologist* 96: 131–41.

Strathern, Andrew (1975), "Veiled speech in Mount Hagen," in Maurice Bloch (ed.), *Political Language and Oratory in Traditional Society.* New York: Academic Press, 185–203.

Struhsaker, T. T. (1967), "Auditory communication in vervet monkeys (*Cercopithecus aethiops*)," in Stuart A. Altmann (ed.), *Social Communication Among Primates.* Chicago: University of Chicago Press, 281–324.

Studdert-Kennedy, Michael (1998), "The particulate origins of language generativity: from syllable to gesture," in James R. Hurford, Michael Studdert-Kennedy, and Chris Knight (eds.), *Approaches to the Evolution of Language.* Cambridge: Cambridge University Press, 202–21.

—— (2000), "Evolutionary implications of the particulate principle: imitation and the dissociation of phonetic from semantic function," in Chris Knight, Michael Studdert-Kennedy, and James R. Hurford (eds.), *The Evolutionary Emergence of Language: Social Function and the Origins of Linguistic Form.* Cambridge: Cambridge University Press.

Tanner, J. E. and Byrne, Richard W. (1996), "Representation of action through iconic gesture in a captive lowland gorilla," *Current Anthropology* 37: 162–73.

Templeton, Alan R. (1993), "The 'Eve' hypotheses: a genetic critique and reanalysis," *American Anthropologist* 95: 51–72.

Tinbergen, N. (1952), "Derived activities: their causation, biological significance, origin and emancipation during evolution," *Quarterly Review of Biology* 27: 1–32.

Tomasello, Michael (1996), "Do apes ape?" in C. Heyes and B. Galef (eds.), *Social Learning in Animals: The Roots of Culture.* San Diego, CA: Academic Press.

—— (2003), *Constructing a Language: A Usage-Based Theory of Language Acquisition.* Cambridge, MA: Harvard University Press.

—— and Call, Josep (1997), *Primate Cognition.* Oxford: Oxford University Press.

—— Nagell, K., Olguin, R., and Carpenter, M. (1994), "The learning and use of gestural signals by young chimpanzees: a trans-generational study," *Primates* 35: 137–54.

—— —— Warren, Jennifer, Frost, G. Thomas, Carpenter, Malinda, and Nagell, Katherine (1997), "The ontogeny of chimpanzee gestural signals: a comparison across groups and generations," *Evolution of Communication* 1: 223–59.

—— and Camaioni, Luigia (1997), "A comparison of the gestural communication of apes and human infants," *Human Development* 40: 7–24.

—— George, B. L., Kruger, A. C., Farrar, M. J., and Evans, A. (1985), "The development of gestural communication in young chimpanzees," *Journal of Human Evolution* 14: 175–86.

—— Gust, D., and Frost, G. T. (1989), "The development of gestural communication in young chimpanzees: a follow-up," *Primates* 30: 35–50.

Turton, David (1975), "The relationship between oratory and the exercise of influence among the Mursi," in Maurice Bloch (ed.), *Political Language and Oratory in Traditional Society*. New York: Academic Press, 163–83.

Tyack, Peter L. and Sayigh, Laela S. (1997), "Vocal learning in cetaceans," in Charles T. Snowdon and Martine Hausberger (eds.), *Social Influences on Vocal Development*. Cambridge: Cambridge University Press, 208–33.

VanSwearingen, Jessie M., Cohn, Jeffrey F., and Bajaj-Luthra, Anu (1999), "Specific impairment of smiling increases the severity of depressive symptoms in patients with facial neuromuscular disorders," *Aesthetic Plastic Surgery* 23: 416–23.

Waal, Frans. B. M. de (1982), *Chimpanzee Politics: Power and Sex among Apes*. New York: Harper and Row.

Wallin, Nils L., Merker, Björn, and Brown, Steven (eds.) (2000), *The Origins of Music*. Cambridge, MA: MIT Press.

Whallon, Robert (1989), "Elements of cultural change in the later Paleolithic," in Paul Mellars and Chris Stringer (eds.), *The Human Revolution*. Edinburgh: Edinburgh University Press, 433–54.

Whiten, Andrew, Goodall, Jane, McGrew, W. C., Nishida, T., Reynolds, V., Sugiyama, Y., Tutin, C. E. G., Wrangham, Richard W., and Boesch, Christophe (1999), "Cultures in chimpanzees," *Nature* 399: 682–5.

Whorf, Benjamin Lee (1956), *Language, Thought, and Reality, Selected Writings*. Cambridge, MA: MIT Press.

Wickett, John C., Vernon, Philip A., and Lee, Donald H. (2000), "Relationships between factors of intelligence and brain volume," *Personality and Individual Differences* 29: 1095–122.

Wilbur, Ronnie Bring (1987), *American Sign Language: Linguistic and Applied Dimensions*. Boston: Little, Brown.

Wolfram, Walt (1976), "Levels of sociolinguistic bias in testing," in Deborah Sears Harrison and Tom Trabasso (eds.), *Black English: A Seminar*. Hillsdale, NJ: Lawrence Erlbaum Associates.

Wrangham, Richard and Peterson, Dale (1996), *Demonic Males: Apes and the Origins of Human Violence*. Boston: Houghton Mifflin.

Wray, Alison (2002), "Dual processing in a protolanguage: performance without competence," in Alison Wray (ed.), *The Transition to Language*. Oxford: Oxford University Press, 113–37.

Yamauchi, Hajime (2001), "The difficulty of the Baldwinian account of linguistic innateness," in J. Kelemen and P. Sosík (eds.), *Advances in Artificial Life: 6th European Conference, ECAL 2001*. Prague: Springer-Verlag, 391–400.

Zahavi, Amot and Zahavi, Avishag (1997), *The Handicap Principle: A Missing Piece of Darwin's Puzzle*. Oxford: Oxford University Press.

Index

Italic numbers denote reference to illustrations or tables

Index

Index

McWhorter, John 238, 239, 242
Mealey, Linda 243
meaning
 in child language 6
 concrete and abstract 132
 conveyed by gesture-calls 50–52
 of earliest words 130
 expansion of 131–3, 223
 referential and emotional 27–9, 42,
  47, 50–3
 referential in sign language 42
 see also propositions
medium, audible and visible 37, 46,
  58, 122–4
Mehler, Jacques 234
Melancon, Thomas F. 243
Mellars, Paul 241
Meltzoff, A. N. 237
mentalese 218
Merker, Björn 240
metaphorics, as a type of
  gesticulation 95
metaphors, as defined by Peirce 93
metrical beat of music and
  poetry 126
Middle Paleolithic 149–150
Miles, H. Lyn 236
Miller, Geoffrey 17, 23, 204–7, 234,
  243, 244
Miller, James D. 240
mimicry,
 by apes 75–6
 selection for 87
 see also imitation
mind reading 215
mind
 of apes and humans 16–7
 designed for language 32
 as an entertainment machine 203,
  207

evolution of 18
and heredity 29–30
transformed by language 47, 49,
  63, 137, 215, 219
 see also conceptualization
mirror neurons 237 n. 75
mirror recognition, by apes 79
Mitani, John 236
mitochondrial DNA 147
modifiers, order in a noun
 phrases 97–8
monkeys
 gelada baboons 57
 rhesus 78
 tamarins 83
 vervets 50–2, 55–6
monolingual demonstration 65–9
Moon, Christine 234
Moore, M. K. 237
morphemes 34, 139
morphology
 def. 248
 needed for speed and clarity
  174
 not needed for thought 91
 origins in early language 174
 and parts of speech 222
motherese 127
motivation 78–82, 84, 92–104 124,
 def. 249
 in child language 118
 and conventionalization 119
 disadvantages of 120
 in gesticulation 96
 lost and gained in language
  change 98
 see also iconicity; indexicality
Mount Hagen 190
Murphy, Jeannine 10
Mursi 190

279